W9-ABF-823

Charlotte Brontë and Defensive Conduct

Charlotte Brontë and Defensive Conduct

The Author and the Body at Risk

Janet Gezari

upp

University of Pennsylvania Press

Philadelphia

Grateful acknowledgment is made to the following:

The National Portrait Gallery London for permission to reproduce a photograph of Charlotte Brontë
Mrs. Audrey W. Hall for permission to reproduce a suspected photograph of Charlotte Brontë
Olwyn Hughes, HarperCollins Publishers, and Faber and Faber Ltd for permission to reprint an extract from "Tulips" from *Sylvia Plath: Collected Poems*, edited by Ted Hughes
The Brontë Society for permission to quote from an unpublished manuscript (Bonnell 98 [7]) in the Museum's collection

Library of Congress Cataloging-in-Publication Data

Gezari, Janet.
    Charlotte Brontë and defensive conduct : the author and the body at risk / Janet Gezari.
        p.   cm.
    Includes bibliographical references (p.   ) and index.
    ISBN 0-8122-3162-7
    1. Brontë, Charlotte, 1816–1855—Knowledge—Psychology.   2. Defensiveness (Psychology) in literature.   3. Conduct of life in literature.   4. Body, Human, in literature.   5. Self in literature.   I. Title.
PR4169.G49   1992
823'.8—dc20   92-22716
                                                                                    CIP

Indignation at literary wrongs I leave to men born under happier stars. I cannot *afford it*. But so far from condemning those who can, I deem it a writer's duty and think it creditable to his heart, to feel and express a resentment proportioned to the grossness of the provocation, and the importance of the object.

—Samuel Taylor Coleridge, *Biographia Literaria*

MY DEAR SIR,—I will tell you why I was so hurt by that review in the 'Edinburgh'—not because its criticism was keen or its blame sometimes severe; not because its praise was stinted (for, indeed, I think you give me quite as much praise as I deserve), but because after I had said earnestly that I wished certain critics would judge me as an *author*, not a woman, you so roughly—I even thought so cruelly—handled the question of sex. I dare say you meant no harm, and perhaps you will not now be able to understand why I was so grieved at what you will probably deem such a trifle; but grieved I was, and indignant too.

—Charlotte Brontë, letter to G. H. Lewes

Contents

Acknowledgments

During the years I have been writing this book, I have benefitted in many ways from the generosity of friends, colleagues, and students at Connecticut College and in the summer school at Tufts. For particularly valued help at different stages, I would like to thank Rick Bogel, John Fyler, Julia Genster, Vanessa Gezari, and Christopher Ricks. I am grateful to Connecticut College for a capstone grant that enabled me to reduce the amount of my teaching in one semester, and to the Society for the Study of Narrative Literature, which provided opportunities for delivering portions of this book at two conferences. I am also grateful to the staff of the Brontë Parsonage Museum, particularly Ms. Kathryn White, for hospitality and kind assistance in answering questions. Like all students of the Brontës, I have profited from the superbly edited Clarendon editions of the Brontës' novels. Quotations from Charlotte Brontë's novels are given parenthetically in my text and refer to book, chapter, and page numbers in the following Clarendon editions: *The Professor*, edited by Margaret Smith and Herbert Rosengarten (1987); *Jane Eyre*, edited by Jane Jack and Margaret Smith (1969); *Shirley*, edited by Herbert Rosengarten and Margaret Smith (1979); and *Villette*, edited by Herbert Rosengarten and Margaret Smith (1984).

1. Introductory: Defending and Being Defensive

The date is 1824, and the six motherless Brontë children, ranging in age from four to ten, have already learned to people their lonely world by studying the magazines and newspapers that come to the Parsonage. Their father, the Reverend Patrick Brontë, thinking his children know more than he has yet discovered they know, suggests a game "to make them speak with less timidity." Each is given a mask and told to "stand and speak boldly" from under its cover. First, he asks Anne, age four, what a child like her most wants. "Age and experience," she intones. It is impossible to say whether she has apprehended the ambiguity of her father's word "wants," which can mean both "desires" and "lacks." Next he asks Emily, nearly six, what to do with her brother, who is sometimes naughty. "Reason with him, and when he won't listen to reason, whip him." Seven-year-old Branwell has an equally ready response to the question of how to know the difference between the intellects of men and women: "By considering the difference between them as to their bodies." "What is the best book in the world?" "The Bible," answers eight-year-old Charlotte. "And the next best?" "The Book of Nature." "What is the best mode of education for a woman?" "That which would make her rule her house well," says nine-year-old Elizabeth. Maria, age ten, has the last word. "What is the best mode of spending time?" "By laying it out in preparation for a happy eternity."

These are brilliantly dull answers, especially because the novels of Charlotte and Emily Brontë, the two most talented of the four who survived into adulthood, challenge the assumptions on which they are based. What is remarkable about the episode, apart from Patrick Brontë's pride in reporting it to E. C. Gaskell, Charlotte Brontë's first biographer, is its evidence of how well his children had already learned to arm themselves for and against adulthood.[1] The mask, a device intended to release the originality of their fledgling spirits, reveals instead the very conditions of culture and language that make flight dangerous. The dramatic formality of the occasion makes each faceless child less individual than representative, like the masked actors on the Greek stage, who have given us one of our words for dissimulation, hypocrisy. Only Emily, whose question is interestingly more practical than those addressed to her siblings, manages an answer at once direct and uncompromising. Confident of her own authority, she challenges her brother's, not only by her willingness to discipline him but also by her implicit refusal of the identity his answer is about to assign her. If woman is, as Branwell follows Pope in thinking, at best "a softer Man," Emily stakes her claim to reason, conventionally a masculine attribute, and to the physical authority required to back it up.

The answers of Anne, Branwell, Charlotte, Elizabeth, and Maria confirm Patrick Brontë's suspicion that his children know more than he has yet discovered they know. The mask game reminds us that although they were isolated from other children and other families in the tiny West Yorkshire village where they grew up, they were by no means isolated from the main ideas about children, education, religion (revealed and natural), and gender current in nineteenth-century England. The mask transforms them into small adults, a promotion related to the one already achieved by naming the tiny, extra upstairs room the "children's study" rather than the nursery. The authority Elizabeth and Maria claim is properly feminine in being domestic and spiritual. The years will not provide Anne with the authority she acknowledges lacking, a matter of experience as well as age. Although Charlotte derives her authority from her Father's books, the Bible and Nature, the first readers of her published novels were quick to recognize in them a formidable challenge to Biblical authority and a dangerous readiness to turn it to her own purposes.

In this paternal game, seeing through masks as speaking from under their cover is already alive to another experience entirely, seeing through masks as seeing what others would hide from us. What Patrick Brontë would hide from his children is in part what he wants to hear, and what the Brontë children know has at least as much to do with their understanding of his expectations as it does with what they have already learned about themselves and their world. Both kinds of knowledge are germane to Charlotte Brontë's life and art. My starting point is the premise that she conducts herself defensively in this mask game and later as a writer, and that her protagonists also adopt a defensive conduct in her novels. Thinking about defending and being defensive opens up a great deal about Charlotte

Brontë and the circumstances of her writing, and thinking about Charlotte Brontë opens up a great deal about defending and being defensive.

In her own time, Charlotte Brontë was reverenced for the feminine nobility with which she endured loneliness, hardship, and deprivation and also censured for writing unfeminine novels that strain against the disguises and confinements of social conventions. In ours, her novels provide a powerfully charged account of the patterns of accommodation and resistance necessary to those who find themselves—largely for reasons of class and gender—on the defensive. Much recent criticism of women writers witnesses our current interest in "the individual subject's shifting alliances as situated in gender and class relations,"[2] but Charlotte Brontë's appeal to readers depends equally on a longer-standing interest on the part of both men and women in the difficulties of conducting an unimpugnable defense of ourselves, a defense at once self-vindicating and free from vindictiveness.

This book connects the consummate skill with which Brontë's novels mediate the cultural conflicts at issue in them to acts of self-defense and self-vindication, and shows how she anchors these acts by representing the body—its organs, senses, and appendages—as the site of social conflict and constraint. Brontë's concern with self-defence and self-vindication does not in itself require this new emphasis on the body. But these two elements of her art—its engagement with acts of self-defense and self-vindication, and its representation of the body as the site of emotional, psychological, and social struggle—are interdependent. This means that the body in Brontë's novels is not, as in Helena Michie's very different construction, distanced from the reader as "a series of tropes or rhetorical codes," an absence Michie postulates to confirm her own preconceived ideology of female experience.[3] I argue instead that Brontë does not so entirely mistake her own enterprise in the well-known letter in which she deprecates Jane Austen as a lady novelist who ignores "what throbs fast and full, though hidden, what the blood rushes through."[4]

As a woman novelist, Brontë strives to reclaim bodies that are "sensibly alive" and pulsing with feeling for the novel. Froma I. Zeitlin suggests that although men "have bodies, to be sure," our gender system assigns "the role of representing the corporeal side of life in its helplessness and submission to constraints" primarily to women.[5] In her only representation of a professional woman artist, the actress Vashti in *Villette*, Brontë comes closest to formulating her own practice as a novelist:

> I have said that she does not *resent* her grief. No; the weakness of that word would make it a lie. To her, what hurts becomes immediately embodied: she looks on it as a thing that can be attacked, worried down, torn in shreds. Scarcely a substance herself, she grapples to conflict with abstractions. (II, 23, 370)

The body—in its availability to hurt as well as caress and in its submission to inevitable constraints—is an organizing motif in both Brontë's novels and this study of them. For Brontë insists on the material possibilities of language, and her novels consistently assert a continuity between language and the physical realm it seeks to represent. As a novelist, she seeks a language that "grapples to conflict with abstractions."

By attending closely to the circumstances of her writing and to her representation of social and emotional conflict in her novels, this book reassesses Charlotte Brontë's achievement as a writer on the defensive. In part, my project is to rehabilitate the notion of defensiveness by suggesting that there are circumstances in which defensive conduct is not only appropriate but creditable. In part, it is to demonstrate how well Brontë understands what she is up against, and how intelligently she defends herself. In both her life and her art, Brontë is alive to the difficulties involved in responding to attacks that are either denied or under-acknowledged and, hence, open any defense to the charge of being defensive in our modern sense of the word: too quick to take offense or covertly aggressive. The analytic deliberateness with which she confronts these attacks has been consistently neglected by her critics. The older view is that her novels are deformed by rage, indignation, and hunger; the newer is that they suppress or repress these feelings. Both ignore the extent to which Brontë's characteristic responses to the world are powerful resources for her art rather than personal difficulties to be surmounted or even deplored.[6] The story she has to tell is one she tells most fully in *Villette*, the novel in which she risks exposing her heroine to the charge of paranoia in order to commit her to unaccommodatingly defensive conduct in her double role as narrated and narrating self. But in all of her novels, Brontë's characters define themselves in terms of their accommodation and resistance to hostile circumstances, characters, and readers. For Brontë, defensiveness is not just self-regarding or self-protective but an engaging enterprise of intelligent and imaginative counter-moves.

This chapter seeks to define the situation of Brontë's writing and clarify the distinction between defending and being defensive by examining three significant occasions for defense in Brontë's life—Gaskell's defense of Brontë in her biography, Brontë's defense of her sisters in her 1850 edition of *Wuthering Heights* and *Agnes Grey*, and Brontë's defense of herself against G. H. Lewes's criticism of *Shirley* in his review of the novel. In attending to Brontë's life in this chapter and others, I am aware that Brontë criticism has been more hampered than facilitated by the kind of interest her life has traditionally solicited. More than a century ago, Henry James courageously attacked the "romantic tradition of the Brontës" which has its basis in "the attendant image of their dreary, their tragic history, their loneliness and poverty of life":

> The personal position of the three sisters, of the two in particular, has been marked, in short, with so sharp an accent that this accent has become for us the very tone of their united production. It covers and supplants their matter, their spirit, their style, their talent, their taste; it embodies, really, the most complete intellectual muddle, if the term be not extravagant, ever achieved, on a literary question, by our wonderful public. The question has scarce been accepted as belonging to literature at all.[7]

Although I see the connections between Brontë's life and her art as always specific and moving, I am not concerned here with the "romantic tradition of the Brontës" with its emphasis on the bleakness of the Yorkshire moors and unrequited love. This makes a more substantial difference to my reading of Brontë's novels than may be evident, especially since I do not always record the biographical connections that have traditionally engaged other Brontë readers. My discussion of *The Professor*, for instance, is not concerned with the novel as a disguised account of Brontë's love for Constantin Héger, but with the relation between the hero's frustrated agency as man and master and Brontë's own frustrated agency as the author of the novel she wrote first but only succeeded in publishing posthumously. My focus throughout is on those engagements in the social world that illuminate Brontë's struggles as a woman of a certain class and a publishing author. They reveal a woman more embattled, contentious, and resilient, though no less passionate, than the familiar trembling soul. Her critics have so far neglected this woman, and her biographers have underdescribed her.

The difficulty of finding a language in which to conduct a conversation between Brontë's culture and ours is already apparent in my choice of a recent word—defensiveness—to identify a social situation that predates it. With the word "defensive," the language arrives by a circuitous route (in this case involving a detour through the more specialized language of psychoanalysis) at a name for what poets and novelists had already well described. Dickens provides one nineteenth-century account of defensiveness in this modern sense. Miss Wade's attempt at self-vindication in *Little Dorrit*, her "History of a Self-Tormenter," conveys both the acute intelligence that decries what people cannot acknowledge or won't openly voice and the touchiness that distorts perception and mocks even the possibility of good intentions. In the passage that follows, Miss Wade describes her schooling by a woman who cared for some children of her own family and some children of other people:

> I must have been about twelve years old when I began to see how determinedly those girls patronised me. I was told I was an orphan. There was no other orphan among us; and I perceived (here was the first disadvantage of not being a fool) that they conciliated me in an insolent pity, and in a sense of superiority. I did not set this down as a discovery, rashly. I tried them often. I could hardly make them quarrel with me. When I succeeded with any of them, they were sure to come after an hour or two, and begin a reconciliation. I tried them over and over again, and I never knew them wait for me to begin. They were always forgiving me, in their vanity and condescension. Little images of grown people![8]

Dickens's representation of Miss Wade as someone who lives to plague herself and others is persuasive. But by labeling her "a self-tormenter," he attributes to her the aggression that is barely concealed in the behavior of others toward her. Her "bad temper" explains her feelings as inadequately as Lockwood's "bad temper" explains his dreams during his first night at Wuthering Heights. As a woman writer, Charlotte Brontë attends more discriminatingly than Dickens to the feelings that are caught up and held up for contemplation in acts of self-vindication like Miss Wade's.

According to the editors of the OED, "defensive" in its current sense has a history that begins in about 1965.[9] No doubt the possession of the word changes as well as registers our relation to the concept in ways I hope to make clear by attending to the way we use it to describe some of our social relations. None of the entries in the OED or its *Supplement* covers our modern sense of "defensiveness," but the *Collins Dictionary of the English Language* has "rejecting criticisms of oneself or covering one's failings." This definition recognizes that defensiveness involves self-interest—one defends someone or something, but one is only defensive about oneself—and it assumes that to act defensively is to admit that one really is indefensible. The failings are real, though they cannot be acknowledged. A willingness to admit fallibility is a good defense against defensiveness, as a recent review from the *London Review of Books* suggests. To turn from the critic William Empson, who "believed that true rigour requires a certain looseness, a recognition of fallibility," the reviewer writes, is "to see, perhaps for the first time, just how defensive [some literary critics] are: sententious, self-absorbed, frightened to leave the pack."[10] But more is at stake in attributions of defensiveness than mere fallibility. When another reviewer says that H. G. Wells is "defensively emphatic" in denying that some other father's affection for his daughter has a sexual dimension, "defensively" clearly implies that Wells is protecting himself against this charge, to which he responds as if it had actually been leveled against him.[11]

The Hite Report on Male Sexuality shows how an apparently reasonable inquiry—"How would you feel if something about you were described as feminine or womanly?"—triggers a range of defensive responses in the men who are being questioned:

> Chagrined. I may appear soft, but I carry a big stick. So watch out.

> Enraged. Insulted. Never mind what women are really like—I know what he's saying: he's saying I should be submissive to him.

Frank Lentricchia, who cites these answers in *Ariel and the Police*, comments sensibly on them: "About two seconds of reflection should be enough to convince most of us that what is offered in *The Hite Report on Male Sexuality* as the representative testimony of contemporary American men is, in fact, representative: our relations with women are problematic, those with ourselves something worse."[12] In both cases, Hite's question is taken as an insult rather than a compliment; moreover, it has the effect of situating the men to whom it is addressed in the position of feminine speakers. Chagrin, a feeling of vexation verging on mortification, is a soft feeling and risks the appearance of femininity in order the more wittily to combat it by rising to so phallic an act of aggression: "I may appear soft, but I carry a big stick." The second response issues in a limper counter-assertion: "I know what he's saying: he's saying I should be submissive to him." The questioner is now explicitly identified as another man from whom the appearance of softness is thought to invite abusive domination, yet both the disclaimer—"Never mind what women are really like"—and the implication of incontrovertible necessity in "should" reveal more than awkward relations with women or deep self-distrust. Both answers suggest the degree to which positioning a speaker as feminine registers that speaker's lack of authority, and so elicits a defensive response.

In such circumstances it can always be argued that no criticism has actually been offered, so that being defensive means something like being touchy or prickly or over-reacting. The OED defines "touchy," an older word than "prickly," as "easily moved to anger; apt to take offence on slight cause; highly sensitive in temper or disposition; irascible, irritable, testy, tetchy." Although you are equally likely to offend the touchy and the prickly individual, contact with someone who is prickly is certain to be painful. The distinction suggests a shift in perspective and emphasis; touchiness implies a receptive vulnerability, but prickliness constitutes an active threat to approaching others. "Over-react" enters the language at about the same time that "defensive" does. According to the *Supplement* to the OED, to over-react is to respond "with excessive force or emotion to a given situation." A 1967 citation brings over-reaction into closer relation to defensiveness by suggesting that over-reactions are "psychologically very revealing."

Our modern use of "defensive" owes a specific debt to the study of defenses and mechanisms of defense in psychoanalysis. In *The Ego and the Mechanisms of Defence* (1946), Anna Freud describes the term *defence* as "the earliest representative of the dynamic standpoint in psychoanalytic theory" and cites Freud's "The Defence Neuro-Psychoses" (1894) as the paper in which the term first appears. Freud uses the term in this and later papers "to describe the ego's struggle against painful or unendurable ideas or affects."[13] The psychological interpretation, in its popular versions, masks relations of social difference that help to constitute the "objective anxieties" that Anna Freud argued were not properly the business of psychoanalytic observation. Defenses against these anxieties, as opposed to defenses against inner drives, may be justified and cannot be "the main focus of attention of clinical observation" because they are "normal, not pathogenic."[14] In *The Language of Psycho-Analysis*, Jean Laplanche and J.-B. Pontalis are also alert to the social as well as the psychological meanings of defensiveness when they insist on the ambiguity of "the term 'defence'": "It connotes both the action of *defending*—in the sense of fighting to protect something—and that of *defending oneself*." Something of value is being defended at the same time that something—internal or external—is being defended against.[15]

It is important to try to say what was lost as well as gained when "defensive" acquired its familiar modern sense and its capacity to register a changed understanding of the social and psychological circumstances to which it refers. In its older sense, the word referred to something made, formed, or carried on for defensive, as opposed to offensive or aggressive, purposes. It could refer to pre-emptively hostile behavior, as it does in Frances Burney's use of the word in 1787 to describe the outcome of a quarrel with a fellow-traveler who has forced his attentions on her: "I was not sorry to have our war end here apparently," she writes after narrating the episode, "though I was obliged to resolve upon a defensive conduct in future, that would prevent any other attack."[16] While registering the unavailability, inappropriateness, or imagined danger of aggressive conduct, Burney's defensive conduct neither masks her anger nor validates the attack that has been made on her. Instead, it proves her honorable determination to hold up her end of the fight. The difficulty that arises with our modern use of "defensive" doesn't only refer to the difficulty of sustaining imputations about someone's unconscious—the imputation, for example, that anyone who describes something about a man as feminine or womanly means to dominate him. It also refers to the way the word is regularly used to foreclose the possibility of an honorable defense of oneself like Burney's by masking the objective anxieties and actual social circumstances that require acts of self-defense and self-vindication.

The relation between the old and new senses of "defensive" resembles the one the undefensive critic Empson exemplifies with a passage in which Proust's Françoise describes the Guermantes as "a great family," and the narrator notes that she has based the family's greatness "at once on the number of its branches and the brilliance of its connections." "A word has two uses normally separate; there is a case where they can be used together; an assertion is added that they normally come together or even are the same."

> What we want to examine is not a speaker accepting extra meanings in a word but a speaker using them to assert a doctrine. However we should recognize that this process will always be somehow near the process of confusion, because he is claiming that the connection is normal since the word is one thing. Also there is commonly an appeal to an outside body of opinion, which adds greatly to the power of this little trick: the idea is 'everybody agrees with me; language itself agrees with me; but you the hearer seem not to know it well enough.' Thus the connection may not only assert a doctrine but give it a specially potable or catching form.[17]

In the case of "defensive," the two senses of the word are no longer separable; in effect, the earlier sense can no longer be distinguished from the modern sense. The doctrine covertly asserted is that to defend oneself is to be defensive. Either whatever criticism is being offered ought to be accepted rather than repelled (and from this it follows that the person being criticized really is indefensible), or no criticism has actually been offered so that someone who responds defensively is over-reacting.

Such a doctrine is especially dangerous to a writer who seemed to others and to herself to need so much defending and whose heroes and heroines are so frequently roused to acts of self-defense and self-vindication. Two famous responses to Brontë, Matthew Arnold's and Virginia Woolf's, focus on her social attitudes and register, in different ways, her defensiveness. Arnold, who said that her mind contained nothing but "hunger, rebellion and rage," accurately identified the prevailing tone of her thought and feeling, but saying so he also marked his objection to her writing as unpleasant, distorted, and self-absorbed.[18] With Arnold's criticism, the old debates about whether anger or its expression is ever warranted are conjoined with the expectation that a woman in particular ought to suppress her anger in order to appear, as Adrienne Rich has it, "calm, detached, and ever charming in a roomful of men where things have been said which are attacks on her very integrity."[19] Virginia Woolf, writing about women and fiction seventy-five years after Arnold, repeats his charge when, comparing *Jane Eyre* and *Pride and Prejudice*, she asserts that "the woman who wrote these pages had more genius in her than Jane Austen; but if one reads them over and marks that jerk in them, that indignation, one sees that she will never get her genius expressed whole and entire."[20] Woolf was responding specifically to Jane Eyre's anticipation of being blamed for her unsentimental assessment of her pupil, Mr. Rochester's ward, in a passage that resonates with Jane's sense that she is going to be unfairly judged. And like Jane, Brontë herself most often imagines her relation to her readers in terms of praise and blame, as in her preface to *Wuthering Heights*, where the ultimate defense of Emily Brontë's probity is her submission to her "creative gift": "If the result be attractive, the World will praise you, who little deserve praise; if it be repulsive, the same World will blame you, who almost as little deserve blame." "What were they blaming Charlotte Brontë for?" Woolf wonders about the passage in *Jane Eyre*. According to Woolf, Austen got "infinitely more said" than Brontë because she wrote "without hate, without bitterness, without fear, without protest, without preaching."

For Woolf, Brontë's books are inevitably "deformed and twisted" by her indignation, but more recent feminist critics like Rich and Elaine Showalter attribute the distortion of the woman, and perhaps of her work, not to her indignation but to its suppression. For Showalter, Woolf's idea that "anger and protest" were "flaws in art" only rationalizes Woolf's own fears in the face of "the punishment that society could inflict on women who made a nuisance of themselves by behaving in an uncivilized manner."[21] Whether or not we blame Woolf, it is impossible to read her criticism of Brontë or for that matter Arnold's without attending to the way in which they turn Brontë's resources as a writer, among them rage, indignation, rebelliousness, and hunger, into difficulties she ought to have surmounted.

These difficulties can be perceived as powerful resources for a great writer, as a comparison of the critical response to Samuel Johnson with these critical responses to Brontë clearly demonstrates. "Promptitude of thought, indeed, and quickness of expression, were among the peculiar features of Johnson," according to Mrs. Thrale: "his notions rose up like the dragon's teeth sowed by Cadmus already clothed, and in bright armour too, fit for immediate battle." Walter Jackson Bate praises this aptitude as "aggressive strength" and remarks as well on Johnson's "personal temptations to make full use" of it: "the irritabilities and impatience of temperament, the eagerness to confute, the large floating dissatisfactions, the physical suffering; all of which he strove so hard to control, though the struggle to do so naturally produced its own further tensions."[22] Bate's language legitimates Johnson's actions just as Arnold's and Woolf's language makes Brontë's actions blameworthy if not unlawful. To make the connection between Brontë's defensive weakness and Johnson's "aggressive strength" is to acknowledge that the energies for resistance, confutation, and conflict will always seem more defensible in the political or military realm where Mrs. Thrale and Bate situate Johnson than in the domestic realm where Brontë, along with other women writers, has so far been located.

In *Keywords: A Vocabulary of Culture*, Raymond Williams shows how appraisive language legitimates as well as describes the attitudes of dominant social groups. A dozen years later, writing on the Brontës in *The English Novel from Dickens to Lawrence*, Williams is at once admiring of Charlotte Brontë's novels and disconcerted by them:

> And I'd then say, finally, that Charlotte stands very obviously at the head of a tradition, in a way that her sister does not; and I think that is history, and significant history, when we come to reflect. For the method of *Villette* is what I called once, coldly, the fiction of special pleading. I mean that fiction in which the only major emotion, and then the relation with the reader, is

that exact stress, that first-person stress: 'circumstanced like me.' The stress is this really: the world will judge me in certain ways if it sees what I do, but if it knew how I felt it would see me quite differently.[23]

With their implicit answer to F. R. Leavis's banishment of Brontë from the "great tradition" of the English novel, Williams's words about her are especially acute in recognizing that Brontë's first-person narrators conduct themselves defensively, and that her novels regularly summon their readers to acts of praise or blame. He suggests the need to rethink these evaluative judgments in relation to interests different from the general interest. The circumstances and feelings of characters like Lucy Snowe are special, rather than general, precisely because they are those of women.

Williams's scrutiny of his own feelings about special pleading is exemplary, for special pleading, a pleading drawn with reference to the particular circumstances of a case, ordinarily means disingenuous or sophistical pleading. Special pleading, a phrase expressing cold disapproval, may, so Williams suggests, warm to praise what it describes. Quentin Skinner explains this situation well:

> To apply any word to the world, we need to have a clear grasp of both its sense and its reference. But in the case of appraisive terms a further element of understanding is also required. We need in addition to know what exact range of attitudes the term can standardly be used to express.[24]

The attitude standardly expressed by "special pleading" sustains a social philosophy according to which judgments of actions and the individual who performs them are supposed to be made without reference to special circumstances. Williams's altered sense of the creditability of special pleading in relation to Brontë's method makes a new claim for the truth of a "first-person stress" and for the truth of feelings more general in the lives of women than in those of men.

*   *   *

The defensibility of special pleading in relation to a woman's life is fundamentally at issue in Gaskell's biography of Charlotte Brontë. When Charlotte Brontë's father and widower asked Gaskell to write a "just and honorable defense" of Brontë,[25] they trusted she would correct the misrepresentations in articles noticing Brontë's death and counter the attacks that followed the publication of *Jane Eyre*. Elizabeth Rigby, later Lady Eastlake, was not the only reader who had vigorously condemned both the book and its author, but her review, appearing in the influential *Quarterly Review* in 1848, is an articulate compendium of the attacks leveled at Currer Bell. The mystery of what one reviewer discriminatingly called the author's "*nom de guerre*" had encouraged biographical speculation and invited prejudice rather than protecting against it, as Brontë had hoped. Rigby's review firmly grounds the hostile response to *Jane Eyre* in issues of class and gender. "Whoever it be," Rigby wrote of Currer Bell, "it is a person who, with great mental powers, combines a total ignorance of the habits of society, a great coarseness of taste, and a heathenish doctrine of religion." Jane Eyre is "a decidedly vulgar-minded woman—one whom we should not care for as an acquaintance, whom we should not seek as a friend, whom we should not desire for a relation, and whom we should scrupulously avoid for a governess. . . ." These are also the censures Rigby directs at the author: ". . . if we ascribe the book to a woman at all, we have no alternative but to ascribe it to one who has, for some sufficient reason, long forfeited the society of her own sex."[26]

Gaskell's instincts about how to mount her defense of Brontë were excellent. Thanking Ellen Nussey for showing her some of Brontë's letters, she writes, "I am sure the more fully she—Charlotte Brontë—the *friend*, the *daughter*, the *sister*, the *wife*, is known, and known where need be in her own words, the more highly will she be appreciated."[27] This ascending sequence of relational titles (the next in the list, conspicuous by its absence, is *mother*) is remarkable only for the place of importance it gives to Brontë's role as sister (greater than that of daughter, though less still than that of wife). But it is eloquent in its contrast to Rigby's sequence, which also ascends from less to more intimate connections. Rigby's sequence gives the place of highest importance to its last term not only rhetorically but syntactically by introducing the variation of a clause in which a positive injunction to do something—scrupulously avoid this woman for a governess—substitutes for the negative constructions that have so far been the pattern. The governess is most likely not a mother and also displaces one, in this sequence as in life, a displacement that implicates Rigby's readers in a reassuring system that conflates moral and class inferiority.

While rebuking Rigby's "want of Christian charity,"[28] Gaskell's *Life of Charlotte Brontë* nevertheless concedes her main premise, that an author who is a woman is constituted less by her work than by her relations with intimate and domestic others. The publication of *Jane Eyre* divides her biography into two volumes, a division that formulates, on the level of structure, Gaskell's paradigmatic bifurcation of Brontë's existence into "two parallel currents—her life as Currer Bell, the author; her life as Charlotte Brontë, the woman." There were "separate duties belonging to each character—not opposing each other; not impossible, but difficult to be reconciled." A man who becomes an author changes his employment, Gaskell writes, but "a woman's principal work in life is hardly left to her own choice; nor can she drop the domestic charges devolving on her as an individual, for the exercise of the most splendid talents that were ever bestowed."[29]

Gaskell's biography argues that Brontë subordinated her own interests to those of others, and its large redemptive and conciliatory success can be measured by the difference it made to Brontë's contemporary readers. Charles Kingsley was one who recorded his appreciation. "Let me renew our long interrupted acquaintance by complimenting you on poor Miss Brontë's 'Life,'" he wrote Gaskell.

> You have had a delicate and a great work to do, and you have done it admirably. Be sure that the book will do good. It will shame literary people into some stronger belief that a simple, virtuous, practical home life is consistent with high imaginative genius; and it will shame, too, the prudery of a not over cleanly though carefully whitewashed age, into believing that purity is now (as in all ages till now) quite compatible with the knowledge of evil. I confess that the book has made me ashamed of myself.[30]

Brontë's sex is the crucial, unspoken fact that provides the basis for Kingsley's response to her novels both before and after reading the *Life*, for the compatibility of genius with domestic duties and of the knowledge of evil with purity become issues only in relation to generally accepted views of women and women's roles. Although novels written by men like Hardy and Dickens were also accused of containing impurities, so that Dickens was moved, in his preface to the third edition of *Oliver Twist*, to defend as an "established truth" the principle that "a lesson of the purest good may . . . be drawn from the vilest evil," he was not moved to defend his own purity or to suspect that his readers had impugned it.[31] The difference in the standards applied to novels by women and novels by men resulted in a situation in which praise for a novel was in no way inconsistent with blame for its author. The review of *Jane Eyre* in the *Christian Remembrancer* is explicit about this:

> There is an intimate acquaintance with the worst parts of human nature, a practised sagacity in discovering the latent ulcer, and a ruthless rigor in exposing it, which must commend our admiration, but are almost startling in one of the softer sex.[32]

Mary Taylor, Brontë's feminist friend, responded very differently from Kingsley to the prospect of Gaskell's *Life*. From New Zealand, where she had recently emigrated, she wrote Ellen Nussey that she could "never think without gloomy anger of Charlotte's sacrifices to the selfish old man [her father]." Her indignation on her friend's behalf is a spirited retort to the prejudices that animate Rigby's and Kingsley's criticisms:

> I wish I could set the world right on many points, but above all respecting Charlotte. It would do said world good to know her and be forced to revere her in spite of their contempt for poverty and helplessness. No one ever gave up more than she did and with full consciousness of what she sacrificed. I don't think myself that women are justified in sacrificing themselves for others, but since the world generally expects it of them, they should at least acknowledge it. But where much is given we are all wonderfully given to grasp at more. If Charlotte had left home and made a favour of returning, she would have got thanks instead of tyranny—wherefore take care of yourself Ellen, and if you choose to give a small modicum of mention of other people, *grumble hard.* [33]

Because she writes so honorably in Brontë's defense, Taylor can negotiate the descent from fervent indignation ("I wish I could set the world right on many points") to homely resentment ("*grumble hard*"). For although indignation may be aroused by a sense of wrong to oneself, it is more often the proper response to injuries done to others; these are injuries about which one can't be too indignant. Resentment is quieter than indignation and more familiar; it is useful for covering those cases in which one feels too much interested for indignation to be appropriate. Mary Taylor feels indignant about Brontë's sacrifices for the sake of her father, but she counsels her friend to resent the use that others would make of her. Taylor's indignation isn't diminished by her beautifully judged acknowledgment of the opposing view ("I don't think myself that women are justified in sacrificing themselves for others"); her vindication of Brontë is more powerful because of it. Her defense of her friend is entirely without defensiveness, both because it understands clearly what it is up against and because the interest the writer defends is her friend's rather than her own.

Gaskell's biography brings Brontë herself before the bar, much as if she were one of her own characters. Withholding her own verdict on her friend at its close, Gaskell summons Mary Taylor as her last witness for the defense. She quotes from one of Taylor's letters to her, a letter that begins by expressing a "strong desire to obtain appreciation" for Brontë and ends with a bitter rebuke:

Yet, what does it matter? She herself appealed to the world's judgment for her use of some of the faculties she had,—not the best,—but still the only ones she could turn to strangers' benefit. They heartily, greedily enjoyed the fruits of her labours, and then found out she was much to be blamed for possessing such faculties. Why ask for a judgment on her from such a world? [34]

In this trial, the public, like Kingsley, should suspect itself: "I confess that the book has made me ashamed of myself." But it is only to this public that Gaskell can appeal if she is to succeed in her largest enterprise, the vindication of Charlotte Brontë. Gaskell's *Life* manages to reproach Brontë's public while offering it the redemption that comes with a change of heart. "Reproach" is to be preferred to blame in this case for the reasons that Empson provides in his analysis of these words. Blame "deals with placing the responsibility; if you can put the blame on someone else you are free." This is the sense in which Brontë herself uses the word in the preface to *Wuthering Heights*, which blames the creative gift, not the artist who is its agent, for what is shocking in the novel. In Empson's analysis, "the tenderness of REPROACH comes from a different kind of mutual feeling; 'I am sorry about this, and you will be sorry when I have made you feel what you have done." [35] Empson doesn't avoid ambiguity in this use of "tenderness," which can signify either a softened attitude toward the object of reproach or the touchiness of the reproacher. "A woman's attitude is one of constant reproach," Simone de Beauvoir writes in her chapter on "Woman's Situation and Character" in *The Second Sex*. She describes the position of the feminine speaker as involving both "distrust of the world as given" and resistance to suffering in it against her will. [36]

To turn from Gaskell's defense of Brontë to two defenses by Brontë herself, her public defense of her sisters in the 1850 edition of *Wuthering Heights* and *Agnes Grey* and her private defense of herself in her correspondence with one of her reviewers, G. H. Lewes, is to engage with the special difficulties involved in defenses of one's own interests or interests very closely connected to them and defenses against attacks that deny their own aggression. Both these defenses are especially vulnerable to the charge of defensiveness. Brontë's critics have largely neglected the 1850 volume, which consists of a "Biographical Notice of Ellis and Acton Bell," an "Editor's Preface" to *Wuthering Heights*, and a small selection of Emily Jane Brontë's poems as well as the two novels. [37] The most poignant irony of the volume is that it originates in Brontë's impulse to separate herself as an author from Emily Brontë and ends in her inability or unwillingness to endure that sundering.

The first thing in the 1850 edition, the "Biographical Notice," begins by deprecating the reviewers' refusal to keep the Bells separate. Brontë's opening—"I am advised distinctly to state how the case really stands"—disclaims both the authorship of her sisters' novels and the initiative for providing the account of them that follows. The second paragraph continues matter-of-factly, although it reveals its uneasiness by referring to the sisters as Ellis and Acton Bell in the same breath as it promises to do away with the mystery surrounding their identities:

> Indeed, I feel myself that it is time the obscurity attending those two names—Ellis and Acton—was done away. The little mystery, which formerly yielded some harmless pleasure, has lost its interest; circumstances are changed. It becomes, then, my duty to explain briefly the origin and authorship of the books written by Currer, Ellis, and Acton Bell.[38]

The story of Emily Brontë's response to her sister's discovery of her poems suggests how deeply divided the impulses behind the "Biographical Notice" must have been:

> My sister Emily was not a person of demonstrative character, nor one, on the recesses of whose mind and feelings, even those nearest and dearest to her could, with impunity, intrude unlicensed; it took hours to reconcile her to the discovery I had made, and days to persuade her that such poems merited publication.[39]

When Brontë then writes about how *Wuthering Heights* came to be attributed to the author of *Jane Eyre*, she both praises her sister's novel and condescends to it:

> We laughed at it at first, but I deeply lament it now. Hence, I fear, arose a prejudice against the book. That writer who could attempt to palm off an inferior and immature production under cover of one successful effort, must indeed be unduly eager after the secondary and sordid result of authorship, and pitiably indifferent to its true and honorable meed. If reviewers and the public truly believed this, no wonder that they looked darkly on the cheat.
>
> Yet I must not be understood to make these things subject for reproach or complaint; I dare not do so; respect for my sister's memory forbids me. By her any such querulous manifestation would have been regarded as unworthy, and offensive weakness.[40]

Two authors' names—Ellis Bell and Currer Bell—are attached to two texts, *Wuthering Heights* and *Jane Eyre*. To identify Ellis as Currer, or Currer as Ellis, is to establish a new set of diacritical relations between these texts, for instance, that of temporal priority, as in Brontë's dismissive reference to *Wuthering Heights* as an "immature production." The imputation that Ellis is Currer aligns the author with the publisher, Thomas Newby, whose motive for publishing will be the "secondary and sordid" one of financial gain, and to resent this is to reproach the reviewers, despite Brontë's disclaimer. Charlotte Brontë's difference from Emily Brontë, a difference related to but not coincident with Currer Bell's difference from Ellis Bell, is the main point of the second paragraph above and of the "Biographical Notice" as a whole. "I have always felt certain that it is a deplorable error in an author to assume the tragic tone in addressing the public about his own wrongs or griefs," Brontë had written several months earlier. And, "If I live, the hour may come when the spirit will move me to speak of [my sisters], but it is not come yet."[41] In telling the story of her sisters' lives, Brontë insists on her difference from them, doing for them what she had refused to do for herself when her publisher asked her to write a biographical preface for one of her own novels and what neither would have done for herself at a time when neither is alive to reproach her for doing it.

The "Biographical Notice" ends with a one-sentence paragraph that marks how reproachful Brontë's tone has become in the course of telling the story of her sisters' lives by forcibly recalling the words with which she began:

> This notice has been written, because I felt it a sacred duty to wipe the dust off their gravestones, and leave their dear names free from soil.[42]

Her plain duty has become "a sacred duty," and the dust that obscures the names on her sisters' gravestones is a new figure for the "obscurity attending those two names." The action that makes it possible to read the names of the dead on a gravestone is itself a simple reminder that the sisters have died and been buried, though so recently as not to suggest any accumulation of dust. But a name is still held in reserve when the biographical notice is signed "Currer Bell." In the final phrases of the notice, reproach sharpens into censure, for "soil" differs from "dust" in a way that vindicates Brontë's use of the word "sacred" to characterize her duty to her sisters: it carries the additional sense of a moral stain that has tarnished their names.

The 1850 volume closes with a selection of poems by Ellis that includes a poem titled "Stanzas" but better known as "Often Rebuked." As a vindication of Emily Brontë, this poem might be called the poetry of special pleading because it establishes a relation to the reader and the reader's judgment that depends on the persuasiveness of the first-person stress:

"circumstanced like me." "Rebuke" differs from "blame" and "reproach" slightly yet firmly, as the poem's first line suggests. To rebuke is "to beat down or force back; to repress or check (a person); to repulse." The citation from *Macbeth* that follows this definition in the OED is apt: "Under him / My Genius is rebuk'd, as it is said Mark Anthonies was by Caesar" (iii, i, 56–57). In the poem, the return is always to a place of origin, to "first feelings that were born with me" (l. 2), both because the feelings cannot pre-exist the one who feels and because they are only awakened by a life on earth (l. 19):

> Often rebuked, yet always back returning
> To those first feelings that were born with me,
> And leaving busy chase of wealth and learning
> For idle dreams of things which cannot be:
>
> To-day, I will seek not the shadowy region;
> Its unsustaining vastness waxes drear;
> And visions rising, legion after legion,
> Bring the unreal world too strangely near.
>
> I'll walk, but not in old heroic traces,
> And not in paths of high morality,
> And not among the half-distinguished faces,
> The clouded forms of long-past history.
>
> I'll walk where my own nature would be leading:
> It vexes me to choose another guide:
> Where the gray flocks in ferny glens are feeding;
> Where the wild wind blows on the mountain side.
>
> What have those lonely mountains worth revealing?
> More glory and more grief than I can tell:
> The earth that wakes *one* human heart to feeling
> Can centre both the worlds of Heaven and Hell.[43]

This poem defends Emily Brontë's decision to take her own nature as a guide rather than following in the footsteps of epic, "high morality," or history. Its second and third stanzas, which connect the "visionary forms" of some "shadowy region" to the "clouded forms of long-past history"—

neither can any longer sustain her—are the least forceful in the poem, for they lack the gerunds and present progressive verbs that are so regularly the rhyme words in the other stanzas and give the poem so many feminine endings. These words best describe the writer's nature: returning, learning, leading, feeding, revealing, and feeling (this last, the poem's penultimate rhyme word, gives additional force to the "feelings" of the first stanza). The justification this poem offers for the writer's following her own bent rather than walking in "old heroic traces" (both well-worn paths and the ropes that connect a draught animal to its load) is like the one Wordsworth gives in the "Prospectus to *The Recluse*": one human heart, and that the poet's, is a richer fund of tragic and ennobling human truth than all the adventures of epic or legendary heroes. But Brontë's "*one* human heart" is more particular than the Wordsworthian Mind of Man. It is the locus of the distinctive individual feelings this poem strives to record and value. The "earth that wakes *one* human heart to feeling" exalts the clay or dust that is the origin and end of a single human life.

The authorship of "Often rebuked, yet always back returning" has been disputed, in part because it is the only poem in the 1850 volume for which no manuscript has ever been known and the only one of the seventeen printed there not taken from one of Emily Brontë's two transcript notebooks. C. W. Hatfield, the best of Emily Brontë's editors, printed it in an appendix to his edition of her poems, believing that it sounded more like Charlotte Brontë and seemed to express her thoughts about her sister rather than Emily Brontë's own thoughts. In fact, the poem expresses thoughts about herself that Charlotte Brontë was also expressing in her letters, especially one to W. S. Williams, her publisher's reader, the previous year: "No matter—whether known or unknown—misjudged or the contrary—I am resolved not to write otherwise. I shall bend as my powers tend," she had written rhymingly.[44] Edward Chitham, the editor of Anne Brontë's poems and the co-editor of the forthcoming Oxford English Texts edition of Emily Brontë's poems, has argued for Emily Brontë's authorship on the grounds that the "general content of the poem is quite characteristic of Emily in certain ways" and that some of its language resembles that of other poems written by her. The suggestion that the "general content" of the poem is "characteristic of Emily in certain ways" is puzzling, since the only poem in which Emily Brontë can be said to engage in self-vindication is "No coward soul is mine." The idea that some of the poem's language resembles that of Emily Brontë's other poems cannot be substantiated: key words and phrases in the poem do not connect it to other poems by Emily Brontë. On balance, resemblances between it and other poems written by Emily Brontë—and the resemblances are not striking—may be the product of Charlotte Brontë's not incompetent attempt to write a poem that Emily Brontë might have written.[45]

What is indisputable is that this poem expresses Charlotte Brontë's deepest feelings about the artist's relation to her audience and the sources of her spiritual and imaginative power. It also makes a case for the portrait of Emily Brontë that emerges from the "Biographical Notice": "Her temper was magnanimous, but warm and sudden; her spirit altogether unbending." The sense of "altogether unbending" is in keeping with the discriminating relation of adverbs in the poem's first line: "Often rebuked, but always back returning. . . ." The strongest argument in favor of Emily Brontë's having written "Often rebuked" is the obvious one that Charlotte Brontë would not have represented her own work as her sister's. But this argument is vitiated by her extensive revisions of the other poems in the volume (she revised nearly a fifth of the lines) and undermined by her deep conviction that it was her duty to act as her sister's "interpreter."[46]

Moved to argue, in the "Biographical Notice," that Emily Brontë "failed to defend her most manifest rights" and that her will "generally opposed her interest," Charlotte Brontë's decision to defend those rights and act in that interest was inevitably complicated. The overall defending strategy of the 1850 volume anticipates Gaskell's in the *Life*: the vindication of Ellis Bell, the author, is made to depend on the vindication of Emily Brontë, the woman. Yet Charlotte Brontë continually resisted this pattern in defending herself, most eloquently in her correspondence with G. H. Lewes, who had reviewed *Shirley* for the *Edinburgh Review*. "Now in this review of 'Shirley,'" Gaskell writes, "the headings of the first two pages ran thus: 'Mental Equality of the Sexes?' 'Female Literature,' and through the whole article the fact of the author's sex is never forgotten."[47] Lewes's review is long and impossible to summarize fairly, for Brontë's quarrel with it is a quarrel with its treatment of the writer's sex and its use of her sex, at every point, to criticize the novel's lack of humor, the coarseness of its style, the sordidness of its heroes, and the falseness of its heroines. Its last paragraph suggests the tone of the review as a whole as well as the premises from which it proceeds:

> Our closing word shall be one of exhortation. Schiller, writing to Goethe about Madame de Stael's *Corinne* [1807] says, 'This person wants every thing that is graceful in a woman; and, nevertheless, the faults of her book are altogether womanly faults. She steps out of her sex—without elevating her-

self above it.' This brief and pregnant criticism is quite as applicable to Currer Bell: for she, too, has genius enough to create a great name for herself; and if we seem to have insisted too gravely on her faults, it is only because we are ourselves sufficiently her admirers to be most desirous to see her remove these blemishes from her writings, and take the rank within her reach. She has extraordinary power—but let her remember that '*on tombe du côté où l'on penche!*'[48]

In a letter to W. S. Williams, Brontë characterized the review as "brutal and savage" and said that it made her feel "cold and sick."[49] At around the same time, she sent Lewes a brief, proverbial message: "I can be on my guard against my enemies, but God deliver me from my friends!" This is apt in indicating not only the strength of her response to the review but her sense of her relation to Lewes. Her previous correspondence with him had given him the character of a friend, she did not doubt that he had written his review in that character, and she knew that she was more defenseless because of the friendship. Lewes was surprised by Brontë's response; probably he thought that she was being defensive in not admitting her faults. "Seeing that she was unreasonable because angry," he wrote Gaskell, "I wrote to remonstrate with her on quarreling with the severity or frankness of a review, which certainly was dictated by real admiration and real friendship; even under its objections the friend's voice could be heard."[50]

Brontë's letter to Lewes justifying her response to the review, is worth quoting in full, for it shows anger's compatibility with reason. Gaskell agreed with Lewes that "the tone" of Brontë's letter was "cavalier," but it is the right tone for a courageous and intelligent defense of what Brontë clearly saw as her own "most manifest rights":

MY DEAR SIR,—I will tell you why I was so hurt by that review in the 'Edinburgh'—not because its criticism was keen or its blame sometimes severe; not because its praise was stinted (for, indeed, I think you give me quite as much praise as I deserve), but because after I had said earnestly that I wished critics would judge me as an *author*, not as a woman, you so roughly—I even thought so cruelly—handled the question of sex. I dare say you meant no harm, and perhaps you will not now be able to understand why I was so grieved at what you will probably deem such a trifle; but grieved I was, and indignant too.

There was a passage or two which you did quite wrong to write.

However, I will not bear malice against you for it; I know what your nature is: it is not a bad or unkind one, though you would often jar terribly on some feelings with whose recoil and quiver you could not possibly sympathise. I imagine you are both enthusiastic and implacable, as you are at once sagacious and careless; you know much and discover much, but you are in such a hurry to tell it all you never give yourself time to think how your reckless eloquence may affect others; and, what is more, if you knew how it did affect them, you would not much care.

However, I shake hands with you: you have excellent points; you can be generous. I still feel angry, and think I do well to be angry; but it is the anger one experiences for rough play rather than for foul play.—I am yours, with a certain respect, and more chagrin,

CURRER BELL

The letter is honest in expressing Brontë's feelings about the review and her thoughts about Lewes, and her resentment of the review doesn't betray her into defensiveness. She rebukes Lewes—"There was a passage or two which you did quite wrong to write"—but withholds a reproach, for Lewes is incapable of understanding her feelings or, even if he could be made to understand them, incapable of caring about them. The last paragraph of the letter holds resistance and accommodation in eloquent balance. Her shaking hands with Lewes is a compliment to him, not only an acknowledgment of his own "excellent points" but an emulation of the particular excellence she mentions, his generosity. But her gesture also insists on her sense of herself as an author, not a woman. With a handshake, she confirms her role as a combatant who claims an equal fellowship with her male critic. At the same time, she remains angry, even in fellowship, and does not resist the nice distinction between simply feeling angry and thinking, as she does in this case, that the anger is to her credit. The salutation not only balances her respect for Lewes against her chagrin but makes good use of the ambiguity of "a certain respect." "I am yours, with a settled and dependable respect," or "I am yours, with a positive, yet restricted degree of respect," or, with a humor characteristically grim and precise, "I am yours, with a respect that it is neither polite nor necessary to define very precisely" (as in "a certain age," or "a certain weight").

Brontë's "respect" is notably different from the "admiration" that Lewes accords her, both in his letter and in the review, for an admirer is not only someone who esteems someone or something but also, according to Johnson's *Dictionary*, "in common speech, a lover." In a review of a novel by a woman writer, the word signals the special combination of wonder, chivalry, and condescension that has often characterized the male critic's attention to the woman writer. The closing thought of Lewes's review—that Brontë "steps out of her sex—without elevating herself above it"—formulates what Mary Ellmann has described as a significant difference between the moral judgments that operate in our thinking about women as opposed to our thinking about men. "Men are not men without effort," Ellmann writes, "and their ideal condition is attained by their *becoming*, but (with luck) remaining, simply men." Women, on the other hand, "unfortunately *are* women," and "their ideal condition is attained by rising above themselves.[51]

Lewes would have Brontë "take the rank within her reach." The exhortation is vague, but what he thinks that rank is may be guessed from his remarks, earlier in the review, about Jane Austen, a writer he admired even more than he admired Charlotte Brontë. Austen is Lewes' example of a woman writer whose art is at once "perfect" and perfectly womanly:

> Her range, to be sure, is limited; but her art is perfect. She does not touch those profounder and more impassioned chords which vibrate to the heart's core—never ascends to its grand or heroic movements, nor descends to its deeper throes and agonies; but in all she attempts she is uniformly and completely successful.

Brontë could only have responded cavalierly to an art that achieves its perfection by limiting its range, and the difficulty with Lewes's "brief and pregnant criticism" of Currer Bell is that he both recognizes her genius and rebukes her for it. What it means for a woman writer not to step out of her sex may be clearest in Lewes' discussion of humor:

> Compare Miss Austen, Miss Ferriar, and Miss Edgeworth, with the lusty mirth and riotous humour of Shakespeare, Rabelais, Butler, Swift, Fielding, Smollett, or Dickens and Thackeray. It is like comparing a quiet smile with the 'inextinguishable laughter' of the Homeric gods!

Lewes's logic here is exactly that of the six-year-old Branwell Brontë, who, asked what was the best way of knowing the difference between the intellects of men and women, answered, "By considering the difference between them as to their bodies." What is the best way of knowing the difference between the humor of women and the humor of men? By considering the difference between a woman's "quiet smile" and the "inextinguishable laughter of the Homeric gods."

Yet Lewes deserves credit for his final sentence. In the review, he had remonstrated against Brontë's pretentious use of French words and phrases in *Shirley*:

A French word or two may be introduced now and then on account of some peculiar fitness, but Currer Bell's use of the language is little better than that of the 'fashionable' novelists. To speak of a grandmother as '*une grand'-mere*,' and of treacle as '*melasse*,' or of a young lady being angry as '*courroucée*,' gives an air of affectation to the style strangely at variance with the frankness of its general tone.

His own French proverb—"*on tombe du côté où l'on penche*"—not only resists translation into English but remains resolutely ambiguous, no less a recognition, then, of Brontë's genius than a criticism of her faults. In French, one can "*tomber bien*" or "*tomber mal*." In English, one might fall on the side where one leans or arrive by taking one's own direction. "*On tombe du côté où l'on penche*." Or, "I shall bend as my powers tend," as Brontë put it. The author who had already, at age ten, written her first book, a present for her youngest sister Anne, and whose question from her father was appropriately a question about the best books, wrote her own best books under the influence of what the poet Stevie Smith calls "anger's freeing power." "I still feel angry, and think I do well to be angry." Often rebuked, Charlotte Brontë was always moved to defend herself and to defend herself against any abrogation of her rights, however friendly its intent.

*   *   *

Brontë's striking a physical attitude in her letter to Lewes—her offering to shake hands with him as a mark of fellowship—is characteristic of her. The body—its organs, senses, and appendages—is intimately and immediately involved in negotiating all Brontë's contacts with the external world. At once the object of affectionate attention and insult and the agency for self-extension and self-defense in the novels, the body is the place where Brontë reveals and enacts her particular relation to the social world. In her earlier and better known professional correspondence with Lewes, Brontë had defended herself against his urgings to emulate Austen, and in a related exchange with W. S. Williams, she opposed her own relation to the body to Austen's:

> Her business is not half so much with the human heart as with the human eyes, mouth, hands and feet; what sees keenly, speaks aptly, moves flexibly, it suits her to study, but what throbs fast and full, though hidden, what the blood rushes through, what is the unseen seat of Life and the sentient target of death—*this* Miss Austen ignores; she no more, with her mind's eye, be-

holds the heart of her race than each man, with bodily vision sees the heart in his heaving breast. Jane Austen was a complete and most sensible lady, but a very incomplete, and rather insensible (*not senseless*) woman, if this is heresy—I cannot help it.[52]

Read figuratively, this criticism raises no interpretive difficulties. Brontë clearly stakes her claim to the new subject matter that she saw herself as mining for fiction. The oppositions between "a complete and most sensible lady" and "a very incomplete, and rather insensible (*not senseless*) woman" and between surface (eyes, mouth, hands, and feet) and depth (the human heart) reveal the gap between a represented social and an unrepresented passional life and anticipate D. H. Lawrence's later attack on the "stable ego" as the basis for the old mode of characterization.

Read with some real attention to the figures Brontë has chosen, however, the passage is differently revealing. Her distinction between "bodily vision" and the "mind's eye," which should be capable of deeper beholdings, can be compared to Johnson's preference for Richardson over Fielding, a preference also grounded in the relation of surface to depth:

> It always appeared to me that he estimated the compositions of Richardson too highly, and that he had an unreasonable prejudice against Fielding. In comparing those two writers, he used this expression: "that there was as great a difference between them as between a man who knew how a watch was made, and a man who could tell the hour by looking on the dial-plate." This was a short and figurative state of his distinction between drawing characters of nature and characters only of manners.[53]

If Roland Barthes is right that "imagery, delicacy, vocabulary spring from the body and the past of the writer and gradually become the very reflexes of his art,"[54] Johnson's choice of a mechanical device for telling time and Brontë's choice of the human body are in themselves revealing. But Brontë's imagery has an additional effect that Johnson's doesn't: it not only permits but requires a literal reading.

Brontë's reading of Austen is penetrating, for she notices what is still underdescribed in Austen's novels, the very real presence in them of human eyes, mouths, hands, and feet. It is Elizabeth Bennett's ankles as well as her eyes that excite Darcy's admiration, especially in the scene in which the muddied hem of her dress draws his view along with the contempt of Bingley's sisters. But the scene in which Sir William Lucas takes her hand and attempts to place it in Darcy's, forcing her to declare herself unwilling to dance, and the one in which Emma Woodhouse gives her hand to Knightley, acknowledging him, for the first time, as a suitable partner, are more than admirably effective in carrying on the business of the human heart: they sound its beat.

Brontë's percipience in impercipience about Austen's art is related to the misleading information she conveys about her own. How is it that Charlotte Brontë studies "what throbs fast and full, though hidden, what the blood rushes through, what is the unseen seat of Life and the sentient target of death"? As Brontë's opposition of Austen's determined (and lady-like) good sense to her own more acute sensibility already suggests, her novels study the "recoil and quiver" of the feelings that animate the body—in anger and indignation as well as love. "Most of our emotions," Darwin writes, "are so closely connected with their expression that they hardly exist if the body remains passive—the nature of the expression depending in chief part on the nature of the actions which have been habitually performed under this particular state of mind."[55] William James extends this, arguing in *The Principles of Psychology* not only that "our whole cubic capacity is sensibly alive; and each morsel of it contributes its pulsations of feeling, dim or sharp, pleasant, painful, or dubious to that sense of personality that every one of us unfailingly carries with him" but that the "moods, affections, and passions" are "in very truth constituted by, and made up of, those bodily changes which we ordinarily call their expression or consequence."[56]

Mary Douglas asserts that "there can be no natural way of considering the body that does not involve at the same time a social dimension." According to Douglas, the "social body constrains the way the physical body is perceived" and "the physical experience of the body" in turn "sustains a particular view of society."[57] My emphasis on a different kind of bodily experience in each novel identifies the specific social constraints of that novel and the kinds of self-extensions and self-defenses at issue in it. My point is not that *Jane Eyre*, for example, contains no hands, stomachs, or voices, or that the other novels ignore the eye that figures so prominently in *Jane Eyre*, but that the hands, the eye, the stomach, and the voice are differently and emphatically present to us in each novel as the bodily site of defenses specific to each novel.

The chapters that follow study what Douglas calls the "continual exchange of meanings between the two kinds of bodily experience so that each reinforces the categories of the other." In the social world of *The Professor*, Brontë's first attempt at a novel for publication and her only novel with a male protagonist, hands figure so largely because the most important social relations the novel explores are contractual and contactual. Hands are instrumental to the hero-narrator's frustrated agency as man and master: they are extended and grasped in aid, shaken to confirm friendly or business connections, raised in anger and enmity, and, often, repulsed or ignored. Hands are moreover essential to work and the main channel for "what throbs fast and full, though hidden" in *The Professor's* most important working relation, that of master and pupil. Brontë's representation of the hand as the locus of both punishing and generous impulses is, I argue in Chapter Two, essential to this novel's analysis of vindictiveness and vindication as twin poles of its hero's struggle for mastery.

Brontë's having begun *Jane Eyre* while her father was undergoing an operation for cataracts, an operation she was compelled to watch, helps explain the prominence of the eye in her second novel, but not the powerful move according to which *Jane Eyre* conceives of the threat to the "eye" as a threat to the "I." Chapter Three reads *Jane Eyre* as Brontë's defense of vision, her own as well as her heroine's. I focus on the exchange of meanings between the novel's generally well understood social and religious vision and the ordinary bodily experience of seeing, as well as being seen by or not seen by, and seeing for others. I argue that Brontë's defense of her heroine's vision in *Jane Eyre* requires Fairfax Rochester's blinding, and I oppose the usual reading of the novel that subordinates the literal value of this event to its metaphorical or symbolic value as castration or unmanning.

Although hunger figures as an event in *Jane Eyre*, it is the central fact and metaphor in *Shirley*, where Brontë explores it as a physical, psychological, social, and political experience. As an organ, the stomach has almost as strong a claim to being "the unseen seat of Life and the sentient target of death" as the heart itself. Like the eye and the hand, it may be active or passive but cannot be impassive in its mediation of vital exchanges between the body and the world. In both *Jane Eyre* and *Shirley*, I argue, a happy ending for the heroine signals not just a fault in each novel's design but a false pretense: defensive conduct is no longer required because the conventional social judgments her heroines have resisted are ones to which they can, after all, accommodate themselves.

Chapter Five explores the idea that *Villette*, written after Brontë had reread and edited *Wuthering Heights* for the 1850 volume, both defends *Wuthering Heights* and defends against it. But in *Villette*, as I argue in Chapter Six, Brontë's signal achievement is to mark the absolute prominence of the voice as the organ of the narrative. A new emphasis on the power that comes with control of the voice, in speech, in silence, and, differently, in writing, is related to this novel's defense of the right to speech and its defense against powerful threats embodied not only in injunctions against speech but in incitements to it, in specific the confessional and the medical and academic examination. The voice is less corporeal than the hands, the eye, or the stomach, but words in *Villette* are remarkably corporeal. They are frequently represented as inked images on paper, school exercises that can be torn in pieces or offered as evidence of plagiarism, and letters that can be enclosed in caskets, thrown like missiles, or sealed in bottles and buried like corpses.

Deprived of any occasion to use her voice during the long vacation, Lucy undergoes a kind of dissolution; she is saved only by the narrative efforts she makes, first in the privacy of the priest's confessional and later in her reports about herself to Dr. John. Accused of having stolen Paul's voice, Lucy is vindicated when she regains her own, although she can only write, not speak, before the two men who present themselves as her examiners. These events begin to suggest *Villette*'s special place among Brontë's novels, for it is not only her last completed work of fiction but the fiction in which she most courageously confronts the divisive impulses toward accommodation and resistance in her life and art. In *Villette*, Brontë undertakes a thorough analysis of her heroine's internal and external anxieties. Like the Vashti, this heroine does not resent her grief but embodies it; by locating what hurts in the actual social world of the novel, she fully authorizes her own efforts to grapple with it.

In my reading of each novel, my aim is to define the kind of attacks to which it responds as well as the form and nature of that response, and to account for the special quality of Brontë's work that derives from her representation of acts of self-defense as defensible, not merely defensive in the modern sense of the word. This being the case, it has seemed appropriate to consider the novels in the order in which they were written and relevant that Charlotte Brontë both shared the sensitivity of other canonical women writers like Virginia Woolf and George Eliot to criticism of their work and differed from them in her avid pursuit of criticism and in the record she left, in her letters, her prefaces, and her novels, of her responses to it. This reading of Brontë's novels is developmental to the extent that it argues, implicitly, that the author's defensive project enlarged in scope and imaginative power during her brief career as a novelist. Yeats's idea that we make rhetoric out of the quarrel with others but poetry out of the quarrel with ourselves suggests why it is that *Villette*, Brontë's supreme achievement of an art of self-vindication, requires neither preface nor dedication.

2. The Master's Hand: Vindictiveness and Vindication in *The Professor*

Self-vindication is immediately an issue in Brontë's first novel. She wrote the preface published with *The Professor* after the publication of *Shirley*, when she hoped Smith, Elder would agree to bring *The Professor* out. It begins with the author's hand and the pen that it wields, "worn down a good deal in a practice of some years. . . . I had not indeed published anything before I commenced 'The Professor'—but in many a crude effort destroyed almost as soon as composed I had got over any such taste as I might once have had for the ornamented and redundant in composition— and had come to prefer what was plain and homely." The preface tells the story of *The Professor*'s rejection because publishers "would have liked something more imaginative and poetical," and this vindication of Brontë's authority as novelist is related to Brontë's vindication of her hero:

> I said to myself that my hero should work his way through life as I had seen real living men work theirs—that he should never get a shilling he had not earned—that no sudden turns should lift him in a moment to wealth and high station—that whatever small competency he might gain should be won by the sweat of his brow—that before he could find so much as an arbour to sit down in—he should master at least half the ascent of the hill of Diffi- culty—that he should not even marry a beautiful nor a rich wife, nor a lady of rank—As Adam's Son he should share Adam's doom—Labour through- out life and a mixed and moderate cup of enjoyment. (3–4)

The preface is deceptively silent about the novel's central romance, the relation of master and pupil, and about Frances Henri, the pupil who becomes William Crimsworth's wife. She is not merely the object of her master's desire; her "ascent of the hill of Difficulty" mirrors his, and the desire that flashes between them is the sign of their shared ambition to rise in a hostile world.

In this chapter, I argue that *The Professor*'s ample experience of rejection and what almost all readers have recognized as its unattractiveness have less to do with the mortification of romance and sensibility that

Brontë herself cites in her preface than with its hero's inability to break the circuit of violence that makes him perpetually both its victim and its agent.[1] For despite Crimsworth's mastery of the whole of his ascent, Frances Henri's mirroring climb, and the presence of a young scion named Victor in the Crimsworth arbor, vindictiveness shadows victory and vindication in *The Professor*. The plot of Brontë's preface to the novel resembles the plot of the novel itself. In *The Professor*, the vindictive acts of others inspire acts of self-vindication that are themselves vindictive.[2]

Issues of defense and defensiveness in *The Professor* are deflected by issues of mastery, and the manuscript of the novel shows that its original title was *The Master*. It is concerned with Crimsworth's profession mainly in relation to his struggle for mastery of himself and others, and Brontë represents the struggle for self-mastery as a defensive and defensible response to being mastered by others. As early as the novel's first chapter, Brontë establishes a wide range of reference for the word "master"; it delimits the realm in which men control property, persons, commercial enterprises, and hired hands. Edward, Crimsworth's older brother, is master of a mansion, a servant, and a mill as well as master of the brother who becomes his second clerk. "I may as well remind you, at the very outset of our connection," he tells Crimsworth, "that 'no man can serve two masters'" (I, II). This allusion to Bunyan's hero's choice between God and Mammon glances ironically at Edward's mammonism and the unavailability of an alternative in the form of hearty assistance to Crimsworth from his aristocratic uncles. But this irony is instrumental to a larger one: Crimsworth's identity as himself the master is incompatible with his dependence on any other. While Christian attributes his self-mastery and his repudiation of an oppressive master to his allegiance to the Lord of the hill, Crimsworth's self-mastery is both means and end. His achievement adapts the soteriology of *The Pilgrim's Progress* to a middle-class nineteenth-century world in which the goal is not the heavenly city but an earthly garden where the reward for self-sufficiency is a competency.[3]

Although Brontë has regularly been identified with Frances Henri, it is *The Professor*'s male protagonist who does double duty as the agent of the woman writer who experiences her own agency as frustrated. Brontë's difficulties in making literature her profession are inscribed in the text as well as the preface of her first novel. In a letter to M. Héger, her beloved Belgian master, in which Brontë addresses her choice of profession, the terms "master" and "professor" appear in a proximity that reveals their very different connotations for her:

> This weakness of sight is a terrible hindrance to me. Otherwise do you know what I should do, Monsieur?—I should write a book, and I should dedicate it to my literature-master—to the only master I ever had—to you, Monsieur. I have often told you in French how much I respect you—how much I am indebted to your goodness, to your advice; I should like to say it in English. But that cannot be—it is not to be thought of. The career of letters is closed to me—only that of teaching is open. It does not offer the same attractions; never mind, I shall enter it, and if I do not go far it will not be from want of industry. You too, Monsieur—you wished to be a barrister—destiny or Providence made you a professor; you are happy in spite of it.[4]

Brontë's knowledge of Héger's professional disappointment contributes to her determination to face her own as she apparently renounces the profession of literature for a career in teaching. But her ambition to be an author—an ambition that twice surfaces as she writes of dedicating a book to Héger and of writing to and of him in English—is just as important as her devotion in this identification of him as "the only master I ever had." To acknowledge his mastery is paradoxically to insist on her own.

In the novel, the issue of literary ambition surfaces in Frances Henri's conflict with Mdlle. Reuter, whose living prototype is Mme. Héger, an obstacle to Brontë's devotion, but whose words are borrowed from Robert Southey, an obstacle to Brontë's ambition. Southey's letter to Brontë, written in 1837 after she had sent him a sample of her poetry and asked for his opinion, is often quoted as evidence of the prejudices she confronted as a woman writer. It begins with some approval of her poems, cautions against high ambitions for them, and then qualifies this advice with specific reference to women:

> I, who have made literature my profession, and devoted my life to it, and have never for a moment repented the deliberate choice, think myself, nevertheless, bound in duty to caution every young man who applies as an aspirant to me for encouragement and advice against taking so perilous a course. You will say that a woman has no need of such a caution; there can be no peril in it for her. In a certain sense this is true; but there is a danger of which I would, with all kindness and all earnestness, warn you. The day dreams in which you habitually indulge are likely to induce a distempered state of mind; and in proportion as all the ordinary uses of the world seem to you flat and unprofitable, you will be unfitted for them without becoming fitted for anything else. Literature cannot be the business of a woman's life, and it ought not to be. The more she is engaged in her proper duties, the less leisure will she have for it, even as an accomplishment and a recreation.[5]

In a letter to Caroline Bowles, Southey speaks of having "sent a dose of cooling admonition to the poor girl whose flighty letter reached me at

Buckland." After mentioning Wordsworth's disgust at a letter from Branwell, which had reached him at about the same time, he writes complacently: "I think well of the sister from her second letter, and probably she will think kindly of me as long as she lives."

Southey was partly right, for Brontë not only marked the cover of his letter to her with the inscription "Southey's advice to be kept for ever" but told Gaskell, years later when a letter from Cuthbert Southey arrived asking permission to print her letter in his father's *Life*, that "Mr. Southey's letter was kind and admirable; a little stringent, but it did me good."[6] Nevertheless, by attributing the laureate's words to Mdlle. Reuter, whose apparent concern for Frances Henri only thinly disguises her own jealousy and ambition, Brontë reveals a more combative response to Southey's advice:

> it appears to me that ambition, *literary* ambition especially, is not a feeling to be cherished in the mind of a woman; would not Mdlle. Henri be much safer and happier if taught to believe that in the quiet discharge of social duties consists her real vocation, than if stimulated to aspire after applause and publicity? (18, 150–51)

Brontë promised Southey, as she later promised M. Héger, she would "never more feel ambitious to see [her] name in print; if the wish should rise, I'll look at Southey's letter, and suppress it."[7] These words recall Wordsworth's at the end of "Resolution and Independence," but despite her resolves, Brontë continued to defend "the dream of creations whose reality I shall never behold"[8] and to record those dreams in writing.

The animus of the preface to *The Professor*, written by the established author of *Jane Eyre* and *Shirley*, has its main source in Brontë's knowledge that only its publication would have vindicated her agency as a writer by making literature her profession rather than the dangerous diversion Southey had warned her against. This helps to explain why the preface Brontë wrote for the novel feels vindictive as well as self-vindicating, especially in its treatment of Crimsworth, whose cup of enjoyment it so grudgingly rations. Etymologically, "vindicate" and "vindictive" stand interestingly to each other. "Vindicate" has its root in the Latin "vindicare," which means both to liberate and to avenge or punish. The Latin "vindicta," which is the root of "vindictive," literally refers to the rod with which the praetor touched the slave who was to be freed and can mean deliverance from something as well as vengeance or punishment. Although acts of vindication may be undertaken without punitiveness, our word "vindictive" is properly applied only to punitive actions. But vindication, and especially self-vindication, is as easily charged with vindictiveness as self-defense is with defensiveness. *The Professor* is Brontë's fullest account of how this happens.

*   *   *

The hand, the appendage that is explicitly instrumental to the writer's agency in the preface to *The Professor*, is also instrumental to all of the novel's important relations. It figures so largely in the first six chapters that it confirms their organic relation to the rest of the novel, despite Brontë's own thoughts about a revision that would eliminate them. In an undated manuscript draft of a preface for a revised version of the novel, she offers a "brief summary" of these chapters that omits Crimsworth's "introduction" to his story, the letter he writes to an old friend, and alters that story by making Crimsworth Edward's half-brother, the son of their father's second wife.[9] These changes are consistent with the judgment of *The Professor* she shared with W. S. Williams when, after the success of *Jane Eyre*, she first suggested that Smith, Elder publish a revised version of *The Professor*:

> A few days since I looked over 'The Professor.' I found its beginning very feeble, the whole narrative deficient in incident and in general attractiveness. Yet the middle and latter portion of the work, all that relates to Brussels, the Belgian school, etc., is as good as I can write: it contains more pith, more substance, more reality, in my judgment, than much of 'Jane Eyre.'[10]

Kathleen Tillotson agrees with Brontë about the feebleness of *The Professor*'s beginning: "The relation between the Crimsworth brothers raises interest but leads nowhere, is dropped after seven chapters, and never recurs; it is a vestigial appendix from the rivalries of Angrian characters."[11] A "vestigial appendix": a supplement to the novel that recalls some earlier stage of its development, or an organic element that no longer performs any useful function. The metaphor is at once attentive and inattentive to *The Professor*'s organic life.

Crimsworth's frustrated efforts to establish his agency as man and master begin with his visit to his vindictive older brother Edward, whose assistance he seeks in becoming a tradesman. Preparing to meet this relation he hasn't seen since childhood, Crimsworth analyzes his feelings:

> . . . I anticipated no overflowings of fraternal tenderness—Edward's letters had always been such as to prevent the engendering or harbouring of delusions of this sort. Still, as I sat awaiting his arrival—I felt eager—very eager—I

cannot tell why; my hand, so utterly a stranger to the grasp of a kindred hand, clenched itself to repress the tremor with which impatience would fain have shaken it. (1, 10)

The hand that clenches itself for lack of a kind hand to hold and is shaken only by impatience establishes Crimsworth's condition as an outcast. By personifying the hand as "a stranger to the grasp of a kindred hand," Brontë draws attention to its action of repression or self-clenching; the hand is Crimsworth's, but it is also itself a center of agency and feeling. Crimsworth's earlier account of the alienation from his wealthy, aristocratic uncles that has driven him to seek Edward's aid also focused on kindred hands. The first chapter of the novel explains his declaration of independence in two ways. First, he says he has rejected their offer of a living in the Church because he is ill-suited to being a clergyman and their hope that he will marry one of his cousins because "not an accomplishment, not a charm of theirs, touches a chord in my bosom" (1, 6). Then he reveals that his motives are the self-vindicating ones engendered in vindictive exchanges, especially those within the family:

> At first, while still in boyhood, I could not understand why, as I had no parents, I should not be indebted to my uncles Tynedale and Seacombe for my eduction—but as I grew up, and heard by degrees of the persevering hostility, the hatred till death evinced by them against my father—of the sufferings of my mother—of all the wrongs, in short, of our house—then did I conceive shame of the dependence in which I lived, and form a resolution no more to take bread from hands, which had refused to minister to the necessities of my dying mother. (1, 8)

Hands that can be extended in kindness can also be withheld in "persevering hostility" or "hatred till death." Although Crimsworth's only practical revenge is to reject his uncles' plans for him, he continues to conceive of his achievement in some relation to this background of social injury. Much later, when Hunsden taunts him with the remark that he was "born with a wooden spoon in [his] mouth," Crimsworth's reply recalls his "resolution no more to take bread from the hands" of his uncles: "I believe you; and I mean to make my wooden spoon do the work of some people's silver ladles—grasped firmly, and handled nimbly, even a wooden spoon will shovel up broth" (22, 206–207). This seems a bold defense of the determination and skill of those who provide for themselves, but the phrase "shovel up broth" betrays the social prejudices Crimsworth shares with his aristocratic uncles.

Crimsworth's family background appears in a letter (Crimsworth's hand, once again) to an old friend, a letter that is unread because the friend is already on his way to a government appointment in one of the colonies. The letter is another powerful image of the self-closed circuit of communication, one that refigures the hand that clenches itself or shovels its own broth when it cannot grasp a kindred hand and will accept no help from kindred hands that are less than kind. By soliciting the attention of a reader who is already unavailable, the unread letter anticipates and may have helped to create Brontë's own first readers, the six publishers who received the manuscript of *The Professor* yet gave no sign of having read it. In Gaskell's phrase, the manuscript came "back upon her hands."[12]

The frustrated agency of Crimsworth's hand in the opening chapters, like the frustrated agency of his creator's in writing an unpublishable novel, calls attention to the long-standing connection between the contactual and the contractual. With our hands, we confirm business arrangements. In our signatures and more largely in our letters, our hands seal our commitments and our feelings. Shaking hands is one of *The Professor's* most important gestures, and Crimsworth twice comments that the gesture is less customary and so more significant for foreigners. When Mdlle. Reuter clasps his extended hand at their first interview, he prides himself on having brought her to allow an intimacy, and after discovering her engagement to Pelet, he shows his own pride by not taking the hand she extends to him. Shaking or not shaking hands with a compatriot also conveys important information: thus, Hunsden's shaking hands with Crimsworth for the first time when he hears that Crimsworth is about to marry beneath himself conveys his sympathy and pity. Hands may be given as well as taken, as in dancing or marriage, and the relation between these two engagements is probably always implicit and regularly explicit. This accounts for the delicate weight of the moment when Emma takes Knightley's hand at the ball at the Crown and for the oppressive weight of Crimsworth's exclusion from the dancing at the ball at Crimsworth Hall, where he watches Hunsden, who "applied for the hand of the fine girl, and led her off triumphant." Brontë gave Frances Henri a "little hand" with "small, taper fingers," like her own, and the variety of ways in which Crimsworth imagines it helps to focus their points of connection, first as master and pupil and later as husband and wife. He dreams of shutting the coins she has paid him for his lessons in that hand, loves the "movement with which she confided her hand to my hand," and, when he proposes marriage, has to be told that he is holding her right hand "in a somewhat ruthless grasp."

Hands are also instrumental to work and violence. When Crimsworth becomes his brother's clerk, he earns his living with his hands, "scraping with a pen on paper, just like an automaton." So Hunsden taunts him. When he leaves Edward's employment he mocks Hunsden's suggestion that he turn for support to his noble uncles: "How can hands stained with the ink of a counting-house, soiled with the grease of a wool-warehouse, ever again be permitted to come into contact with aristocratic palms?" (6, 51). He decides to become a tradesman because he is unwilling to put himself in his uncles' hands, and his becoming a tradesman makes him untouchable. In their final confrontation, Edward tries to horsewhip Crimsworth after accusing him of publicly complaining about "the treatment you receive at my hands. You have gone and told it far and near that I give you low wages and knock you about like a dog" (5, 48). When Crimsworth breaks Edward's gig-whip and threatens to have him up before the magistrate, Edward "seemed to bethink himself that after all, his money gave him sufficient superiority over a beggar like me, and that he had in his hands a surer and more dignified mode of revenge than the somewhat hazardous one of personal chastisement" (5, 45). What he has "in his hands" is the master's capacity to deprive his workers of their means of support. Crimsworth's last act before leaving Edward's counting-house is the cool one of drawing on his gloves, a gesture that sustains his claim to be his brother's social equal as well as his superior in temper and manners.

*   *   *

Crimsworth's struggle against the mastery of his older brother has a sexual as well as a social meaning, for the man who can be mastered risks his male identity as well as his social place. Brontë explores the frustration of her hero's male agency by means of a succession of triangles that configure Crimsworth's conflict with Edward, as later with other masterly men, as a competition for mastery of a woman—Edward's wife, the ladies who frequent Crimsworth Hall, and the Crimsworths' mother. A mother is always connected to her son's establishment of his male identity, both as the first object of his desire and as an element of the primary identity that precedes his separation from her. The first principle is essential to Freud's analysis of early male development; Nancy Chodorow powerfully examines the second. She argues that "because of a primary oneness and identification with his mother, a primary femaleness, a boy's and a man's core gender identity itself—the seemingly unproblematic cognitive sense of being male—is an issue. A boy must learn his gender identity as being not-female, or not-mother."[13]

The Crimsworths' mother survives only in the portrait of her as a desirable, young woman, and this image can be possessed, as the living mother cannot be. But since it can be possessed by only one brother at any one time, possession comes to signify one brother's mastery of the other. In this version of the son's Oedipal relation to his mother, the father hardly exists. In Edward's home, the mother's portrait "had the benefit of a full beam from the softly shaded lamp," while the father's portrait, mentioned only this once, is "in the shade" (1, 14). First hung over the mantelpiece in Edward's dining room, the mother's portrait is bought by Hunsden in a bankruptcy sale of Edward's possessions and then insultingly bestowed upon William. Crimsworth's neglect of his mother's portrait later (he shoves it under his bed and does not mention it again) is explained partly by Hunsden's humiliation of him; partly by Edward's financial failure, which has the same meaning as possession of the portrait, thereby making it redundant as a signifier; and partly by Crimsworth's success in transferring his affection from his mother to Frances Henri. As if to confirm this aspect of a healthy Oedipal development, Frances Henri is often pictured in Crimsworth's mother's pose, sitting quietly as if in a portrait, with her head on her hand in a "thinking attitude" she can retain "a long time without change" (19, 167–68).

Crimsworth contrasts his own image with Edward's, as he sees both reflected in the mirror that hangs over Edward's mantelpiece, as if they too were portraits:

> As an animal, Edward excelled me far—should he prove as paramount in mind as in person I must be a slave—for I must expect from him no lion-like generosity to one weaker than himself; his cold, avaricious eye, his stern, forbidding manner told me he would not spare. Had I then force of mind to cope with him? I did not know—I had never been tried. (2, 16)

Edward establishes his masculinity not only by possessing the mother's portrait but by being physically different from her. Later Crimsworth marks his own resemblance to his mother, who has "bequeathed to me much of her features and countenance—her forehead, her eyes, her complexion" (3, 24), and Hunsden confirms the connection in class terms: the mother was thought to have married beneath herself by marrying a tradesman and, while Edward is a tradesman by choice, Crimsworth is one only by default. According to Hunsden, "there is Aristocrat written on the [mother's] brow and defined in the figure" (3, 26) and "ugly distinction" in Crimsworth's own features and figure (4, 37).

Crimsworth's connection to his mother is at once comforting as a sign of his social superiority to his brother and threatening as a sign of his feminine dependence on male relations. Invited along with Edward's other clerks to a party at Crimsworth Hall, he is "introduced to none of the band of young ladies who, enveloped in silvery clouds of white gauze and muslin sat in array against me. . . ." Dependent on his brother for support, he is not only isolated but vulnerable to humiliation. Surrounded by a "group of very pretty girls with whom he conversed gaily— Mr. Crimsworth, thus placed, glanced at me, I looked weary, solitary, kept-down—like some desolate tutor or governess—he was satisfied" (3, 23). The manuscript of *The Professor* shows that Brontë originally wrote "kept down like some desolate governess" and later inserted the phrase "tutor or." Margaret Smith observes this interpolation and concludes that it shows "how inadequately she realized [Crimsworth's] masculinity,"[14] but such a reading not only assumes that a writer's early thinking has a special claim to authenticity but fails to catch the quality of the revision Brontë made. By simply substituting "like some desolate tutor" for "like some desolate governess," she might have lent some support to Smith's guess that she suspects herself. Her revision is one proof of Brontë's consistent understanding that class figures more importantly than gender: tutor and governess are occupations that equally signify dependence in a household. The titles differ from each other primarily in specifying the sex of the individual who performs the occupation, and sexuality is also part of what dependence denies to both the tutor and the governess by a process *Jane Eyre* examines more fully. Crimsworth longs to be introduced to "some pleasing and intelligent girl" in order to show that he is "an acting, thinking, sentient man," but he turns away "tantalized" and seeks instead the portrait of his mother, "a softened and refined likeness" of himself (3, 24). His comparison of himself to a "desolate tutor or governess" suggests the difficulty with which *he* realizes and asserts his masculinity. He feels himself unmanned in his competition with the brother who is his master.

This rivalry between the Crimsworth brothers shares some of the features of a contest between a brother and sister, for, like a sister, Crimsworth seeks to prove that his physical difference from his brother is difference merely, not inferiority. "Had I been in anything inferior to him," Crimsworth writes, he would not have hated me so thoroughly, but I knew all that he knew and, what was worse, he suspected that I kept the padlock of silence on mental wealth in which he was no sharer. If he could have once placed me in a ridiculous or mortifying position, he would have forgiven me much, but I was guarded by three faculties; Caution, Tact, Observation; and prowling and prying as was Edward's malignity, it could never baffle the lynx-eyes of these—my natural Sentinels. Day by day did his Malice watch my Tact, hoping it would sleep, and prepared to steal snake-like on its slumber, but Tact—if it be genuine—never sleeps. (4, 31)

In the earlier passage in which Crimsworth admitted to Edward's superiority as "an animal," he warned himself not to expect "lion-like generosity" from him. This passage answers the question he then asked: "Had I then force of mind to cope with him?" By making Edward "snake-like," not "lion-like," Crimsworth asserts not only his mental but his animal superiority. Edward's attempts to penetrate his brother's defenses are partly attempts to elicit an offensive response, but Crimsworth's tact, the faculty for saying or doing the right thing, is also a sense of touch so refined that it makes him untouchable.

Hunsden Yorke Hunsden mediates Crimsworth's relation to Edward and also displaces Edward as Crimsworth's rival and model. Like Edward, Hunsden has no trouble recommending himself to his dancing partner at Crimsworth Hall, "a tall well-made, full-formed, dashingly-dressed young woman, much in the style of Mrs. E. Crimsworth" (3, 27). But, like Crimsworth himself, he is more refined and sensitive than Edward, as a result of either his gentleman's education or his ancient Yorkshire lineage. While Edward is connected only to a mill, Hunsden is connected to a wood; at the close of the novel, he and Crimsworth are landed neighbors. Hunsden's most obvious function in the early chapters is to hasten Crimsworth's confrontation with Edward and his departure from England, but he also plays a role in Crimsworth's establishment of his identity as man and master. He does this by complicating the simple model of sexual difference in terms of which Edward's superior physical strength calls Crimsworth's masculinity into question. For Hunsden, who has mostly played the role of strong male to Crimsworth's weak female, turns out to be physically more feminine than either Edward or Crimsworth:

. . . I was surprised now, on examination, to perceive how small and even feminine were his lineaments; his tall figure, long and dark locks, his voice and general bearing had impressed me with the notion of something powerful and massive; not at all—my own features were cast in a harsher and squarer mould than his. I discerned that there would be contrasts between his inward and outward man, contentions too, for I suspected his soul had more of will and ambition than his body had of fibre and muscle. Perhaps in these incompatibilities of the "physique" with the "morale" lay the secret of that fitful gloom; he *would* but *could* not and the athletic mind scowled scorn on its more fragile companion. As to his good looks, I should have liked to have a woman's opinion of that subject; it seemed to me that his face might produce the same effect on a lady that a very piquant and interesting, though scarcely pretty, female face would on a man. I have mentioned his dark locks—they were brushed sideways above a white and sufficiently expansive forehead—his cheek had a rather hectic freshness—his features might have done well on canvass [*sic*] but indifferently in marble—they were plastic; character had set a stamp upon each; expression re-cast them at her pleasure—and strange metamorphoses she wrought, giving him now the mien of a morose bull and anon that of an arch and mischievous girl; more frequently the two semblances were blent, and a queer, composite countenance they made. (4, 35)

Like Crimsworth's, Hunsden's strengths are more moral than physical, for he has a powerful will and ambition and a soft, feminine body, one lacking "fibre and muscle." The reference to a woman's opinion of Hunsden's "good looks" operates by means of a curious reversal. Socially, femininity means sexual attractiveness to men: the "very piquant and interesting, though scarcely pretty, female face" would be judged feminine or not according to whether the man who looks at it finds it sexually attractive. But masculinity has no analogous social meaning: socially, masculinity mostly means acceptability to other men.

The Hunsden this passage describes is a study of incompatibilities rather than a coherent whole. Caught and fixed in the process of metamorphosis, he is more fabular than real, a man who has sometimes the "mien of a morose bull" and sometimes that of "an arch and mischievous girl," as if the legendary Minotaur were to have been a daughter instead of a son. Marriage figures again as a metaphor for the union of social incompatibilities in a later passage, which Brontë also removed from the manuscript of *The Professor*:

I can only say that the face [or form?] and countenance of Hunsden Yorke Hunsden Esq resembled more the result of a cross between Oliver Cromwell and a French grisette, than anything else in Heaven above or in the Earth beneath.[15]

Both the text and the additional manuscript descriptions of Hunsden suggest how complicated Brontë's representation of gender is. The manuscript passage in particular suggests the relation between gender and class uncertainties that has already figured in Crimsworth's comparison of himself to both a governess and a tutor. Terry Eagleton, who sees Hunsden's importance in the novel in relation to the marriage of "identifiably bourgeois values with the values of the gentry or aristocracy," is helpful in showing why Crimsworth has such difficulty in assigning Hunsden a fixed place in the social order. For unlike Crimsworth, whose inheritance is half bourgeois, half aristocratic, Hunsden is one of Carlyle's "'natural aristocrats': cultivated gentlemen sprung from a long line of Yorkshire lineage who combine a settled paternalist tradition of 'blood' and stubborn native pride with a rebellious, independent spirit of anti-aristocratic radicalism." [16] Both Hunsden's gender and his class are unstable, even though his economic independence keeps him from being, like Crimsworth, mastered on either score. Brontë's description of Hunsden suggests that neither gender nor class can be fixed, except by an act of abstraction, and then only in the flux of changing relations to others.

*   *   *

While Crimsworth's role as an English teacher in a foreign country provides new occasions for enjoying the same vindictive triumph he felt when he refused his maternal uncles' patronage or severed his connections with his brother, it also shows him profiting from socially sanctioned forms of oppression which he has so far opposed. The first six chapters of *The Professor* can't defend him against the charge of being racist, bigoted, and misogynist in Belgium, but they help to make the case that these hardened forms of oppression are a consequence of his feeling of powerlessness rather than the cause of his vindictiveness. The controlling metaphors in the novel's first chapter with a Belgian setting are physiognomy and painting. The first positions Crimsworth as an objective observer who translates physical features, the land's and those of its natives, into moral meanings; the second as someone well trained to appreciate beauty. Both metaphors will be important to Crimsworth's representation of his Belgian pupils, and both are explicit in his account of the first Belgian he meets, a Flemish housemaid:

> . . . she had wooden shoes, a short red petticoat, a printed cotton bed-gown, her face was broad, her physiognomy eminently stupid; when I spoke to her in French, she answered me in Flemish, with an air the reverse of civil, yet I thought her charming; if she was not pretty or polite, she was, I conceived, very picturesque; she reminded me of the female figures in certain Dutch paintings I had seen in other years at Seacombe-Hall. (7, 58)

This passage is alive with prejudice. Crimsworth claims a scientific warrant for assessing the housemaid's intelligence even before she speaks; when her speech to him is hostile, he establishes his control over the situation by consigning her to a Dutch painting. With "charming" and "very pic-turesque," he asserts his own superior social standing to justify his con-descension toward the housemaid. His familiarity with Dutch paintings suggests it, and his reference to the privileges of a childhood in Seacombe-Hall insists on it.

The science of physiognomy, like that of phrenology to which it is closely related, was prejudicial by definition and in practice. In nineteenth-century England, phrenology attracted working-class support because it suggested a form of social distinction based on biology rather than birth.[17] By focusing attention on latent faculties, it could minister to philosophies of self-improvement. But biological determinism is, as Stephen Jay Gould demonstrates at some length, essentially "a *theory of limits*."[18] A popular nineteenth-century introduction to the subject, the *New Illustrated Self-Instructor in Phrenology and Physiology*, grounds physiognomy in the famil-iarity of social and racial prejudice:

> That nature has instituted a science of Physiognomy as a *facial* expression of mind and character is proclaimed by the very instincts of man and animals. Can not the very dog tell whether his master is pleased or displeased, and the very slave, who will make a good, and who a cruel master—and all by the expres-sions of the countenance? The fact is, that nature compels all her productions to proclaim their interior virtues—their own shame, even—and hoists a true flag of character at their masthead, so that he who runs may read.
>
> Thus, all apples both tell that they possess the apple character by their apple shape, but what *kind* of apple—whether good, bad, or indifferent—by their special forms, colors, etc.; all fish, not only that they are fish, but whether trout or sturgeon, and all humans that they are human by their outline aspect. And thus of all things.[19]

Gould is interested in physiognomy because of its widespread influence on the treatment of groups, especially racial groups: "It takes the current status of groups as a measure of where they should and must be (even while it allows some rare individuals to rise as a consequence of their for-tunate biology)."[20] Brontë herself would not have expressed Crimsworth's views of Belgians,[21] but the novel fails to provide any individuals who call his stereotypes into question. The novel's posthumous publication after the *Life* probably discouraged contemporary reviewers from attending to these elements of *The Professor*, and modern critics have mostly ignored them.[22] *Villette*, though subject to some of the same criticisms as *The Pro-*

fessor, as Harriet Martineau recognized in her review of the novel, not only focuses on the Roman Catholic training of Lucy's pupils rather than their race but complicates what Martineau called Currer Bell's "passionate hatred of Romanism" in a variety of ways.[23]

In a novel so much concerned with the education of foreigners, Crimsworth's prejudices are especially remarkable. Still smarting from the punishment of Edward's drudgery and the humiliation of his scorn, he controls his pupils with calculated displays of anger and derives considerable satisfaction from humiliating them. Like Heathcliff, he responds to social oppression by becoming an oppressor, but unlike him, he feels persistently compelled to vindicate himself. Since he does this by repeating the lessons he has learned about foreigners, Roman Catholics, and women, self-vindication hardens into a set of general principles, the principles of racism, religious bigotry, and misogyny. In his view, the moral and mental depravity of his pupils justifies his actions: "Their intellectual faculties were generally weak, their animal propensities strong; thus there was at once an impotence and a kind of inert force in their natures; they were dull, but they were also singularly stubborn, heavy as lead and like lead, most difficult to move" (7, 67).

Because education can only hope to move, not lead, these pupils, Crimsworth is a tyrannical teacher:

> I offered them but one alternative; submission and acknowledgement of error or ignominious expulsion. This system answered—and my influence, by degrees, became established on a firm basis. "The boy is father to the Man," it is said, and so I often thought when I looked at my boys and remembered the political history of their ancestors: Pelet's school was merely an epitome of the Belgian Nation. (7, 68)

The tone is self-congratulatory, the reasoning circular. Crimsworth visits the faults of Belgian fathers on their sons at the same time as he derives the moral character of the fathers from that of the sons. His allusion to "My Heart Leaps Up" is also an allusion to the *Immortality Ode*, for which these lines serve as epigraph, for Crimsworth recalls Wordsworth's idealization of the child only to deny it. As Elisabeth Jay points out, the idea of the *Immortality Ode* is "totally incompatible with the Evangelical's vision of the child, who was taught to lisp from its earliest years the confession, 'Lord, I am vile, conceiv'd in sin.'"[24] Crimsworth's later decision to send his own son to Eton to have "the leaven of the offending Adam . . . if not *whipped* out of him, at least soundly disciplined" (25, 266) accords with this tradition, which Brontë brilliantly satirizes in the Brocklehurst episodes of *Jane Eyre*. But the references to "intellectual faculties" and "animal propensities" indicate that the heritage of this educational philosophy is scientific as well as Evangelical, a doctrine of limits more compatible with discipline than education.

Crimsworth's female pupils are Continental, not Belgian, and they elicit his antipathy to Roman Catholicism:

> I know nothing of the arcana of the Roman-Catholic religion and I am not a bigot in matters of theology, but I suspect the root of this precocious impurity, so obvious, so general in popish Countries, is to be found in the discipline, if not the doctrines of the Church of Rome. I record what I have seen—these girls belonged to, what are called, the respectable ranks of society, they had all been carefully brought up, yet was the mass of them mentally depraved. So much for a general view, now for one or two selected specimens. (12, 98)

One of the "selected specimens," eighteen-year-old Aurelia Koslow, has "a vindictive eye" with which she seeks to draw Crimsworth's attention:

> . . . as I take my seat on the estrade, she fixes her eye on me, she seems resolved to attract and, if possible, monopolize my notice: to this end, she launches at me all sorts of looks, languishing, provoking, leering, laughing; as I am found quite proof against this sort of artillery—for we scorn what, unasked, is lavishly offered—she has recourse to the expedient of making noises; sometimes she sighs, sometimes groans, sometimes utters inarticulate sounds, for which language has no name. . . . (12, 99)

Crimsworth asserts that his role as professor in a girls' school has enabled him to see women as human rather than angelic, but such passages not only represent sexual provocation as an attack but brutalize Crimsworth's female pupils, making them less human than animal.

Mdlle. Reuter, the mistress of these pupils, reenacts Aurelia Koslow's experience, first seeking to master Crimsworth and then becoming the abject recipient of his scorn. Their relations begin with concealment on his part and attempts at penetration on hers as she seeks to discover, like Edward, "where her mind was superior to mine—by what feeling or opinion she could lead me" (10, 90). But Crimsworth succeeds in penetrating Mdlle. Reuter's enclosure: he sees the garden that so tantalized him when he was kept from it by the boards over his window; he sees and shakes hands with Mdlle. Reuter herself, a personified garden with her "nut-brown" hair and her cheeks the color of the "bloom on a good apple" (9, 79); and he enters "her sanctum sanctorum" when he assumes his teaching responsibilities (10, 83). The sentimental eroticism of these images recalls the melodramatic eroticism of Crimsworth's conflict with Edward. The theme of both conflicts is erotic domination:

> He flourished his tool—the end of the lash just touched my forehead. A warm excited thrill ran through my veins, my blood seemed to give a bound, and then raced fast and hot along its channels. . . . (5, 43)

As Crimsworth concentrates his energy on defending himself from his pupils, he grows susceptible to their mistress's arts:

> Still she persevered and at last—I am bound to confess it, her finger, essaying, proving every atom of the casket—touched its secret spring and for a moment—the lid sprung open, she laid her hand on the jewel within; whether she stole and broke it, or whether the lid shut again with a snap on her fingers—read on—and you shall know. (12, 105)

This passage introduces a strain of imagery that contrasts sharply with the pastoral garden that has so far figured in Crimsworth's representation of Mdlle. Reuter's seductive appeal. The professor's jewel is both like and different from the bank account that figures in George Eliot's description of her scholar's disillusionment with love:

> Poor Mr. Casaubon had imagined that his long studious bachelorhood had stored up for him a compound interest of enjoyment, and that large drafts on his affections would not fail to be honoured; for we all of us, grave or light, get out thoughts entangled in metaphors, and act fatally on the strength of them.[25]

George Eliot's criticism of Casaubon is poignant in its sense of Casaubon's blankness about the difference between his emotional and his financial transactions, a blankness the narrator of *Middlemarch* attributes to a literal-mindedness that does not take account of the ground of difference that prevents the vehicle of any metaphor from being entirely assimilated to its tenor. But unlike George Eliot with Casaubon, Brontë credits Crimsworth's idea of his heart as a jewel, and his idea that hearts and jewels can be stolen or broken in similar ways. Crimsworth's metaphor, together with the little allegorical narrative in which it figures, suggests that the preservation of his emotional capital is not only instrumental to but interchangeable with his material achievement.

Crimsworth does not acknowledge M. Pelet, the employer who is already secretly engaged to Mdlle. Reuter, as his model and only barely acknowledges him as a rival, but it is Pelet who first rouses and then continues to stimulate Crimsworth's desire for Mdlle. Reuter, tempting him to believe that her appearance of being "all form and reserve" with him is only a disguise. Later Pelet's desire for his Zoraïde will be heightened as much by his suspicion that Crimsworth also desires her as by his knowledge that she desires Crimsworth. Crimsworth is already far advanced in his calculations of the advantages of a marriage to Mdlle. Reuter, calculations that show him to himself in a position of mastery like Pelet's, when he looks out of his bedroom window, unboarded after the young ladies in Mdlle. Reuter's school have become his pupils, and overhears his two employers talking about their upcoming marriage and joking about Crimsworth's boyish passion.

The adultery Crimsworth contemplates after Pelet's marriage to Mdlle. Reuter constitutes the most obvious erotic triangle in *The Professor*. John Maynard discusses it in *Charlotte Brontë and Sexuality*, which argues that Brontë's novels examine "fully the complexities of sexual experience, especially the experience of sexual awakening or unfolding." When Crimsworth imagines that a "modern French novel" will be "in full process of concoction" unless he removes himself from M. Pelet's house, Maynard remarks that

> the extraordinary thing is that this plot in which he would be helplessly caught up, this fictive structure that he dissociates himself from entirely as a dirty French import, has himself as sole author and agent. Only his continuing desire for Zoraïde can make it happen. And of this his judgment is so quick and decided we feel he avoids facing what he is saying: "I was no pope—I could not boast infallibility" (ii, 90). As before, a process of reason follows that substitutes for honesty about his sexual feelings.[26]

Maynard's description of what Crimsworth imagines as "a dirty French import" itself suggests a tone of mind that Maynard insufficiently recognizes and incompletely dissociates himself from. The idea that only Crimsworth's "continuing desire for Zoraïde can make it happen" and that Crimsworth lacks but will later gain the capacity to "acknowledge and deal honestly with his sexual desires" proceeds from two assumptions. One is that Crimsworth's attraction to Mdlle. Reuter can be understood as something he needs to resist and outgrow if he is to be happily married in the end. The other is that desire is a straight line joining a desiring subject and his object.

In *Deceit, Desire, & the Novel*, René Girard argues that the desiring subject always imitates another's desire and that this pattern is central to the tradition of the European novel.[27] In Girard's triangles, the vectors of desire do not mount from rival subjective centers to collide in a common object but rather take a deflected course to their object, which is only valuable by virtue of the deflection. Because a desiring subject's bond with his rival is more powerful than his bond with the one who is desire's object, the idea of the triangle as an implicitly hierarchical figure with an apex and a base (susceptible, of course, to substitutions and rotations) gives place to the idea of it as a figure for describing concealed lines of force.

It would be difficult to find a novel in which romantic and erotic triangles did not play some role. Jane Eyre's relation to Rochester is triangulated by both Bertha Rochester and Blanche Ingram, and Shirley is at once Caroline's best friend and her competitor for Robert Moore's attention. Dr. John and Paul Emanuel occupy positions in several of *Villette*'s proliferating triangles, and Lucy discovers a rival in almost every woman who appears. But the triangles in *The Professor* are more various than those in the other novels (one involves his mother, another his child), and they more closely resemble Girard's in giving greater value to the relation between rivals than to that between either rival and the object of his desire. These differences follow from what is at stake in *The Professor*, the hero's vindication as man and master. Relations between men in *The Professor* are competitive, humiliating, and violent, and Crimsworth's relation to Frances Henri is problematic because it is both an escape from these conflictual intensities and a reformulation of them.

Crimsworth is more honest about his sexual than his vindictive feelings, and although Mdlle. Reuter's physical attractions are a necessary incitement to adultery they are not, in themselves, sufficient. Only Pelet's importance to Crimsworth can account for the violence of his reaction to the discovery that Mdlle. Reuter and M. Pelet are engaged:

> I did not, it is true, like my position in his house, but being freed from the annoyance of false professions and double-dealing I could endure it, especially as no heroic sentiment of hatred or jealousy of the Director distracted my philosophical soul—he had not I found wounded me in a very tender point, the wound was so soon and so radically healed, leaving only a sense of contempt for the treacherous fashion in which it had been inflicted and a lasting mistrust of the hand which I had detected attempting to stab in the dark. (20, 181)

The "false professions" are professions of friendship, and Crimsworth's reference to his "philosophical soul" comports oddly with his sense that he is the victim of a murderous and cowardly attack. The vindictiveness animating this passage finds little justification in Crimsworth's narration of the events that have occurred, for these suggest that Mdlle. Reuter and

Pelet coldly toy with his feelings with a view to their own amusement, not that they conspire to assassinate him.

Crimsworth's discovery of Mdlle. Reuter's compact with Pelet reverses the vectors of desire in the novel. Determined no longer to allow Mdlle. Reuter access to his "jewel," Crimsworth meets her approaches with "no respect, no love, no tenderness, no gallantry . . . nothing but scorn, hardihood, irony" (13, 113–14). The result is a redistribution of power. Several chapters later, he acknowledges the reversal of their earlier roles:

> Next day when I saw the Directress and when she made excuse to meet me in the corridor and besought my notice by a demeanour and look subdued to Helot humility, I could not love, I could scarcely pity her. . . . I had ever hated a tyrant and behold the possession of a slave, self-given, went near to transform me into what I abhorred! There was at once a sort of low gratification in receiving this luscious incense from an attractive and still young worshipper and an irritating sense of degradation in the very experience of the pleasure. When she stole about me with the soft step of a slave—I felt at once barbarous and sensual as a pasha—I endured her homage sometimes, sometimes I rebuked it—my indifference or harshness served equally to increase the evil I desired to check. . . . (20, 183–84)

The reference to "the soft step of a slave" recalls an earlier conversation between Crimsworth and Pelet in which Pelet fanned Crimsworth's desire for Mdlle. Reuter and described the probable outcome of a passion for her: "I am mistaken if she will not yet leave the print of her stealing steps on thy heart, Crimsworth" (11, 94). The difference between the scorn Crimsworth earlier felt for what "unasked, is lavishly offered" and the "sort of low gratification" he feels here is not primarily a matter of increased self-consciousness—of Crimsworth's recognizing his own desire. Rather, it signifies what is at stake in his relation with Mdlle. Reuter. By becoming a tyrant rather than a suitor, Crimsworth acquires the self-mastery that Mdlle. Reuter relinquishes.

Meanwhile, Crimsworth seems to collude with Mdlle. Reuter to punish Frances Henri, the Anglo-Swiss teacher of lace-mending who becomes his pupil soon after he spurns Mdlle. Reuter. Mdlle. Reuter recognizes Frances as a rival for Crimsworth, dismissing her from her post at the pension, forbidding her access to him when she comes with a letter, and refusing to give Crimsworth her address, and Frances sees Mdlle. Reuter primarily as an obstacle, determined to keep her isolated as a Protestant, subordinate as a teacher of lace-mending, and separated from the man she loves. But Mdlle. Reuter is also Frances's model, for what she is, Frances wishes to become: mistress of herself and of a school.

The jewel within the casket, Crimsworth's image for the heart that Mdlle. Reuter "laid her hand on" (12, 105), is recalled in his image for Frances Henri when he finds her after weeks of fruitless looking, in the Protestant cemetery, where she is visiting her aunt's grave: "here was my lost jewel dropped on the tear-fed herbage, nestling in the mossy and mouldy roots of yew-trees!" (19, 167). The "lost jewel" is first of all Frances herself, but it is also Crimsworth's buried affective life. The economic terms he chooses to represent that affective life in this central passage, as in the preface Brontë wrote for the novel, are imbued with religious fervor. What Crimsworth finds in the cemetery is the treasure Mdlle. Reuter tried to steal from him. Because it is still intact in its burial place, Crimsworth can confer it and not some diminished or different thing:

> I loved the movement with which she confided her hand to my hand; I loved her, as she stood there, penniless and parentless, for a sensualist—charmless, for me a treasure, my best object of sympathy on earth, thinking such thoughts as I thought, feeling such feelings as I felt, my ideal of the shrine in which to seal my stores of love; personification of discretion and forethought, of diligence and perseverance, of self-denial and self-control—those guardians, those trusty keepers of the gift I longed to confer on her—the gift of all my affections. . . . (19, 168–69)

The emphasis here is all on saving, and Crimsworth is no longer (as at the beginning of the novel) empty handed. Frances is at once a "treasure" and the container of one, not a casket but a "shrine in which to seal my stores of love." The affections are guarded by the virtues that make for self-sufficiency: discretion, forethought, diligence, perseverance, self-denial, and self-control—Crimsworth's virtues as well as those of Frances Henri and Mdlle. Reuter, the novel's exemplary businesswoman. Preceded by Frances's acknowledgment of Crimsworth as "Mon Maître" and followed by Crimsworth's acknowledgment of her as "my pupil," this passage formulates the master-pupil relation as reciprocal recognition and sacramental economic achievement.

Crimsworth's indifference and impenetrability are ideally suited to sustaining his self-mastery and heightening the desire of both Mdlle. Reuter and Frances Henri, yet he responds very differently to them. In his view, Mdlle. Reuter's humility is the product of "morbid illusions,—'Que le dédain lui sied bien!' I once overheard her say to her mother: 'Il est beau comme Apollon quand il sourit de son air hautain'" (20, 184)—but Frances Henri's humility is evidence of mutual "regard":

and my wife she shall be—that is, provided she has as much—or half as much regard for her master as he has for her. And would she be so docile, so smiling, so happy under my instructions if she had not? Would she sit at my side when I dictate or correct, with such a still, contented, halcyon mien? (19, 176–77)

Frances Henri, who bitterly resents Mdlle. Reuter's deceit and domination, thrives under Crimsworth's discipline and receives it gratefully.

*   *   *

Modern critics have unhesitatingly condemned the master-pupil relation in Brontë's novels as psychologically or politically incorrect.[28] One of Brontë's best contemporary critics, W. C. Roscoe, thought Frances Henri Brontë's "most attractive female character," but noted she suffered "the ordinary fate" of Brontë's heroines:

> Miss Brontë was a great upholder of the privileges of her sex, yet no writer in the world has ever so uniformly represented women at so great a disadvantage. They invariably fall victims to the man of strong intellect, and generally muscular frame, who lures them on with affected indifference and simulated harshness; by various ingenious trials assures himself they are worthy of him, and, when his own time has fully come, raises them with a bashaw-like air from their prostrate condition, presses them triumphantly to his heart, or seats them on his knee, as the case may be, and indulges in a condescending burst of passionate emotion. All these men are in their attachments utterly and undisguisedly selfish, and we must say we grudge them their easily won victories over the inexperienced placid little girls they lay siege to. . . . [29]

Roscoe's "affected indifference and simulated harshness" perfectly describe Crimsworth's treatment of Frances Henri, treatment largely justified, in Crimsworth's and Frances Henri's view, by his role as master.

Their relation, seen from the point of view of the female pupil, is the subject of the poem called "Master and Pupil" included in *The Professor*. It is attributed to Frances, and Crimsworth overhears her reading it aloud when he visits her in her rooms. In the poem, the pupil toils on, always seeking out the "longest task, the hardest theme," even though the master "begrudged and stinted praise" and "Even when his hasty temper spoke." Her reward is his recognition of her achievement, but she discovers that ambitious desires cannot be divorced from erotic ones. Having desired that which the master possesses, she acknowledges that she wants also to possess him. It would be as true to say that she discovers the frustration of her ambitious desire, in that what she desires is the prestige she attributes to the master, as that what she discovers is a sexual desire she has all along been unwilling to admit:

> At last our school ranks took their ground,
>   The hard-fought field I won:
> The prize, a laurel-wreath was bound
>   My throbbing forehead on.
>
> Low at my master's knee I bent,
>   The offered crown to meet;
> Its green leaves through my temples sent
>   A thrill as wild as sweet.
>
> The strong pulse of Ambition struck
>   In every vein I owned;
> At the same instant, bleeding broke
>   A secret, inward wound.[30]

The pupil's masochism is inextricably linked to her ambition to be the master. The victorious woman warrior, her "throbbing forehead" crowned with the poet's laurel wreath, experiences her "strong pulse of Ambition" as a bleeding wound. The wound reveals not only sexual desire but the violence of the competitive compact between pupil and master, victim and persecutor.

All Brontë's masterly men have themselves been victims, an experience that helps them to identify their female counterparts with themselves. This identification also explains the disciplined dissimulation necessary to keep the master from becoming the slave and the toggling of roles that occurs. John Kucich emphasizes the idealized self-concentration of the master, the inviolability of the slave, and the reversibility of mastery and slavery that "makes them transient positions of combat—neither one more attractive than the other. . . . No one's autonomy and distance is diminished. What we are left with is the expansion of self-concentrated desire itself, without its inhering in any fixed interpersonal relationship."[31] Crimsworth makes Frances Henri into a replica of himself, and she accepts his humiliation of her not because she enjoys suffering but because the pupil's suffering is the concomitant of her desire for the master's prestige. Writing about the compact between master and slave, Girard argues that the "dividing line between sickness and health is always arbitrary": "No one can say where a repulsive masochism begins and so-called 'legitimate' ambition and noble hunger for what is risky leave off."[32]

For Frances, there is no necessary contradiction between her proto-feminist determination to have a working life and earn an income of her own and her self-abasement before Crimsworth, her "so-called 'legitimate' ambition" and her "repulsive masochism." As an idealized version of a sadomasochistic relation, the master-pupil relation in Brontë's novels can be distinguished from the master-slave relation it so much resembles, the relation to Mdlle. Reuter that Crimsworth describes as degrading though still pleasurable, primarily by the reciprocity of its roles. Although Crimsworth is alternately desiring and desired in his relation to Mdlle. Reuter, first the humble suitor who is violated by his mistress and then the tyrant who disdains the offerings of his slave, these roles are not repeatedly reversible, and once Mdlle. Reuter admits her desire, Crimsworth no longer desires her. But Crimsworth only maintains his position as Frances Henri's master by continual reproofs and a wary dissimulation of his feelings. He acknowledges the truth of the master's identification with his pupil in a passage that reveals more fully than any other Brontë's insight into the sexual suggestivity of the schoolroom and the prurience of power:

> The reproofs suited her best of all: while I scolded she would chip away with her pen-knife at a pencil or pen; fidgeting a little, pouting a little, defending herself by monosyllables, and when I deprived her of the pen or pencil, fearing it would be all cut away, and when I interdicted even the monosyllabic defence, for the purpose of working up the subdued excitement a little higher, she would at last raise her eyes and give me a certain glance, sweetened with gaiety, and pointed with defiance, which, to speak truth, thrilled me as nothing had ever done; and made me, in a fashion (though happily she did not know it), her subject, if not her slave. (19, 177)

In his role as professor, Crimsworth not only corrects exercises but, in his words, insists "with decision on the pupil taking your arm and allowing himself to be led quietly along the prepared road" (7, 68). But education in *The Professor* involves management more than guidance, and mostly the management of unruly pupils. When he handles Frances Henri's work after catching her in the act of reading "Master and Pupil" aloud, Crimsworth exhibits a rare tenderness:

> . . . we met as we had always met, as Master and pupil, nothing more. I proceeded to handle the papers, Frances, observant and serviceable, stept into an inner room, brought a candle, lit it, placed it by me; then drew the curtain

over the lattice, and having added a little fresh fuel to the already bright fire, she drew a second chair to the table and sat down at my right hand, a little removed. The paper on the top was a translation of some grave French author into English, but underneath lay a sheet with stanzas; on this I laid hands. Frances half rose, made a movement to recover the captured spoil, saying that was nothing; a mere copy of verses. I put by resistance with the decision I knew she never long opposed, but on this occasion her fingers had fastened on the paper; I had quietly to unloose them; their hold dissolved to my touch; her hand shrunk away; my own would fain have followed it, but for the present I forbade such impulse. (23, 217)

The disclaimer with which the passage begins ("We met as we had always met, as Master and pupil, nothing more") is paradoxically undermined and sustained by what follows. On the one hand, the passage can be said to describe a much more intimate relation than that of master and pupil; the setting is as different as possible from the classroom because of its privacy, its informality, and the comforting domesticity of candle, bright fire, and closed curtain. On the other, it describes the intimacy essential to the relation of master and pupil as Brontë idealizes it. Frances sits at Crimsworth's "right hand," a placement that at once acknowledges her importance and her kind of importance. Their attention is directed not at each other but at the writing she has produced and which Crimsworth now handles. The pupil's work, her writing, triangulates the relation of master and pupil. The most powerful phrase in the passage is the reference to Crimsworth's laying hands on Frances's manuscript, for it recalls Mdlle. Reuter's violation of Crimsworth's hidden heart ("she laid her hand on the jewel within") and simultaneously expresses the violence of Crimsworth's gesture ("Frances half rose, made a movement to recover the captured spoil") and its sacramental connotations. These attach not just to the professor but also to the work of his pupil's hands. Her "fingers had fastened on the paper" (a gesture that again recalls Mdlle. Reuter's "finger, essaying, proving every atom of the casket"), but the contest of hands that follows suggests the sexual pleasure of loosening and dissolving while insisting on the interchangeability of the roles of master and pupil. The pupil not only challenges her professor's control but tempts him to follow her lead.

*   *   *

In the last part of the novel, Brontë uses Hunsden Yorke Hunsden to reconstitute the patterns of rivalry and displacement by means of which

Crimsworth finally confirms his agency as man and master, for he is Crimsworth's model as Mdlle. Reuter is Frances Henri's. What Hunsden is, Crimsworth wishes to become: an English landowner who does not need to work with his hands. During Crimsworth's stay in Belgium, Hunsden repairs his family's damaged fortunes through trade and settles into a life of landed leisure. Hunsden is repeatedly pressed into service as Crimsworth's rival, and his treatment of Crimsworth is transparently vindictive. In a letter to Crimsworth, full of the gossip of Crimsworth's impending marriage to Mdlle. Reuter, Hunsden calls attention to his rivalry with Crimsworth and the mercenary motives behind Crimsworth's desire for Mdlle. Reuter:

> Won't I have a look at her when I come over? And this you may rely on, if she pleases my taste, or if I think it worth while in a pecuniary point of view, I'll pounce on your prize and bear her away triumphant in spite of your teeth. (21, 193)

Visiting Crimsworth shortly after Mdlle. Reuter's marriage to Pelet, he abuses him as one who is unable to "communicate pleasure or excite interest" (22, 204) and delivers the mother's portrait, bought at a bankruptcy sale of Edward's effects. The letter that accompanies the portrait takes particular delight in demeaning any pleasure Crimsworth might have taken in the gift:

> There is a sort of stupid pleasure in giving a child sweets, a fool his bells, a dog a bone. You are repaid by seeing the child besmear his face with sugar; by witnessing how the fool's ecstasy makes a greater fool of him than ever; by watching the dog's nature come out over his bone. In giving William Crimsworth his Mother's picture, I give him sweets, bells and bone, all in one; what grieves me is, that I cannot behold the result; I would have added five shillings more to my bid if the auctioneer could only have promised me that pleasure. (22, 209-10)

Finally, Crimsworth presses Hunsden into service as his rival for Frances Henri. Hunsden admires her but warns Crimsworth not to be "vain-glorious. Your lace-mender is too good for you but not good enough for me: neither physically nor morally does she come up to my ideal of a woman" (24, 243). In another displacement in the novel's last chapter, Hunsden reveals his own womanly ideal, or its "shadow," the miniature portrait of Lucia, the woman he would have liked to marry but "*could* not." Frances guesses that Lucia was an actress whom Hunsden could not marry because she broke "social chains." Hunsden denies nothing, asking only whether Frances doesn't feel her "little lamp of a spirit wax very pale beside such a girandole as Lucia's" (25, 262). A woman who can be possessed only in an image, Lucia has a particular relation to Crimsworth's dead mother and a particular difference from her, for the mother's portrait is publicly displayed, but the portrait of Lucia is closely held and finally held out with a purpose. Hunsden's possession of both images and his power to put both to punishing use identifies him as the novel's most masterly man.

At the end of the novel, the William Crimsworths have achieved their small competency. Retired from their teaching duties, they are living in England, in their own home, on a plot of land adjacent to Hunsden's estate. To this peaceful setting, the Crimsworths bring their only child, a boy, like the child of Jane and Rochester. But Victor Crimsworth isn't perfunctorily displayed as the natural consequence of ten years of married life and then dismissed, a nameless and featureless heir. The son and heir of parents of mixed backgrounds and mixed fortunes, Victor powerfully reactivates the rivalries between Frances and Crimsworth, Frances and Hunsden, and Crimsworth and Hunsden and the familial, social, political, and educational conflicts that make *The Professor* Brontë's most insidiously violent novel. Hunsden accuses Frances of making a "milk-sop" of the boy, and she accuses him of ruining him with "his mutinous maxims" (25, 263). "Victor has a preference for Hunsden—full as strong as I deem desirable—being considerably more potent, decided and indiscriminating than any I ever entertained for that personage myself," Crimsworth writes (25, 267). The novel attempts to resolve these conflicts in its last action. Victor's dog, given to him by Hunsden and named Yorke after him, is bitten by an apparently rabid dog and shot by his father.

Although the dog's name and provenance clearly connect it to Hunsden, it has a ghostly connection to Crimsworth too, since he has been repeatedly figured as a dog in situations of violent discipline.[33] In his confrontation with Edward, Edward accused him of complaining publicly of

> the treatment you receive at my hands. You have gone and told it far and near that I give you low wages and knock you about like a dog. I wish you were a dog! I'd set to this minute, and never stir from the spot till I'd cut every strip of flesh from your bones, with this whip. (5, 43)

"I have no doubt in the world that you are doing well in that greasy Flanders," Hunsden writes in his first letter:

> I know this, because you never write to anyone in England. Thankless dog that you are! I by the sovereign efficacy of my recommendation, got you the

place where you are now living in clover and yet not a word of gratitude, or even acknowledgment have you ever offered in return; but I am coming to see you, and small conception can you, with your addled aristocratic brains, form of the sort of moral kicking I have, ready packed in my carpet-bag, destined to be presented to you immediately on my arrival. (21, 192)

The dog whose "nature come[s] out over his bone" also figures in the humiliating letter that accompanies Crimsworth's mother's portrait, together with the fool and the child, and it is latent in Hunsden's raillery on the subject of Mdlle. Reuter: "If she pleases my taste, or if I think it worth while in a pecuniary point of view, I'll pounce on your prize and bear her away triumphant in spite of your teeth"(21, 193).

Edward's use of "dog" places Crimsworth as a dependent creature, and the wish that he were a dog so that he could be brutally flayed suggests the frustration Edward feels at having to acknowledge his brother's human claims. Hunsden's use of "dog" is more ambiguous, compacting the most common eighteenth-century sense of a dog as a cynical rogue, in part a "rib digging term of affection" or admiration (Hunsden also imagines himself as doglike), with disgust: the dog is "thankless," greedy, and always craven whether being thrown a bone or kicked by its master.[34] The surprise, then, of finding an actual dog in the novel is partly the surprise of its being so unlike the dogs that have figured in the characters' imaginations: "It grew to a superb dog whose fierceness, however, was much modified by the companionship and caresses of its young master" (25, 263). In this the dog resembles Victor more than either Crimsworth or Hunsden, for Victor has a temper, "a kind of electrical ardour and power" that Hunsden calls spirit and that Frances mollifies ("and by love Victor can be infallibly subjugated").

Crimsworth's killing of Victor's dog is at once perfectly vindictive and perfectly self-vindicating, vindictive because it expresses Crimsworth's hostility to Hunsden, Victor, and himself, and self-vindicating because the dog is rabid, and has to be killed to prevent its harming others. But the dog is inadequate as scapegoat, inadequate in particular to the task of ridding the novel of vindictiveness. Instead, its killing marks the repetition according to which Victor takes his father's place on the hill of Difficulty and reenacts his punishing achievement:

> Victor learns fast. He must soon go to Eton, where, I suspect, his first year or two will be utter wretchedness: to leave Me, his Mother and his home will give his heart an agonized wrench—then the fagging will not suit him—but emulation, thirst after knowledge—the glory of success will stir and reward him in time. (25, 265–66)

Crimsworth's idea of education as a conjunction of ennobling ambition and suffering also brings Victor's experience into relation with his mother's. But by compacting the idea of salutary punishment with that of infectious violence, the conclusion of *The Professor* points to the heavy cost, not the glorious reward, of the struggle for self-mastery.

The image of the superb mastiff cub, shot "where he lay licking his wound," dominates the end of *The Professor*. In her draft preface for the novel, Brontë analyzed her hero:

> I had the pleasure of knowing Mr. Crimsworth very well—and can vouch for his having been a respectable man—though perhaps not altogether the character he seems to have thought he was. Or rather—to an impartial eye—in the midst of his good points little defects and peculiarities were visible of which he was himself excusably unconscious—An air—a tone of his former profession lingered over & round him—a touch of the pedagogue—unobtrusive but also unmistakable—Besides his houshold [*sic*] thought him infallible and this naturally inclined other people to look out for failings—which as he was human and erring—or course they found. . . . [35]

Crimsworth's inability to admit fallibility, the "defects and peculiarities" of which he is "unconscious," argues for Brontë's consciousness that her hero is open to the charge of defensiveness. Brontë's doubts about Crimsworth made her also doubt *The Professor*'s "general attractiveness," yet she remained confident that the part of the novel that relates to Brussels was "as good as I can write." [36] Her progress toward *Villette*, in which she wrote better, required her to reconstitute the experience of her English teacher in Brussels by removing the shadow of vindictiveness from her character's triumphant self-vindication. At the same time, she also manages to make Lucy Snowe's acts of self-defense undefensive by having her admit not just fallibility but genuine defects and peculiarities. "As to the character of 'Lucy Snowe' my intention from the first was that she should not occupy the pedestal to which 'Jane Eyre' was raised by some injudicious admirers," she wrote in a letter to Ellen Nussey. "She is where I meant her to be, and where no charge of self-laudation can touch her." [37]

3. In Defense of Vision: The Eye in *Jane Eyre*

When Rochester disguises himself as a gypsy fortune-teller and forecasts Jane's destiny, he prefers looking at her face to looking in her palm and pays particular attention to her eyes:

> The flame flickers in the eye; the eye shines like dew; it looks soft and full of feeling; it smiles at my jargon: it is susceptible; impression follows impression through its clear sphere; when it ceases to smile, it is sad; an unconscious lassitude weighs on the lid: that signifies melancholy resulting from loneliness. It turns from me; it will not suffer farther scrutiny; it seems to deny, by a mocking glance, the truth of the discoveries I have already made,—to disown the charge both of sensibility and chagrin: its pride and reserve only confirm me in my opinion. The eye is favourable. (II, 4, 251)

Like "amiable," "favourable" looks in two directions. A favorable eye is one that wins favor as well as one that confers it. In fortune-telling, a favorable eye is also propitious, boding well for a particular design. Such discriminating attention to the operations of the eye is a distinguishing feature of the novel Brontë began writing in Manchester, where her father was being treated for cataracts and where the manuscript of *The Professor* "came back upon her hands, curtly rejected by some publisher, on the very day when her father was to submit to his operation."[1] *Jane Eyre* registers these two events—the denial of Brontë's vision as a writer and the threat to her father's sight—not only in one of its central events, the blinding of Rochester, but also in its representation of seeing, being the object of sight, and looking as the essential forms of relatedness at every stage of Jane Eyre's experience.

In what follows, I look closely at Jane's being looked at punishingly by others and lovingly by Rochester, and at Jane's own looking, ahead at a prospect or prospects, at Rochester, and finally for him. The language Brontë uses to describe the facts of perception supports J. L. Austin's observation that these facts are "much more diverse and complicated than has been allowed for" and that "our ordinary words are much subtler in their uses, and mark many more distinctions, than philosophers have realized."[2] The distinctions Brontë's language marks in *Jane Eyre* are crucial to understanding the trajectory of this novel's plot, its main events, and its most important narrative effects. This chapter deliberately takes up questions other readers of the novel have addressed during the last century, but it also seeks to redress the balance between the generous attention devoted to *Jane Eyre*'s plot and the scanty attention devoted to its verbal texture. In it I argue that defense is widened and deepened in Brontë's second novel, widened in the greater range of oppositions in which the heroine engages and deepened by a new sense that what one defends against is inside as well as out.

In casting *Jane Eyre* as Brontë's defense of vision, I am concerned with vision in all of its usual senses, which I take to be bounded by ordinary, bodily sight, on the one hand, and, on the other, by the truth-telling associated with visionary experience as set over or against ordinary sight. The genius of *Jane Eyre* does not consist merely of contrasting these different operations of the eye, as Brontë does in the juvenilia, but of providing the fullest possible account of their conflict, convergence, and inter-animation. In *Jane Eyre*, Brontë sets out to defend her heroine's view against the tyrannical views of others—those of individuals and institutions like the family, the school, and the Church—and discovers the dangers of any totalizing vision. After all, the man Jane marries loses his sight, and even at the novel's end, when he recovers a portion of it, it is only to see according to Jane's tuition. Brontë connects Rochester's blindness to acquisition of insight and to punishment, but it is above all a necessary concomitant of the novel's relentlessness in establishing Jane's point of view as not merely dominant but exclusive, either obliterating or containing all others.

The eye is *primus inter pares* and has a tendency to tyrannize over the other senses and over other eyes. Perhaps because it is at once the most vulnerable of our senses and the one most necessary to our own defense, *Jane Eyre* is more corporeal than *The Professor*, and attacks on the body—wounding, maiming, and incarceration—figure more largely in its plot. The danger to Brontë's father's eyes as she began to write *Jane Eyre* is intimate with her own history of endangered sight. She had long been anxious about her eyesight, always weak and represented by her as an obstacle to a career as a writer, perhaps even as a punishment for her ambition to become an author. "Formerly I passed whole days and weeks and months in writing, not wholly without result," she had written, not wholly without pride, in a letter to M. Héger two years earlier, for Southey and Coleridge—two of our best authors, to whom I sent certain manuscripts—were good enough to express their approval, but now my sight is too weak to write.—Were I to write much I should become blind. This weakness of sight is a terrible hindrance to me.[3]

Her simulation of blindness in order to write differently connects eyesight and anxiety about writing, and makes her father's condition, as he lay in a darkened room with his eyes bandaged, a hideous travesty of one she had eagerly sought. She wrote her early tales with her eyes closed, and she frequently suggests that some refusal of ordinary sight is required for access to "the divine, silent, unseen land of thought." In the autobiographical fragment known as the "Roe Head Journal," she represents herself as both visible and visionary, juxtaposing the ordinary sight of those around her to her own transcendent seeing. With her eyes shut, she sees those who gape at her.

> Wiggins might indeed talk of scriblomania if he were to see me just now— encompassed by the bulls, (query cows of Bashan) all wondering why I write with my eyes shut—staring, gaping hang their astonishment. . . . [4]

Mary Taylor, describing her first view of Brontë, wrote that she was "so short-sighted that she always appeared to be seeking something, and moving her head from side to side to catch a sight of it. . . . When a book was given her, she dropped her head over it till her nose nearly touched it, and when she was told to hold her head up, up went the book after it, still close to her nose, so that it was not possible to help laughing." Later, she presented the same appearance while she was writing the drafts of her novels. She wrote on "bits of paper in a minute hand, holding each against a piece of board, such as is used in binding books, for a desk," a "plan" that was "necessary for one so short-sighted as she was."[5]

This conjunction of anxiety about sight and anxiety about writing is already visible and may be audible in the heroine's surname. The usual pronunciation of it calls attention to Jane's relation to *air*, which David Lodge considers in his account of the war of elements in the novel,[6] and to *heir*, reminding us that Jane succeeds to her uncle's property when she claims her proper name, renouncing the false name of Elliott, which has hidden her relation to her cousins at Moor House. But *Eyre* is a name that Brontë may have pronounced and certainly would have seen in some relation to the "eye" it includes.[7] Multiple associations are at work in one sentence in the novel that invokes the air/Eyre pun: "You are a beauty in my *eyes*, and a beauty just the *desire* of my heart—delicate and *aerial*," Rochester tells Jane (II, 9, 326; italics mine). The only clue in the text to the pronunciation of the name is ambiguous, for Adele asks Jane's name and, being given it, declares it unpronounceable: "Aïre? Bah! I cannot say it" (I, 11, 122). The umlaut appears in the Clarendon edition and has its authority from Brontë's manuscript, but the first three editions of the novel (and all later versions before the Clarendon edition) omitted it, thereby helping to establish the literary tradition that has determined the usual pronunciation. But the pronunciation of "Aïre" is closer to "eyer" than "air" and has the additional attraction of its punning relation to "ire" as well as to the French "haïr." "Never was there a better hater," as the anonymous reviewer for the *Christian Remembrancer* was the first to remark. "Every page burns with moral Jacobinism."[8] Finally, the name glances at Brontë's Irish background, and perhaps through it at a threat to the established order just as formidable as that of the dispossessed Jacobites.

Virginia Woolf astutely noted that *Jane Eyre*'s most evident narrative effect is the indivisibility of narrator and narrative, seer and seen. "The writer has us by the hand, forces us along her road, makes us see what she sees, never leaves us for a moment or allows us to forget her. At the end we are steeped through and through with the genius, the vehemence, the indignation of Charlotte Brontë."[9] In Woolf's account, Jane is visible to us and to herself largely by virtue of what she sees, and Woolf connects the terrific force of *Jane Eyre* to the narrowness of this vision. "The drawbacks of being Jane Eyre are not far to seek. Always to be a governess and always to be in love is a serious limitation in a world which is full, after all, of people who are neither one nor the other." Put this way, these limitations will seem to be merely aspects of the social construction of the novel's heroine and narrator, rather than contingencies of vision itself. But it is these contingencies that constitute Jane Eyre as a genuinely new social subject for the novel.

Seeing in *Jane Eyre* opens up questions of power, property, and propriety in ways that help to explain this novel's eccentric relation to the tradition of the English novel and justify its perennial interest for feminist critics.[10] When, in the compelling opening chapters of *Jane Eyre*, Jane is denied not only a place within the family circle but the right to look, first at the book she has taken with her into the window-seat, then at her attacker, the punishable impropriety of her so looking deserves more notice than it has had. In her analysis of how Jane's withdrawal to the window-seat of the breakfast room places her as the "marginalized individualist," Gayatri Spivak points out that the reader becomes Jane's "accomplice" because both are reading. Spivak's reading of this episode is fecund in its choice of words, for "accomplice" already suggests that Jane is guilty of some crime. According to Spivak, this crime may be her preservation of "her odd privilege" because she never does "the proper thing in its proper place. She cares little for reading what is *meant* to be read: the 'letter-press.' *She* reads the pictures."[11]

This subtle impropriety is associated with more formidable ones. The pictures in Bewick stimulate visions more engaging than those presented by either the interior of Gateshead Hall or the landscape outdoors, and such looking itself resists being kept in one's proper place by appropriating both a book and a prospect. Jane's punishment for so looking is the primal act of violence in the novel and makes explicit the act of dispossession behind her oppression. John Reed wounds her in the head when he hurls his book and these words at her: "You have no business to take our books: you are a dependant, mama says; you have no money; your father left you none . . ." (I, 1, 7). His insult connects Jane's proper place to one of its main indicators, a proper name, the name of Eyre rather than Reed. Jane's only connection to property is through her mother, also a Reed, and she will not own her proper place in the world until she has owned her proper name, becoming the heir to her paternal uncle's property by renouncing the alias Jane Elliott. The novel thus provides its own compacted version of the social ideology Elizabeth Rigby's notorious review of *Jane Eyre* makes explicit:

> If these times puzzle us how to meet the claims and wants of the lower classes of our dependants, they puzzle and shame us too in the case of that highest dependant of all, the governess—who is not only entitled to our gratitude and respect by her position, but, in nine cases out of ten, by the circumstances which reduced her to it. For the case of the governess is so much harder than that of any other class of the community, in that they are not only quite as liable to all the vicissitudes of life, but are absolutely supplied by them. There may be, and are, exceptions to this rule, but the real definition of a governess, in the English sense, is a being who is our equal in birth, manners, and education, but our inferior in worldly wealth. Take a lady, in every meaning of the word, born and bred, and let her father pass through the gazette, and she wants nothing more to suit our highest *beau idéal* of a guide and instructress of our children. We need the imprudencies, extravagancies, mistakes, or crimes of a certain number of fathers, to sow that seed from which we reap the harvest of governesses.[12]

Rigby's "real definition of a governess" precisely defines Jane Eyre, not yet a governess but destined to become one. Jane's anger at her social displacement is the impulse to narrative, both the stories of cruel and wicked emperors she flings back at John Reed and the story of herself she tells her aunt, Mr. Lloyd (the apothecary who is called in after her fit in the Red Room), and, later at Lowood, Miss Temple.

In Jane's scene with John Reed, the eye is not only the object of punishment but its agent, the instrument which, together with the hand, is required to deliver punishment. Later, Jane will describe Mrs. Reed's eye as "cold" and "composed": "That eye of hers, that voice, stirred every antipathy I had" (I, 4, 39). Even in death, her eye is "flint," not flesh, under "its cold lid" (II, 6, 301). The Dowager Lady Ingram has "a fierce and hard eye: it reminded me of Mrs. Reed's" (II, 2, 215). St. John has an "ever-watchful" eye that threatens like a blade: "so keen was it, and yet so cold" (III, 8, 507).

Brontë describes the eye's use as weapon most fully in the scene in which Brocklehurst brands Jane a liar. The Lowood scenes have always been admired for their power, but they have hardly been appreciated for the humor that makes them so different from the earlier scenes of Jane's martyrdom at Gateshead Hall. Brontë's punning use of *pupil* in the scene at Lowood when Brocklehurst makes his first visit after Jane's arrival anticipates Sylvia Plath's in "Tulips," especially in its sense of the patient-pupil's terrible vulnerability in exposure.

> They have propped my head between the pillow and the sheet-cuff
> Like an eye between two white lids that will not shut.
> Stupid pupil, it has to take everything in.[13]

Unlike Plath, Brontë empowers the pupil, who has herself to be taken in: "Suddenly his eye gave a blink, as if it had met something that either dazzled or shocked its pupil" (I, 7, 73). She describes actual visual experience precisely, for the pupils constrict when the eye is either dazzled by light or exposed to an unpleasant stimulus. The sight that causes Brocklehurst's defensive blink is both bright and shocking, a pupil named Julia Severn, whose offense is to have naturally curled, red hair. The submerged pun on "pupil" surfaces in Brontë's recognition that the pupil's subversiveness is, after all, natural. When Brocklehurst makes all the pupils stand and face the wall so that he can examine the backs of their heads, the "looks and grimaces with which they commented on this manoeuvre" are their defense against it, even though their eyes are invisible to Brocklehurst. The general punishment—"All those top-knots must be cut off"—precedes Jane's particular punishment when she unluckily draws "every eye" by dropping her slate. "'A careless girl!' said Mr. Brocklehurst, and immediately after—It is the new pupil, I perceive.'"

> "Ladies," said he, turning to his family; "Miss Temple, teachers, and children, you all see this girl?" Of course they did; for I felt their eyes directed like burning-glasses against my scorched skin. (I, 7, 75–76)

The burning-glass, which may be either a lens or a mirror, concentrates the sun's rays. Brocklehurst's eye acts as a lens that focuses the vision of the teachers and pupils on Jane and makes it punishing, but it also acts as a mirror that burns Jane with her reflection in these other eyes. Seeing in them "the 'other side' of her own power of looking,"[14] she feels their sight as a scorching touch.

Jane's punishment is both preceded and followed by that of Helen Burns, whose name connects her to light and marks her as Lowood's chief martyr. Helen's eyes are the focus of Jane's characterization of her: she seems to see "by a light invisible to [Jane's] eyes" (I, 6, 63). When Helen has to stand in the middle of the school-room, her "sight seems turned in," Jane says, "gone down into her heart: she is looking at what she can remember, I believe; not at what is really present" (I, 5, 58). After Brocklehurst brands Jane a liar, Miss Scatcherd literally brands Helen, making her wear a piece of pasteboard on which the word "Slattern" is written "in conspicuous characters" (I, 8, 86). This scene, and the one of Jane's humiliation by Brocklehurst, have an analogue in *David Copperfield*, which appeared two years after *Jane Eyre* and, despite Dickens's disclaimers, may have been influenced by it. For when David arrives at school, he too is made to wear a placard that commemorates his one overtly aggressive act, the attack on his stepfather, Mr. Murdstone, who viciously beat him for not learning his lessons: "Take care of him. He bites."

But David's sign is interestingly different from Helen's and Jane's. For one thing, Helen does not wear her placard on her back, like David, but on her "large, mild, intelligent, and benign-looking forehead," in close proximity to her eyes, which see the looks of others. Bound "like a phylactery," the placard demonically travesties the words that Deuteronomy instructs God's chosen people to wear as frontlets between their eyes.[15] At the same time, the placard singles Helen out as one chosen for glory, a word Brontë always associates not just with exaltation but with light, for the passage from Deuteronomy also orders that God's words be written on the doorposts and gates of one's house, and Helen's placard recalls the inscription on the stone-tablet above the door into the Lowood schoolroom: "Let your light so shine before men that they may see your good works, and glorify your Father which is in heaven." Helen's philosophy aligns her with the Lowood inscription, for she opposes the "ill usage" that "brands its record on [the] feelings" to "the impalpable principle of life and thought" transmitted by the Creator to the creature: "whence it came it will return; perhaps again to be communicated to some being higher than man—perhaps to pass through gradations of glory, from the pale human soul to brighten to the seraph!" (I, 6, 67). When Jane is punished, Helen advises her to disregard the world's scorching vision, but Jane's project is both smaller and larger than Helen's. It is not to irradiate the world's vision of her with a more powerful inner light but to correct that vision by making her own eyes her world's lens and its glass.

Two sentences, one imperative, one indicative, compose David's sign. The admonition is ambiguous, as Alexander Welsh remarks, couching a hope as well as a warning: "The sign is a portent as well as a stigma. 'Take care' can mean either beware or cherish, and it comes to mean both."[16] The ambiguity in part accounts for our sense that the injustice to David is smaller than the injustices to Helen and Jane, and indeed, the scene in *David Copperfield* is more pathetic than tragic. The single noun on Helen's sign, with its copula elided, doesn't accuse her of untidiness only. Its slander is impurity, perhaps even the sexual impurity that "slattern" regularly connotes in its most familiar application to women, and in throwing the placard into the fire, Jane rejects the imputation and indicts the institution that is blind to the holy light emanating from her friend. The charge against Jane is just as terrible, for lying is equally central to a sense of identity. This episode questions Jane's whole relation to language, the past, her story of it, and her knowledge of and in the world, for what she is said to have lied about is specifically her life with Mrs. Reed. Much later, lying on her death-bed, Jane's wicked aunt will finally tell the truth that she, not Jane, has been deceitful in denying Jane her proper place.

But this discussion of the schoolroom scene does not fully explain its force in the novel. When Jane sees herself being seen and feels her visibility as the burning touch of a hundred concentrated looks, she experiences the negative inversion of what Merleau-Ponty calls "the undividedness of the sensing and the sensed,"[17] the at-oneness of becoming visible for oneself by virtue of the sight of things that is the essence of her own power in the novel. Her defense against this power, here vested in others and turned against her, takes two specific forms: she annexes two new realms of expression, beginning her study of both French and drawing. Specifically, she learns the first two tenses of *être*, and she sketches a cottage. Patricia Yaeger connects Jane's destruction of a word when she throws Helen's placard into the fire with the new relation to language that is marked by her learning French. According to Yaeger, Jane's mastery of the tenses of "être" evokes a "sonority" in her name, "revealing 'Eyre' as a cognate for the verb 'to be.'"[18] This says too much and not enough. Jane's mastery of two tenses, presumably the present and the passé composé, is richly implicative. It provides a way out of the confinement of Brocklehurst's copulative—"this girl is—a liar!"—by supplying the minimal conditions for narrative, the possibility of a significant temporal relation, of a verbal formulation like the one attached to David rather than the simple nouns, "slattern" and "liar." Jane's sketch of a cottage marks a complementary new agency for her eye in space, and Jane is the only Brontë heroine whose art is visual and celebrates the visible world. At Lowood, Jane begins to acquire the skill that will enable her to make visible to others what she has seen. Having said so much, Jane has nothing to add. Although the novel devotes another chapter to her next eight years at school, it gives no further information about what she learns there.

✳   ✳   ✳

And where is Mr. Rochester?

He comes in last: I am not looking at the arch, yet I see him enter. I try to concentrate my attention on these netting-needles, on the meshes of the purse I am forming—I wish to think only of the work I have in my hands, to see only the silver beads and silk threads that lie in my lap; whereas, I distinctly behold his figure, and inevitably recall the moment when I last saw it: just after I had rendered him, what he deemed, an essential service—and he, holding my hand, and looking down on my face, surveyed me with eyes that revealed a heart full and eager to overflow; in whose emotions I had a part. How near had I approached him at that moment! What had occurred since, calculated to change his and my relative positions? Yet now, how distant, how far estranged we were! So far estranged, that I did not expect him to come and speak to me. I did not wonder, when, without looking at me, he took a seat at the other side of the room, and began conversing with some of the ladies.

No sooner did I see that his attention was riveted on them, and that I might gaze without being observed, than my eyes were drawn involuntarily to his face: I could not keep their lids under control: they would rise, and the irids would fix on him. I looked, and had an acute pleasure in looking,— a precious, yet poignant pleasure; pure gold, with a steely point of agony: a pleasure like what the thirst-perishing man might feel who knows the well to

which he has crept is poisoned, yet stoops and drinks divine draughts nevertheless. (II, 2, 217–18)

The old convention that love enters the soul or heart through the eyes
is consistent with recent experimental evidence that couples in love spend
more time looking at each other than do other couples, and that pupil
dilation can be produced both by sexually arousing stimuli and by pupil
dilation in the person looked at.[19] What is remarkable about *Jane Eyre*'s
representation of the activity of the eyes in courtship is partly its positioning a woman as a subject seeing her lover as "the beautiful object." According to Freud, the gaze is male, and many feminist critics have agreed.
The classic feminist account of this male gaze is Luce Irigaray's:

> . . . the prevalence of the gaze, discrimination of form, and individualization
> of form is particularly foreign to female eroticism. Woman finds pleasure
> more in touch than in sight and her entrance into a dominant scopic economy
> signifies, once again, her relegation to passivity: she will be the beautiful
> object.[20]

Jane Eyre controverts this idea that a woman finds visual pleasure primarily in being visible or that a woman who gazes takes on masculine
qualities. "I looked, and had an acute pleasure in looking," Jane says. Criti-
cizing the conventional exclusion of women from visual pleasure, Teresa
de Lauretis argues that the "project of feminist cinema is not so much 'to
make visible the invisible,' as the saying goes, or to destroy vision altogether, as to construct another (object of) vision and the conditions of
visibility for a different social subject."[21] *Jane Eyre* does this partly by
refusing the logic of opposition that characterizes Irigaray's formulation:
male vs. female eroticism, subject vs. object, active vs. passive, sight vs.
touch. An acute pleasure is one that acts keenly on the senses, and not only
pleasures but a penetrating sight, a high, sharp, or shrill sound, and a
pungent taste are properly said to be acute. Jane's eye is favorable because
it gazes feelingly back at Rochester. Her sight is at once touched and
touching.

Jane Eyre goes further by reconceiving sight so that the very terms
subject and object are false to the experience of Jane and Rochester. If Jane
Eyre is fully embodied as an agent in this account of her visual pleasure,
where is Mr. Rochester? Not relegated to passivity, for Jane's active eye is
not only receptive but vulnerable. Even when seeing occurs in only one
direction—"I might gaze without being observed"—it always occurs with
a full recognition of the "human reciprocity lurking within the situation."[22]

The polarities of human reciprocity in *Jane Eyre* are the nightmare of the scorching by burning-glass, the lens or mirror that turns sight at or against the one who sees and is seen, and the dream of a loving visibility in which the eye is at once the organ of sight and sight's best object.

Without yet looking at Rochester, Jane "distinctly behold[s]" him, first as he presently appears and then in memory as he appeared when she last looked at him while he looked at her "with eyes that revealed a heart full and eager to overflow; in whose emotions I had a part." This conventional image of reciprocated love as an eager outflow from the eyes stands behind Rochester's description of Blanche Ingram's smiles:

> I was talking of ladies smiling in the eyes of gentlemen; and of late so many smiles have been shed into Mr. Rochester's eyes that they overflow like two cups filled above the brim: have you never remarked that? (II, 4, 249)

The unpleasantness of the phrase, "ladies smiling in the eyes of gentlemen," comes from its suggestion that sights can be both assaulting and intrusive. Blanche "sheds" her smiles, sloughing them off like dead things, into eyes grotesquely figured as cups, overflowing because they cannot contain an emotion in which they do not share. Blanche's eyes don't figure at all in Rochester's vision; they don't talk to his eyes, they don't correspond. But Rochester calls Jane's eyes into play when he asks her whether she has "never remarked" this assault of smiles on eyes. Later in the same scene when he uses the protection of his gypsy disguise to scrutinize Jane's face, he redeems the smile by locating it where it belongs, in a corresponding eye, which not only "looks soft and full of feeling" but "smiles" (II, 4, 251).

When Brontë describes Jane's "acute" visual pleasure in Rochester as "a precious, yet poignant pleasure; pure gold, with a steely point of agony," she recovers much of the history of the word *poignant*, which is not only sometimes a synonym for "acute" but like it is alive to the interanimation of the senses:

> 1. Of weapons, or other pointed material objects: Sharp-pointed, piercing. *Obs.* b. *fig.* Of the eye or look: Piercing, keen. 2. Sharp, pungent, piquant to the taste or smell. 3. Painfully sharp to the physical or mental feelings, as hunger, thirst, a pang, an affront; also said of a state of feeling, as grief, regret, despair. b. Stimulating to the mind, feelings, or passions; pleasantly or delightfully piquant. 4. Of words or expressions: Sharp, stinging; severe; also pleasantly keen or pointed, piquant.

The passage in *Jane Eyre* remembers the word's wide range of reference, its linking of the senses to each other as well as to the feelings and passions. It does not spiritualize sight, traditionally the noblest of the senses, but associates it with touch when it is reciprocal and with hunger and thirst because of the sharpness of its cravings. Jane's contradictory sensations convey the dangerous eroticism of her visual pleasure in looking at Rochester.

Brontë is wonderfully resourceful in using the language of perception in *Jane Eyre*. Some of these words are so familiar to us that we tend to take them for granted, expecting them to go about their work quietly. But sleeping meanings, like the pun in "pupil," may wake and startle: "Oh, that is the light in which you view it!" Rochester says to Jane, after she has responded to a piece of his life story, directing our attention to the known effect that changes in lighting have on an appearance. "Well, I must go in now; and you too: it darkens" (I, 15, 179). Suddenly Jane's lightness and Rochester's darkness emerge as contrasting elements, and Rochester seems as unable to sustain Jane's bright view of himself as he is to hold the sun in the sky.

Other ambiguities are inherent in the familiar nouns and verbs themselves, and point to insights of the kind to which J. L. Austin has directed our attention. In *A Comprehensive Grammar of the English Language*, Randolph Quirk notes that English has "special agentive perception verbs" for the senses of sight and hearing, but lacks them for touch, smell, and taste. Both "look (at)" and "listen (to)" are "agentive and dynamic and describe an intentional activity."[23] But this account of "looking" and "looking at" is complicated by the way that "look" as both verb and noun refers ambiguously to the dynamic activity of looking and to an appearance:

> How stern you look now! Your eyebrows have become as thick as my finger, and your forehead resembles, what, in some very astonishing poetry, I once saw styled, "a blue-piled thunder-loft." That will be your married look, sir, I suppose? (II, 8, 330)

Contrasting Rochester's "look of native pith and genuine power" with the looks of his noble guests, Jane again invokes both senses of "look." Her lack of "sympathy in their appearance, their expression," means that "while they would pronounce Mr. Rochester at once harsh-featured and melancholy-looking," she wonders "to see them receive with calm that look which seemed to me so penetrating" (II, 2, 219). Both Rochester's look and Rochester's looking are poignant.

In explaining her reluctance to look at Rochester, Jane twice uses the verb "look at" to describe actions that are intentional, but she needs the deep equivocation of the noun "look" to express the reciprocity of seeing that is a consequence of his marriage proposal. This is Jane on the morning after:

> While arranging my hair, I looked at my face in the glass, and felt it was no longer plain: there was hope in its aspect, and life in its colour; and my eyes seemed as if they had beheld the fount of fruition, and borrowed beams from the lustrous ripple. I had often been unwilling to look at my master, because I feared he could not be pleased at my look; but I was sure I might lift my face to his now, and not cool his affection by its expression. I took a plain but clean and light summer dress from my drawer and put it on: it seemed no attire had ever so well become me; because none had I ever worn in so blissful a mood. (II, 9, 324)

Traditionally, the beloved's eyes are said to be a mirror in which the lover beholds at once his beloved's heart and his own image.[24] Rochester's eyes are present to Jane as "the fount of fruition," but the mirror in this scene is a real one, and the dramatized exchange is between Jane's own eyes, imaging and imaged there. When Jane says that her "eyes seemed as if they had beheld the fount of fruition," the difficulty of deciding whether the eyes are those looking at her out of the glass or those with which she looks at her reflected image is compounded by our awareness that what her eyes are doing is beholding or, in another image for the same activity, borrowing light from light, light being the precondition for being able to see at all. On first reading, the noun "look" in "I had often been unwilling to look at my master, because I feared he could not be pleased at my look" seems to mean the action of looking, and Jane's reference to not cooling Rochester's affection "by expression" forwards this sense. But in its connection with the attention to Jane's appearance that follows, her putting on the dress that best becomes her ("become" is a quiet pun, and "light" in the phrase "light summer dress" borrows "beams from the lustrous ripple" of the "fount of fruition"), "look" also refers to Jane's personal aspect. The slide from Jane's looking at Rochester to Rochester's looking at Jane, or to Rochester's looking at Jane looking at Rochester, recapitulates the unbroken perceptual circuit already established as Jane looks at her own look in the mirror. Jane's own image is not a love-object any more than is Rochester's. Both arouse admiration, but neither is fixed by it into mindless unresponsiveness.

Rochester's admiration frees Jane's glance, but to look at Rochester is also to submit to constraint. The sentence I have already quoted in the context of my discussion of Jane's surname—"You are a beauty in my eyes, and a beauty just the desire of my heart—delicate and aerial"—is an equivocation because what it asserts is a subjective, private truth that must not entirely deny its objective correlative and public consequence: "I will make the world acknowledge you a beauty, too." Jane herself, firmly in possession of a loving eye, invokes and then abolishes such equivocations:

> "A loving eye is all the charm needed: to such you are handsome enough; or rather, your sternness has a power beyond beauty." (II, 7, 307–8)

> Most true is it that "beauty is in the eye of the gazer." My master's colourless, olive face, square, massive brow, broad and jetty eyebrows, deep eyes, strong features, firm, grim mouth—all energy, decision, will—were not beautiful, according to rule; but they were more than beautiful to me: they were full of an interest, an influence that quite mastered me,—that took my feelings from my own power and fettered them in his. I had not intended to love him: the reader knows I had wrought hard to extirpate from my soul the germs of love there detected; and now, at the first renewed view of him, they spontaneously revived, green and strong! He made me love him without looking at me. (II, 2, 218–19)

Both passages distinguish features that are beautiful "according to rule" from those that are "more than beautiful" because of the interest they arouse and the influence they exert. In the first passage, the ambiguity of whose "loving eye" is "all the charm needed" (Jane's? Rochester's?) reminds us that "the eye that reveals a heart full and eager to overflow" can charm a viewer, before it establishes that the eye in question belongs to the viewer, who half creates what she sees. This Romantic truth about perception is complicated in the second passage by a larger sense of the vulnerability inherent in sight. Jane cannot keep from looking at Rochester (the verb here is agentive and dynamic but describes an unintentional activity), and since she loves what she sees, it is Rochester who seems more active, even when he chooses not to look at her. "He made me love him without looking at me" relocates the agency of "I might gaze without being observed." At the same time, Jane's identification of her love for Rochester as a vigorous, healthy plant transfigures the metaphor of the germs of love, ambiguously animal or vegetable, and hints also at disease, a dangerous growth that has to be extirpated. This is love that comes as inevitably as the leaves to the trees.

*   *   *

The novel formulates the change in what Jane sees after seeing Bertha Rochester as a change in prospects or in what she now has to look forward to. The word "prospect" appears twenty-three times in *Jane Eyre*, eleven of these in the plural,[25] when it usually refers to expectations of having, or lacking, money and property. "I should wish her brought up in a manner suiting her prospects," Mrs. Reed tells Mr. Brocklehurst, "to be made useful, to be kept humble" (I, 4, 36). Later, when Jane inherits her uncle's fortune, St. John Rivers will caution her against too hastily giving most of it away to him and his sisters. He approaches the subject of Jane's altered prospects with a series of alliterating words—possess, pounds, place, prospects—that charts the crucial relations:

> . . . you do not know what it is to possess, nor consequently to enjoy wealth: you cannot form a notion of the importance twenty thousand pounds would give you; of the place it would enable you to take in society; of the prospects it would open to you. . . . (III, 7, 494)

As the word "open" indicates, even when "prospects" refers to a future presented to the mental vision, the sense of a spectator looking out at a landscape from a vantage point is close at hand.

Jane uses "prospect" to refer to an expectation or hope, as in the prospect of a new situation, a journey, death, or breakfast, but the novel also continually registers her state of mind in terms of her physical situation before a landscape in prospect. On her wedding evening, Jane tells Rochester, "I cannot see my prospects clearly to-night, sir; and I hardly know what thoughts I have in my head. Everything in life seems unreal." Rochester's response is at once direct and deceiving, for it takes Jane's "prospects" to refer only to what she sees, not to what she hopes and expects. She should, he says, put her faith in what she can touch, not what she can see—"I am substantial enough:—touch me"—and she should focus on the vision that is near instead of the distant prospect that is indeterminate:

> He held out his hand, laughing: "Is that a dream?" said he, placing it close to my eyes. He had a rounded, muscular, and vigorous hand, as well as a long, strong arm.
> "Yes; though I touch it, it is a dream," said I, as I put it down from before my face." (II, 10, 352)

Rochester's "rounded, muscular, and vigorous hand" and his "long, strong arm" are in one sense what is most real to Jane and in another only a fantasy or "dream." His gesture, which she describes with such evident visual pleasure, produces a blindness that Jane has already imagined as the consequence of her loving Rochester too much:

> My future husband was becoming to me my whole world; and, more than the world: almost my hope of heaven. He stood between me and every thought of religion, as an eclipse intervenes between man and the broad sun. I could not, in those days, see God for his creature: of whom I had made an idol. (II, 9, 346)

This image of Jane as the earth and Rochester as the moon, interposing itself between her and the broad sun of religion to block her view, makes an absolute division between Jane's spiritual and material worlds. The latter, which should be transparent, not only providing access to the spiritual world but taking its main meaning and value from it, is opaque and obliterating, for Rochester not only obscures Jane's view of the sun but deprives her of the light necessary to sight itself. To prefer the visible to the invisible world is, as Jane recognizes, idolatry, which is preeminently a sin of the eye, a worship of material things or false appearances. "Turn away mine eyes from beholding vanity," the psalmist implores (Ps. 119:37). If Jane's gesture of taking Rochester's hand from before her eyes portends the actual loss of that offensive limb, it may also be that in loving Rochester too much she is already implicated in his crime. "An adulterer," Saint Jerome says, "is he who is too ardent a lover of his wife."[26]

As someone who has been assigned an unimportant place in the social hierarchy, a place that denies, as we have seen, not only the power of her vision but its propriety, Jane repeatedly seeks an eminence from which she can survey the world with a vision that is comprehensive, wide-ranging, and proprietary. Soon after her arrival at Lowood, when she remarks that its garden is surrounded with "walls so high as to exclude every glimpse of prospect" (I, 5, 54), she correlates the school's physical isolation from the rest of the world with the limitations it imposes on its pupils' expectations. Later she takes visual pleasure "in a prospect of noble summits girdling a great hill-hollow, rich in verdure and shadow; in a bright beck, full of dark stones and sparkling eddies" (I, 9, 88). Looking out from her window at Lowood after Miss Temple's marriage, her eye seeks the distant prospect, but everything bounded by the "hilly horizon" now seems "prison-ground, exile limits" (I, 10, 100). At Thornfield, she enjoys the "calm prospect" of far off hills, "not so lofty as those round Lowood, nor so craggy, nor so like barriers of separation from the living world" (I, 11, 120), but before long, she is climbing those three staircases and looking out from the attic trapdoor, longing "for a power of vision which might overpass that limit" (I, 12, 132).

Jane's inability to see her prospects clearly on the eve of her wedding succeeds to a painfully clear vision of them when the discovery of Bertha Rochester interrupts her marriage ceremony. She acknowledges this climactic reversal in a brilliant passage that reveals the degree to which the plot of the novel is indebted to what M. H. Abrams has described as the plot of Christian history. This plot, Abrams writes, is "right-angled: the key events are abrupt, cataclysmic, and make a drastic, even an absolute difference." St. Augustine's *Confessions* provides the most influential model for the shape that this history typically assumes in Western autobiography and for the central importance of conversion in its plot. The mental experience Augustine records is "one of chiaroscuro, discontinuity, and sudden reversals" culminating in "a new identity, described metaphorically as the end of the old creature and the beginning of the new."[27] This is the shape of St. John Rivers's history, as he describes how his doubts about his decision to enter the ministry concluded in his dedication to missionary work:

> After a season of darkness and struggling, light broke and relief fell: my cramped existence all at once spread out to a plain without bounds—my powers heard a call from heaven to rise, gather their full strength, spread their wings and mount beyond ken. God had an errand for me. . . . (III, 5, 462)

The imagery of flight has already been associated with Jane's longing for a power of vision that might overpass limits, and the call from heaven to St. John's powers has a close analogue in the call to Jane from Rochester that will free her from St. John's grasp: "It was *my* turn to assume ascendancy. *My* powers were in play, and in force"(III, 9, 536). But the sudden reversal in Jane's history that most closely resembles St. John's conversion is an anti-conversion, a moment when darkness falls as Jane contemplates the prospect opened to her by her knowledge of another Mrs. Rochester:

> I was in my own room as usual—just myself, without obvious change: nothing had smitten me, or scathed me, or maimed me. And yet, where was the Jane Eyre of yesterday?—where was her life?—where were her prospects?
>
> Jane Eyre, who had been an ardent, expectant woman—almost a bride— was a cold, solitary girl again: her life was pale; her prospects were desolate. A Christmas frost had come at mid-summer: a white December storm had whirled over June; ice glazed the ripe apples, drifts crushed the blowing roses; on hay-field and corn-field lay a frozen shroud: lanes which last night blushed full of flowers, to-day were pathless and untrodden snow; and the

woods, which twelve hours since waved leafy and fragrant as groves between the tropics, now spread, waste, wild, and white as pine-forests in wintry Norway. My hopes were all dead—struck with a subtle doom, such as, in one night, fell on all the first-born in the land of Egypt. I looked on my cherished wishes, yesterday so blooming and glowing; they lay stark, chill, livid—corpses that could never revive. I looked at my love: that feeling which was my master's—which he had created; it shivered in my heart, like a suffering child in a cold cradle; sickness and anguish had seized it: it could not seek Mr. Rochester's arms—it could not derive warmth from his breast. Oh, never more could it turn to him; for faith was blighted—confidence destroyed! Mr. Rochester was not to me what he had been; for he was not what I had thought him. I would not ascribe vice to him; I would not say he had betrayed me: but the attribute of stainless truth was gone from his idea; and from his presence I must go: *that* I perceived well. When—how—whither, I could not yet discern: but he himself, I doubted not, would hurry me from Thornfield. Real affection, it seemed, he could not have for me; it had been only fitful passion: that was balked; he would want me no more. I should fear even to cross his path now: my view must be hateful to him. Oh, how blind had been my eyes! How weak my conduct! (II, 11, 373–74)

This begins with an acknowledgment of sameness—Jane is "just myself, without obvious change"—yet the difference between yesterday's Jane and today's is that between radically opposed states of mind, one supplanting the other with a suddenness that violates the natural order. A midsummer landscape that has been blighted by a frost is nothing like a winter landscape, any more than a girl who has been a woman is anything like one who still has her maturity before her. The inverted syntax of the clause that climaxes the increasingly malign progression of unnatural effects that Jane describes ("on hay-field and corn-field lay a frozen shroud") models the reversal that is the passage's main theme. The truth that Jane has not been physically injured, not "smitten," "scathed," or "maimed," is both balanced and exceeded by the truth to feeling her three questions register: "where was the Jane Eyre of yesterday?—where was her life?—where were her prospects?" The echo of Jane's earlier question—"And where was Mr. Rochester?"—as well as the clear reference to Rochester's subsequent fate—*he* will be smitten, scathed, and maimed—connect Jane to her lover, whose distance from her, now legally enforced, makes these new prospects visible.

Doreen Roberts, who comments on this passage, suggests that "the dissociation-projection technique" that is the fundamental representational mode of the passage as a whole and the strong "sense of drama going on not just within but around the heroine" prevent a reader from recognizing immediately that the passage describes "an inner landscape, not an external scene."[28] This blurring of the boundaries between inner and outer worlds has been a regular element of the novel's representation of Jane's state of mind and is connected, as we have seen, to the range of reference of the word "prospect" itself. Here a rhetorical set piece that claims its power and place by virtue of all that precedes it intensifies the connections between Jane's prospect and her prospects:

> Jane Eyre, who had been an ardent, expectant woman—almost a bride—was a cold, solitary girl again: her life was pale; her prospects were desolate.

The adjectives describing Jane as she was, "ardent" and "expectant," with their connotations of sexual readiness, cannot be applied to the landscape, but those describing her as she is, "cold," "solitary," and "pale," apply almost as well to the world outside as to Jane herself. The quiet assertion that "her prospects were desolate" completes the convergence of landscape and mindscape.

Like Milton's God, Jane sees not just a future in prospect but all times simultaneously. She evokes vast reaches of time and space in her opposition of June and December, her references to Christmas and to the plagues visited upon Egypt's first-born, and her contrast between a tropical and a wintry Norwegian climate. Her "frozen shroud" anticipates the images of the next three sentences, which represent her hopes, wishes, and love for Rochester as infant corpses littering the ground. Margaret Homans argues that both Emily and Charlotte Brontë "articulate thematically a daughter's bond to and identification with a vulnerable or vanished mother (often figured as Mother Nature)," but in this passage, Jane shares this identification with Rochester, here a mother who is both abandoning and abandoned by an infant that cannot seek his arms or "derive warmth from his breast." Homans rightly perceives that the "transitory experience of being a mother is the central and recurring metaphor for the abundant sense of danger in *Jane Eyre* (just as the plot of *Wuthering Heights* turns on the main character's death in childbirth and her subsequent transformation into a ghost),"[29] but the psychic death that threatens Jane here is not the one attending childbirth that Homans so fully explores, an apprehended subordination of the mother's self to that of husband or child or the symbolic eradication of that self in an act of self-duplication. It is a psychic death imagined from the daughter's point of view and associated specifically with a separation from the mother that feels like self-murder. This separation, like Persephone's from Demeter, is compelled rather than chosen, yet the mother, who also suffers, is held responsible, for her cradle and breast are cold. This is the other side of the daughter's dilemma, her anger at the mother with whom she identifies, an anger almost impossible to express. In what follows, Jane defends herself against her anger at Rochester, the absenting mother, by blaming herself.

The sentence that begins with the words "Oh, never more" marks a transition from descriptive to discursive writing. The passage proceeds with a resounding litany of negative constructions, one or more in every sentence until the last, brief three. These sentences also rely heavily on syntactic inversion, parallelism and antithesis, repetition and anaphora. Margot Peters, who suggests (on the basis of a random sampling) that nearly half of Brontë's sentences involve some inversion, attributes this habit not only to her "poetic sense" but to "a taste for distortion, a certain contrariness, a delight in negativeness and reversal that can be called perverse."[30] In this passage and elsewhere, inversion is sometimes awkward but not perverse. Brontë characteristically uses word order for emphasis, either by placing the most important word or phrase first or by interrupting a normative syntactic progression, and Jane's word order in this passage partly represents her effort to be as precise as she can in analyzing her feelings and Rochester's. The placement of the phrase "to me" in "Mr. Rochester was not to me what he had been" gives it a prominence in keeping with the novel's concern throughout with where the truth of perception is to be located.

Jane avoids blaming Rochester by faulting her idea of him and by focusing less on what he now is than on what he is no longer. "Mr. Rochester was not to me what he had been; for he was not what I had thought him" acknowledges the deception Rochester has practiced but at the same time takes some responsibility for it: not "what he seemed" but "what I had thought him." The verbs in the carefully balanced clauses of the next sentence remind the reader that Jane is attempting not only an understanding of what has happened but a repeatable narrative of it:

> I would not ascribe vice to him; I would not say he had betrayed me: but the attribute of stainless truth was gone from his idea; and from his presence I must go: *that* I perceived well.

The awkwardness of "but the attribute of stainless truth was gone from his idea; and from his presence I must go"—a sentence that bears little relation to idiomatic English—derives not only from the prominence accorded to the abstract nouns but from Jane's need to excuse Rochester by nearly excusing him from her sentence. The chiasmus whose perfect balance requires the use of the objective genitive "his idea" rather than "my idea of him" ("from his idea" and "from his presence") helps to make the connection between Jane herself and the very attribute—"stainless truth"—she has regularly claimed as her own: if "stainless truth" is gone, Jane must go also. The use of the term "view" instead of the more usual "sight" recalls its near synonym "prospect," and the phrase "my view" (rather than "the view of me") recalls "his idea" and creates a syntactic parallelism that perfectly expresses the equipollence of Jane's sense that if she now sees a less attractive Rochester, Rochester now sees a less desirable Jane. The phrase permits an alternative reading that takes "view" to refer not to Jane herself but to the prospect she has just described. This reading partly relies on the extent to which Jane, in this passage and in the novel as a whole, is identified with her view, so that to look in Jane's eyes is to look out of them too. It is striking how little Jane blames Rochester for her situation. "I should fear even to cross his path now: my view must be hateful to him" locates the animus of her thoughts elsewhere and beautifully anticipates her return to Thornfield Hall seeking a view of Rochester and the closing views of the novel when she gazes on Rochester's behalf.

As Jane retraces her steps through "the very fields through which I had hurried, blind, deaf, distracted, with a revengeful fury tracking and scourging me, on the morning I fled from Thornfield," she looks "forward to catch the first view of the well-known woods":

> "My first view of it shall be in front," I determined, "where its bold battlements will strike the eye nobly at once, and where I can single out my master's very window: perhaps he will be standing at it—he rises early: perhaps he is now walking in the orchard, or on the pavement in front. Could I but see him! . . . Who would be hurt by my once more tasting the life his glance can give me?—I rave: perhaps at this moment he is watching the sun rise over the Pyrenees, or on the tideless sea of the south." (III, 10, 541–42)

What strikes Jane's eye when she peeps from behind one of the pillars of the gate in the orchard wall, a "sheltered station" from which "battlements, windows, long-front—all" are at her "command," is only the blackened ruin that is Thornfield after the devastating fire. The ruin is itself a portent of Rochester's own ravaged body: "You are no ruin, sir," Jane will later insist. But the passage is more than portentous, for its language works to generate the very image of Rochester's visage. *Front* inevitably suggests Rochester's noble forehead, and the "bold battlements" that "strike the eye" all but require the reciprocal agent and object of sight, "my master's very window." The window is an old figure for the eyes, and it naturally produces Jane's next image of the man himself: "perhaps he will be standing at it." The sun is also important in this passage and perhaps recalls Rochester's earlier displacement of the source of heavenly light—"he rises early"—before it gathers up the two main consequences of Rochester's blindness: his glance can no longer give life to Jane, and all sunrises are invisible to him.

When Jane arrives at Ferndean and actually crosses Rochester's path, her experience is like and different from the one she has just had at Thornfield. She had compared her experience at Thornfield to that of a lover who steals upon his mistress hoping to catch a glimpse of her face while he himself remains unseen and then is driven wild by the discovery that the mistress is not asleep but "stone-dead." Rochester is not stone-dead, but he is, in the words of the innkeeper from whom Jane has requested his story, "stone-blind." Both these compounds attend to the conjunction between a stone and the absence of feeling that operates in the familiar phrases "eye of stone" and "heart of stone." An eye of stone is one that cannot weep. "Howl, howl, howl! O! you are men of stone," Lear cries out at Cordelia's death. "I stayed my step, almost my breath," Jane says, "and stood to watch him—to examine him, myself unseen, and alas! to him invisible!" (III, ii, 551). But there is all the difference in the world between a lover who is stone-blind and one who is stone-dead, for although Rochester cannot see Jane, he can feel her presence and respond to her feeling for him.

The immediate cause of Jane's return to Rochester is her having heard his call while she was at Moor End, an occurrence that has been criticized repeatedly as improbable or facile. But in insisting that Rochester actually called out to Jane and heard her reply, the novel only revises, in Carlylean fashion, the definition of a miracle and corrects our usual understanding of it as a violation of natural laws:

> "But is not a real Miracle simply a violation of the Laws of Nature?" ask several. Whom I answer by this new question: "What are the Laws of Nature? To me perhaps the rising of one from the dead were no violation of these Laws, but a confirmation; were some far deeper Law, now first penetrated into, and by Spiritual Force, even as the rest have all been, brought to bear on us with its Material Force."[31]

"This is not [superstition's] deception, nor [its] witchcraft: it is the work of nature," Jane avers. "She was roused, and did—no miracle—but her

best" (III, 9, 536). Leslie Stephen's "awkward question" about the implications of Rochester's communication with Jane still rankles:

> What would Jane Eyre have done, and what would our sympathies have been,
> had she found that Mrs Rochester had not been burnt in the fire at Thorn-
> field? That is rather an awkward question. Duty is supreme, seems to be the
> moral of the story; but duty sometimes involves a strain almost too hard for
> moral faculties.[32]

The only answer to Stephen's question is that the renewed communication
between Jane and Rochester presumes Jane's restored view of her own
prospects, which, radically reversed when the wedding to Rochester is
interrupted, are again radically reversed both by what she sees—she is now
an heiress—and by what she can't yet see—Bertha Rochester is dead.[33]

The last chapters of the novel emphasize the difference Rochester's
blindness makes. One passage compares his countenance to a lamp once
lit by the faculty of sight and now quenched:

> His countenance reminded one of a lamp quenched, waiting to be relit—and
> alas! it was not himself that could now kindle the lustre of animated ex-
> pression: he was dependent on another for that office! I had meant to be gay
> and careless, but the powerlessness of the strong man touched my heart to
> the quick: still I accosted him with what vivacity I could:—
> "It is a bright, sunny morning, sir," I said. "The rain is over and gone, and
> there is a tender shining after it: you shall have a walk soon."
> I had wakened the glow: his features beamed. (III, 11, 562)

The countenance illumined by the eyes is implicitly likened to the lustrous
shining of nature on a bright, sunny morning, and the very transformation
that Jane sees and describes for Rochester is the transformation of his
features that her description effects. Like the sun itself, Jane rekindles the
glow of "animated expression" despite his lightless eyes, making his features "beam." When Rochester says that "all the melody on earth is concentrated in my Jane's tongue to my ear," he says that his sense of hearing
has replaced his sense of sight—light has been translated into melody—
because Jane's descriptions of what she sees must substitute for what he
himself used to see. Yet his choice of the word "tongue" to refer to Jane's
faculty of speech, her power of articulation or description, appropriates
for hearing precisely that which it ordinarily lacks. Because we hear without being heard, hearing is not an exchange, a reciprocal activity like
touching. When Rochester refers to hearing Jane speak as having her

"tongue to my ear," he assimilates hearing to touch, and thus through touch to reciprocal seeing as well.

Jane's summary of her relation to the blind Rochester in the novel's last chapter idealizes their seeing together by seeing as one:

> Mr. Rochester continued blind the first two years of our union: perhaps it was that circumstance that drew us so very near—that knit us so very close; for I was then his vision, as I am still his right hand. Literally, I was (what he often called me) the apple of his eye. He saw nature—he saw books through me; and never did I weary of gazing for his behalf, and of putting into words the effect of field, tree, town, river, cloud, sunbeam—of the landscape before us; of the weather round us—and impressing by sound on his ear what light could no longer stamp on his eye. (3, 12, 576–77)

In this passage, "vision" functions as "look" so often has, referring at once to both the agency of perception and its object. As what Rochester sees—Jane herself—the word has two obviously contradictory meanings, for a vision may be either a thing actually seen, or, as is more apt when the perceiver is blind, something seen otherwise than by the ordinary sight, a revelation. The aphorism that follows again compacts the agency of sight with what is seen: "Literally, I was (what he often called me) the apple of his eye." Jane is figuratively the apple of Rochester's eye because she is his most cherished object of sight or vision and also, as she says, literally the apple of his eye, the pupil that sees. The use of the phrase "apple of the eye" to refer to both the pupil of the eye and a cherished object is very old (the OED gives 885 as the date when each first appears), and Brontë profits here from a venerable insight embodied in ordinary language. Yet this apotheosis of reciprocity according to which the eye is what it sees does not dispel the poignancy of Jane's first view of a blinded Rochester: "I stayed my step, almost my breath, and stood to watch him—to examine him, myself unseen, and alas! to him invisible" (III, 11, 551). Nor does it compensate for what has been lost, the reciprocity th. de-pends on simultaneously seeing and being seen and that figures so largely in the courtship of Jane and Rochester. Rochester's housekeeper's words to Jane when she arrives at Ferndean—"I don't think he will see you . . . ; he refuses everybody" (III, 11, 553)—have a grim humor. Their merely social and figurative sense collides with their literal sense: the blind man is someone who is seen by everyone but himself as well as someone to whom everyone is invisible.

*   *   *

Rochester's marriage to Bertha makes an obstacle to his marriage to Jane that only Bertha's death can remove, but all the plot of the novel requires is that death, not Rochester's blinding and maiming. Moralists of one camp have justified these events as acts of divine retribution. According to the host of the grimly named "The Rochester Arms," some say Rochester's injuries are "a just judgment on him for keeping his first marriage secret, and wanting to take another wife while he had one living . . ." (III, 10, 548). Rochester himself interprets his loss of eye and limb as divine vengeance:

> Divine justice pursued its course; disasters came thick on me: I was forced to pass through the valley of the shadow of death. *His* chastisements are mighty; and one smote me which has humbled me for ever. You know I was proud of my strength: but what is it now, when I must give it over to foreign guidance, as a child does its weakness? (III, 11, 571)

This is a harsh justice, but no harsher than that adduced by moralists of other camps, who attribute vengeance to Brontë rather than her God. D. H. Lawrence thought that sex in *Jane Eyre* had become

> something slightly obscene, to be wallowed in, but despised. Mr. Rochester's sex passion is not 'respectable' till Mr. Rochester is burned, blinded, disfigured, and reduced to helpless dependence. Then, thoroughly humbled and humiliated, it may be merely admitted.[34]

Freud's well-known establishment of a substitutive relation between the eye and the penis has served both these lines of interpretation. In "The Uncanny" (1919), he maintains that the study of dreams, fantasies, and myths shows that the anxiety about going blind is often a substitute for the fear of being castrated and adduces the myth of Oedipus, whose self-blinding is a "mitigated form of the punishment of castration—the only punishment that was adequate for him by the *lex talionis*."[35] Richard Chase first used the phrase "symbolic castration" in reference to *Jane Eyre* in a once influential mythic reading of the novel, which argues that the context for Brontë's imputed recoil from Rochester's forceful sexuality is the Victorian cult of domestic love.[36]

Later critics of *Jane Eyre* have not dispelled Lawrence's and Chase's closely related objections to it, and the blinding and maiming of Rochester remains a particularly thorny crux in the novel. Feminist critics whose readings of the novel are currently more influential have not disagreed with the meaning of what happens to Rochester but differ about what we are to make of it, rather as C. S. Lewis disagreed with F. R. Leavis about Milton: "It is not that he and I see different things when we look at *Paradise Lost*. He sees and hates the very same that I see and love."[37] Thus feminist critics have seen Rochester's blinding and maiming as a kind of handicap that gives Jane a fair chance in a patriarchal world (Sandra M. Gilbert and Susan Gubar); as the "inevitable sufferings necessary when those in power are forced to release some of their power to those who previously had none" (Carolyn Heilbrun); or as "the terrible condition of a relationship of equality" (Helene Moglen). Moglen puts this in a contemporary perspective: "the reduction of Rochester's virility and the removal of them both from contact with society are necessary to maintain the integrity of the emergent female self."[38]

Modern criticism of Brontë's most popular novel reads like a family of narratives; each transmutes the novel into a somewhat different, plausible parable. Feminist critics in particular are open to the compliment both St. John Rivers and Rochester offer Jane herself in what G. Armour Craig calls "perhaps the grimmest joke in the book": "You delight in sacrifice." "The subterranean sadism is all too rich, and the imagery is sometimes so gross that the reader must laugh if he does not close his eyes and skip."[39] Lewis thought that his disagreement with Leavis belonged to a realm outside of literary criticism. "We differ not about the nature of Milton's poetry, but about the nature of man, or even the nature of joy itself."[40] Brontë's critics differ not about the nature of *Jane Eyre* but about the nature of men and women, and the cultural conditions that cripple their relations. According to Lawrence and Chase, Brontë embraces a Victorian sexual code when she makes "sex passion" safe for domestic consumption. According to Brontë's feminist critics, she rebels against the relations of power in her culture by giving Jane an absolute advantage.

Defending Brontë against the charge of a complacent or cowardly sadism can mean denying or mitigating Rochester's sacrifice, as Gilbert and Gubar do: "Apparently mutilated, he is paradoxically stronger than he was when he ruled Thornfield, for now, like Jane, he draws his powers from himself, rather than from inequity, disguise, deception."[41] John Maynard, who rejects a Freudian reading of the novel without entirely rejecting "an implication of castration" in Rochester's injuries, takes this line in *Charlotte Brontë and Sexuality*. Although Maynard sees Brontë as Lawrence's precursor, he quickly dismisses what Lawrence saw as Brontë's vicious indictment of sex:

In a novel the symbols should be given proper relative weights. First, we are not encouraged to overstress the element of castration. Rochester has received a blow but is anything but sexually impotent when Jane sees him. Brontë, if anything, seems to intend a blow to his arrogance that does not touch his psyche more deeply. His pride in taking his own way in life, his willingness to deceive Jane rather than confide in her, these are to be excised, not his essential masculinity. Second, the maiming is presented as serious, but capable of amelioration. One of Rochester's eyes will have some of its power restored; his depression and lack of brightness is almost immediately relieved by Jane's presence.[42]

Maynard so mitigates the horror of what happens to Rochester—it's "serious, but capable of amelioration," and Jane is such a cheering influence—that he induces a real longing for what Nabokov jeeringly called the application of Greek myths to our private parts. This is a reading that believes the loss of one's hand and eyesight is a blow to arrogance "that does not touch the psyche more deeply" and accepts the notion of an "essential masculinity" synonymous with sexual potency.

Rochester's blinding and maiming make an absolute difference to his relations with Jane, and so to what we make of *Jane Eyre*. We can recover this difference only by refusing to rewrite Brontë's narrative according to the Freudian "master code of Ur-narrative" that has been proposed as its "ultimate hidden or unconscious *meaning*"[43] and by paying close attention to the specificity of what happens to Rochester. The literal sense of his blindness—his inability to see—has a claim to our attention beyond that of any figurative sense, including the imputation of castration. To regard Rochester's blindness as merely a symbol of his castration is to miss the particular power of vision in *Jane Eyre*. That this is so need not obscure the novel's investment in eyes and hands as the instruments of sexual desire or its continual representation of hands and eyes as agents and objects of erotic pleasure and erotic vulnerability.

The novel explicitly invokes blinding and maiming, as many readers have noticed, on the morning after Jane's interrupted wedding:

> "Let me be torn away, then!" I cried. "Let another help me!"
> "No; you shall tear yourself away; none shall help you: you shall, yourself, pluck out your right eye; yourself cut off your right hand: your heart shall be the victim; and you, the priest, to transfix it" (3, 1, 379)

The editors of the Clarendon *Jane Eyre* provide the following note on this allusion to Matthew 5:27–32:

As Joseph Prescott has pointed out (*Letterature Moderne* (Bologna), ix.6, December 1959), these verses, which the girls of Lowood School learn by heart in Ch. vii, form a commentary on the eventual destiny of Mr. Rochester. Guilty of adultery in his heart (and in a sense of putting away his wife), he loses one eye and one hand. Apparently it is his left eye which remains sightless (p. 577, l. 24, taken in conjunction with p. 558, l. 30). About his hand there is an inconsistency: p. 552, l. 16 states that he lost his left hand, but on p. 577, l. 1, Jane states that she is 'still his right hand'.[44]

What readers have failed to notice is what Jane's voice actually says about blinding and maiming. According to the Bible, these punishments are both preferable and appropriate to adultery, but in Jane's agonized meditation, self-mutilation is the *consequence* of leaving Rochester, that is, of refusing adultery. In *Jane Eyre*, the Biblical prophylactic against sexual indulgence is at one with the felt deprivation of it. This connection is confirmed when Jane, viewing her desolate prospects after the interrupted wedding, identifies her own state of mind by describing the "smitten, scathed," and "maimed" body of nature and when Rochester's least adulterous act, the attempt to save Bertha's life, reproduces these events in him. For both Jane and Rochester, then, the events that separate them—Jane's having to leave Thornfield because of the existence of another Mrs. Rochester and Rochester's responsibility to preserve that existence—constitute acts of self-mutilation.

This blasphemous inversion of the prohibition against adultery supports the charge of more than one contemporary reviewer that *Jane Eyre* was "immoral or antichristian."[45] T. S. Eliot, writing about the literature of the twelfth century, marks the "essential congruity" of religion and blasphemy. In order for blasphemy not to be "feeble," Eliot writes, devotion must not be deficient.[46] Blasphemy in *Jane Eyre* ordinarily involves an inversion of the hierarchy of material and spiritual things that values Jane's profane experience above religious experience or deflects the current of religious feeling so that it flows through Jane's relationship with Rochester. In the terms of Jane's own eclipse metaphor, the broad sun of religion is not only blocked from view by Rochester but made the ground against which he figures more distinctly. Thus, when Jane learns that he had indeed called out to her on the very night his anguished cry tore her from St. John Rivers, she echoes Mary's words when the shepherds tell her that her infant is the Christ—"I kept these things then, and pondered them in my heart" (III, 11, 573).[47] In its most insistent use of a Biblical allusion, the novel repeatedly invokes the words from the close of Revelation that are quoted in St. John's letter to Jane at the close of the novel:

> "My Master," he says, "has forewarned me. Daily he [*sic*] announces more distinctly,—'Surely I come quickly;' and hourly I more eagerly respond,— 'Amen; even so come, Lord Jesus!'" (III, 12, 579)

Awaiting Rochester's return on their wedding eve, Jane cries out: "I wish he would come! I wish he would come!" (II, 10, 350). Futilely resisting Jane's decision to leave him on the day after the interrupted wedding, Rochester gives her words back to her: "Of yourself, you could come with soft flight and nestle against my heart, if you would: seized against your will, you will elude the grasp like an essence—you will vanish ere I inhale your fragrance. Oh! come, Jane, come!" (III, 1, 406). The response Rochester hears in Jane's voice when he mysteriously summons her back to him is "I am coming: wait for me!" (III, 11, 572). As these allusions suggest, Brontë imagines the earthly marriage of Jane and Rochester in terms of the heavenly one in Revelation but not as a symbol of "man's striving for Christian reward."[48] The blasphemy the novel all but utters is that the earthly reward Jane and Rochester enjoy eclipses St. John's "incorruptible crown," so that the broad sun of religion is their marriage's corona.

When, towards the end, Jane speaks of herself as Rochester's "right hand," the figure carries not only its usual sense of indispensable helper or aid—Rochester's weakness makes it necessary for Jane to do for him "what he wished to be done"—but the additional sense of a recovered wholeness. To the extent that this is persuasive, it is so because self-mutilation is the novel's central metaphor for the separation of Jane from Rochester. Jane's benediction on their marriage—"No woman was ever nearer to her mate than I am: ever more absolutely bone of his bone, and flesh of his flesh" (III, 11, 576) confirms Rochester's urging to it: "We must become one flesh without any delay, Jane: there is but the license to get—then we marry—" (III, 11, 570). The allusion to Genesis is especially apt, for both the story of Eve's creation and the story of Jane and Rochester's separation involve a literal dismemberment. When, after their marriage, Rochester regains his sight in one eye, there is a further advance in the direction of a literal restoration that is strongly associated with, if not literally caused by, the marriage itself.

The confusion about which hand Rochester has actually lost, the impulse to take Jane's words literally as well as figuratively, is faithful to the convergence of literal and figurative language in this passage and elsewhere in the novel. According to Margaret Homans, whose subject is literal language in women's texts, the literalization of figures occurs "when some piece of overtly figurative language, a simile or an extended or conspicuous metaphor, is translated into an actual event." In Homans's view, such literalizations are a staple feature of women's writing and connect "female linguistic practices" with "danger and death."[49] But for Brontë, the literalization of figures might be better understood as a defense of the imagination that reveals, or answers to, a pragmatic skepticism about its insights. The truth of imagination is confirmed when it achieves expression in the "real" world. Rochester's injuries literalize and authenticate the horror of his separation from Jane, and his dependence on her eyes when he has actually lost his own sight literalizes and authenticates his earlier figurative blindness to what she sees. When what was figurative is translated into an actual event, the invisible becomes visible.

The blinding of Rochester not only makes visible the invisible consequences of Jane's separation from him. It also completes the triumphant progress of a heroine who has been denied the right to look and punished by the looks of others. It makes her vision not only *primus inter pares* but (literally) exclusive. In the marriage of Jane and Rochester, Jane's vision becomes the whole of the visible world, and Brontë idealizes Jane and Rochester's "perfect concord" at the cost of the reciprocity that has been the defining attribute of their relation. This is a limitation in a marriage or in a novel that has set out to oppose the totalizing view of others.

The account of Jane's married life with Rochester is not memorable.[50] It involves neither the "reduction of Rochester's virility" nor "the removal of them both from contact with society" that Moglen saw as "necessary to maintain the integrity of the emergent female self." Instead, there are rounds of visiting that rely on the absence of Adele, a female child whose education recapitulates the one imposed on Jane, who sends her to a school that will turn her into "a pleasing and obliging companion: docile, good-tempered and well-principled." When Jane's own child is born, she denies her agency in the event, emphasizing instead the boy's patrimony: "When his first-born was put into his arms, he could see that the boy had inherited his own eyes, as they once were—large, brilliant, and black" (III, 12, 577). When "his first-born" is "put into his arms," Jane becomes as invisible in the transaction as she can be, while being naturally an accessory to it.

In the end, Brontë parries the risk of enshrining Jane's vision by these verbal acts of self-effacement. When the independent vision that has been Jane's best defense against social convention comes actively to condone it, the rebellious heroine's resistance is reconstituted as accommodation. By reinstating Jane into a society where all see alike, by restoring Rochester's vision, and by making Jane herself so invisible, Brontë undermines the novel's defense of Jane's oppositional and proprietary view and its still more powerful defense against the exclusion of women from visual pleasure and authority.

4. The "Mental Stomach" in *Shirley*: Digesting History

> Digest, v. *fig.* and *transf.* (from the digestion of food).
> To bear without resistance; to brook, endure, put up with; to "swallow, stomach."
> To comprehend and assimilate mentally; to obtain mental nourishment from.

The first words spoken in *Shirley* are a demand for food: "More bread!" They do not come from the starving workers in Robert Moore's woollen mill but from a hulking Irish curate, who addresses them to a fellow curate's landlady.

> "Cut it, woman," said her guest; and the "woman" cut it accordingly. Had she followed her inclinations, she would have cut the parson also; her Yorkshire soul revolted absolutely from his manner of command. (I, 1, 11)

These impositions by an overbearing foreign gentleman on a Yorkshire working-class woman who suppresses her ready response to them sound the main themes that *Shirley*'s readers have consistently charged the novel with failing to connect.[1] In Mrs. Gale, gender, class, and regional motives coincide, and her conflict with the curate reveals the deep relation between oppressive social distinctions and physical violence. "She would have cut the parson also." Her impulse is to make this young blade feel the edge of her knife and to affect not to see or know him, as if she were socially what she is morally, his superior.

Most readers will not need to be persuaded that food in *Shirley*'s opening scene has political and psychological as well as social valency. "Both perspectives," Stanley Cavell writes, are "interested in who produces food and in how food is distributed and paid for."[2] All three perspectives are interested in how much food is available, and in who provides and serves it. Six-year-old Abraham Gale's complaint when his mother's spice-cake disappears into the curates' bellies registers the throbbing protest of the novel's hungry workers and sounds the note of lamentation that is distinctive to *Shirley*: "He lifted up his voice and wept sore." The curates, blind mouths of a predatory Church, lack the authority that Abraham has here, by virtue of his patriarchal name and the Biblical diction that describes his plight. Brontë's sympathies in this primal conflict are solidly with Mrs. Gale, whose name suggests both a strong wind and the outcry proper to her kind.

As a novel that takes the ominous condition of England as its subject, *Shirley* has regularly been criticized as politically unimaginative and lacking in unity. Raymond Williams excluded it from his list of mid-nineteenth-century industrial novels in *Culture and Society*, and, more recently, Catherine Gallagher excludes it from hers "because industrial conflict in *Shirley* is little more than a historical setting and does not exert any strong pressure on the form."[3] Brontë's decision not to consider the plight of women operatives, a popular subject in industrial novels—*Shirley* mentions and refuses to consider that of children—follows from her proposition that the condition of leisured middle-class women and that of lower-class working men is homologous. As other readers have remarked, *Shirley* presses the hunger of jobless men who cannot feed their families into relation with that of middle-class women who lack meaningful work outside the home and whose lives are trammeled up in frustrated romantic attachments or overlooked by them. Gilbert and Gubar establish this connection, but see "the wrath of workers" as doing "the work of destruction for all those exploited, most especially . . . for those women famished for a sense of purpose in their lives."[4] Such a reading connects the novel's industrial and domestic plots, but only by making literal starvation a metaphor for psychic distress while reducing the workers to the status of psychological projections. Their hunger is subordinated to that of the women, whose political agents or "doubles" they become, according to a strategy that Gayatri Spivak has sharply criticized in her attempt to rehabilitate Bertha Rochester as a social subject.[5] These two complaints—that the novel fails to connect its disparate elements, chiefly its industrial and its feminist plots, and that industrial conflict is so inadequately apprehended as to be merely a historical setting rather than a problematic within which the most serious concerns of the novel can be situated—are necessarily related and deserve further consideration.

In this chapter, I argue that relations between famished workers and famished women in *Shirley* are more complex and contradictory than other readers have indicated, as are the pressures exerted in both directions by

Brontë's representation of them. "A Word to the 'Quarterly,'" the preface Brontë wrote for the novel (her publisher discouraged her from printing it), reveals not only how sharply she had been stung by Elizabeth Rigby's review of *Jane Eyre* but her own sense of the new novel's project and of how *Shirley* might defend its author against Rigby's charge, quoted at the start of the preface: "The tone of mind and thought which has overthrown authority and violated every code, human and divine—abroad—and fostered Chartism and Rebellion—at home—is the same which has written 'Jane Eyre.'"[6] *Shirley* was well underway by the time Brontë read the *Quarterly* review and wrote her preface, and the novel's historical background is Luddite, not Chartist, agitation, but its most evident political project is to resist violent change. The plot of *Shirley* serves this project well by settling the conflict between masters and workers too easily. The forces marshaled against the workers are more powerful than they need to be, the workers' leaders are self-serving and sinister, and the three punctuating Luddite events—the attacks on Robert Moore's new frames at the start, on his mill at the center, and on his life towards the end—are largely ineffectual. Moreover, the only practical answer to the difficulties of its workers that *Shirley* imagines very fully is kindness on the part of mill owners and others in a position to alleviate the distresses of unemployment.

For these reasons, *Shirley* may seem to recommend a version of social or benevolent paternalism, and so to resemble other nineteenth-century contributions to the industrial debate more closely than it does. But social paternalism is a doctrine grounded in faith in the family as "an enclave in which the virtues of benevolence, cooperation, and selflessness take refuge and survive,"[7] and the patriarchal family does not function either metaphorically as a model or metonymically as a school of social reform in *Shirley*. Instead, the novel consistently portrays familial relations, particularly those between husbands and wives and fathers and daughters, as coercive and distortive.[8] This is importantly so even when patriarchal relations are characterized by benevolence, as in the Reverend Matthewson Helstone's insistence that his ailing niece take a vacation instead of a job.

When *Shirley* makes familial relations a model for social relations, it imagines a nourishing mother, not a benevolent father, and figures the possibility of what might be called social maternalism rather than social paternalism. One difficulty with this way of putting things is that the nourishing mother/nursing infant dyad models symbiotic or undifferentiated interaction rather than a social relationship. But in Brontë's view, the fall into the social world always issues in violence, so that the rhythm of *Shirley*'s narrative is jerky, like that of organic life itself in *Beyond the Pleasure Principle*. In *Shirley*, as in the Freudian plot, the death instincts are more potent than the life instincts, and the novel repeatedly enacts retreats from the future it foresees and the present it brings into being in an effort to restore the tranquillity that Brontë associates with an earlier state of things.[9] The repeal of the Orders in Council at the end of the novel is one such retreat. It implies that the crises of both Caroline Helstone and Robert Moore's workers have been created by the Orders, which deprived England of foreign markets for its cloth and the mill-owner of his freedom of action, and can be resolved by their repeal. Paradoxically, the repeal is a reversal or undoing that bolsters the faith in progress associated with a heroic bourgeoisie and formulated by Moore himself, whose watchword is "Forward!" Progress is the theme of Moore's prediction of the future his mill will bring to birth in the novel's last chapter:

> Caroline, the houseless, the starving, the unemployed shall come to Hollow's mill from far and near; and Joe Scott shall give them work, and Louis Moore, Esq., shall let them a tenement, and Mrs. Gill shall mete them a portion till the first pay-day. (III, 14, 738)

The novel ends with a retreat into a more distant past, a past as sentimentally remembered as Moore's future is sentimentally conceived. The narrator imagines a future industry-scape "ambitious as the Tower of Babel," and his housekeeper's last words recall a pastoral landscape that ceased to exist long before the action of the novel began.[10] Moore's battle-charge is in tension not only with his opposition to England's ongoing war with France but with the novel's own investment in backward motion.

Shirley's defense against historical progress is clear in the psychological as well as the political strategies it recommends to its women and workers. Their survival and fulfillment depend on a willingness to relinquish power to men and masters that the novel consistently formulates as a regression into an earlier, unfallen social reality associated with both infancy and a pre-industrial agricultural and barter economy. To a greater degree than any other Brontë novel, *Shirley* relies on the resources of fantasy, melodrama, and myth to resolve "unresolvable social contradictions." I borrow the phrase from Fredric Jameson, who (following Lévi-Strauss's rules for interpreting the art of the Caduveos) argues that narrative form is "an ideological act in its own right, with the function of inventing imaginary or formal 'solutions' to unresolvable social contradictions."[11] In this chapter, I want to show that each of *Shirley*'s formal solutions to unresolvable social contradictions participates in a single psychological and political pattern and that Brontë's decision to treat a sequence of known events in *Shirley*, real because they are part of a historical record, forces a re-inscription of the novel's own narrative contract.

In the novel's paradigmatic fantasy, Caroline Helstone, *Shirley's* central character, nearly dies from inanition after Robert Moore abandons her, but her regress is halted at infancy when she recovers her long-lost mother, whose name—Mrs. Pryor—signals the pattern in which she participates. Caroline's story conjoins two powerful wishes: they are that complete dependence, the entire abnegation of self, will be rewarded by a "shower of manna" and that a regression to infancy, in which the child recovers her earliest relation to the world as nourishing mother, will really bring that world back into being. Shirley's variant on this pattern is a lesser regress involving her financial divestiture and her translation from property owner back into the pupil who marries her former master. Shirley's activity as a reciter and writer of mythic narratives belongs to this pattern; her stories of the Titan Eve and the marriage of Genius and Humanity evoke primordial worlds where women were more vital, more satisfied. William Farren, the novel's representative worker, loses a job in the textile mill but finds one first as a peddler and then as a gardener on Hiram Yorke's ancient estate. The attempted assassination of Robert Moore not only releases the aggressive impulses that have found no adequate expression in Farren's protest or Caroline's wasting illness but also infantilizes and feminizes him. The virago Mrs. Horsfall, Moore's nurse when he is invalided, teaches him "docility"; she "turned him in his bed as another woman would have turned a babe in his cradle."

In a letter written after the publication of *Jane Eyre*, G. H. Lewes warned Brontë "to beware of melodrama" and exhorted her "to adhere to the real."[12] Melodrama is among the evasions that *Shirley's* narrator explicitly deprecates at the novel's start:

> If you think, from this prelude, that anything like a romance is preparing for you, reader, you never were more mistaken. Do you anticipate sentiment, and poetry, and reverie? Do you expect passion, and stimulus, and melodrama? Calm your expectations; reduce them to a lowly standard. Something real, cool, and solid, lies before you; something unromantic as Monday morning, when all who have work wake with the consciousness that they must rise and betake themselves thereto. It is not positively affirmed that you shall not have a taste of the exciting, perhaps towards the middle and close of

the meal, but it is resolved that the first dish set upon the table shall be one that a Catholic—ay, even an Anglo-Catholic—might eat on Good Friday in Passion Week: it shall be cold lentiles and vinegar without oil; it shall be unleavened bread with bitter herbs and no roast lamb. (I, 1, 7–8)

At once strident and defensive, this recalls Brontë's preface to *The Professor*, but the idea that reading is like eating is specific to *Shirley*, and the familiarity of the comparison should not obscure the originality of this representation of reading as eating under its disciplinary aspect. The experience of reading *Shirley*, and the experience of its characters, is more like digestion than eating, and especially like the digestion of what is deemed wholesome because it is so evidently unappetizing. This passage is heavily revised in manuscript, and Brontë's rejected variants show she had digestion in mind when she sought the appropriate adjective to describe her novel. In one manuscript variant, she announces that readers need a change: "something—what you would call—*slow* is more (wholesome) [salutary]—something real (and severe and) [cool and solid ⟨and heavy of digestion⟩—something] unromantic as Monday Morning. . . ."[13] With its strong narrative movement from working Mondays to ritual Fridays and through the courses of a meal, this passage is implicitly concerned with the progress of human history. Brontë does not admit the possibility of the body's protest against its food, a protest in which the stomach would rebel by ejecting its contents, because digestion and protest are mutually exclusive. To do the one is not to do the other. Digestion is ambiguously active and passive, both an operation one performs and a process to be endured, an ambiguity that is reflected in the two contradictory figurative senses of digest, both "to obtain mental nourishment from" and "to brook, endure, put up with; to 'swallow, stomach.'" "Stomach" is also ambiguous, meaning both to endure or tolerate and, well into the nineteenth century, to resent or be offended at. In this warning to its readers, *Shirley* presents history as the story of bodies in pain, both the incarnated God's, fixed to the cross, and the eater's, racked by digestive agonies.

*   *   *

Mary Cave is *Shirley*'s emblem, as Helen Burns is *Jane Eyre*'s and Miss Marchmont is *Villette*'s.[14] Brontë positions these characters at the threshold of each novel, and each dies, not in place of the heroine but in a death that can be seen as a defensive displacement of powerful anxieties. The threat Miss Marchmont embodies for Lucy is another version of the living death or live burial later associated with the novel's haunting nun; her pathologically inconclusive mourning over her dead lover, marked by confinement and physical inaction, approximates Lucy's melancholic or depressive state of mind for most of the novel.[15] Helen Burns embodies the threat of premature death for Jane, as well as the bargain according to which the sense of error, first imposed by the world on the child, is internalized in return for the promise of forgiveness in another world in relation to which the value of this one is depleted. Jane resists this threat at the start, but her contest with St. John Rivers reactivates it. This contest has its main point in Jane's refusal to prefer death to life, the next world to this one, and St. John's Master to her own.

Each name is itself emblematic. Mary Cave is a warning (*cave* Mary) for Caroline, who takes Mary Cave's place in Helstone's house, because she blurs the boundaries between sickness and health, life and death. Death hardly changes her: from a "girl with the face of a Madonna; a girl of living marble; stillness personified," she becomes "a still beautiful-featured mould of clay left, cold and white, on the conjugal couch." Taken together, Mary Cave's Christian and family names suggest both holy virginity and a hollow place or underground opening like a grave. The obsolete adjective "cave," which means "waning," beautifully expresses Mary's progress and associates her with the moon, a traditionally feminine, dark, heavenly body. Long dead at the time of her appearance in the novel, Mary Cave serves partly to explain the antipathy between the men who were rivals for her, Hiram Yorke and Matthewson Helstone, whom she married "for his office's sake":

> and when she one day, as he thought, suddenly—for he had scarcely noticed her decline—but as others thought, gradually, took her leave of him and of life, and there was only a still beautiful-featured mould of clay left, cold and white, on the conjugal couch, he felt his bereavement—who shall say how little? Yet, perhaps, more than he seemed to feel it, for he was not a man from whom grief easily wrung tears. (I, 4, 62)

With a face that expresses no feeling (she either has or pretends to have none), Mary Cave represents not only a feminine ideal but a female fate, and the word "left" in "left, cold and white, on the conjugal couch" ambiguously suggests both "remaining" and "abandoned." Yet Helstone's inability to feel, or perhaps to express his feelings, marks him as another victim of socially imposed standards of behavior, not just their agent. Because neither her character nor the cause of her death can be determined, Mary Cave's life is a blank that can be filled by anyone's story. The neighborhood supplies her with a broken heart and a brutal husband. Mrs. Pryor says she was spiritless (II, 1, 247), and Robert Moore calls her only "a fair, regular-featured, taciturn-looking woman" (II, 7, 613). For Caroline, she figures the silence that is ambiguously conventional or natural to women.

Summarizing Freud's writings on the "profound silence" of women, Sarah Kofman dilates on the consequences for psychoanalytic narrative:

> Because woman does not have the *right* to speak, she stops being *capable or desirous of speaking*; she "keeps" everything to herself, and creates an excess of mystery and obscurity as if to avenge herself, as if striving for mastery. Woman *lacks sincerity*; she dissimulates, transforms each word into an enigma, an indecipherable *riddle*. [16]

Mary Cave's story suggests that women will go to any lengths not to make a claim for themselves, thereby disrupting the order of their faces or their lives. Her silence, which Caroline Helstone imitates when Robert Moore abandons her, marks her desire for that perfect tranquillity for which the price is nothing less than life itself. Yet despite Caroline's silence, her story is not "an indecipherable *riddle*." "Disappointed love never in its bitterest working perpetrated a hundredth part of the mischief it produced in the delicate frame of Caroline Helstone," wrote the anonymous reviewer for *The Times*. "We confess that, looking upon the skeleton and withered form of Miss Helstone in bed, we could on no rational theory account for the abiding fever and continued atrophy." [17] There may be no "rational theory" to account for Caroline's wasting illness, and women may never have died of broken hearts so often in life as in fiction, but the most powerful fantasy in *Shirley* is the one according to which Caroline's story undoes Mary Cave's by making prosperity and happiness rather than death the reward for a woman's silence.

Unlike Mary Cave's decline, Caroline's has a sharply demarcated beginning. Brontë represents the change in her prospects when Robert withdraws his affection from her as a sudden shift in genre, thereby giving her heroine's story affinities with her own development as a novelist. Until that time, Caroline sits "listening to a tale, a marvelous fiction; delightful sometimes, and sad sometimes; almost always unreal"; at that time, "the true narrative of life" commences. This narrative has justly been called "one of the bitterest pieces of Victorian prose": [18]

A lover masculine so disappointed can speak and urge explanation; a lover feminine can say nothing: if she did the result would be shame and anguish, inward remorse for self-treachery. Nature would brand such demonstration as a rebellion against her instincts, and would vindictively repay it afterwards by the thunder-bolt of self-contempt smiting suddenly in secret. Take the matter as you find it: ask no questions; utter no remonstrances: it is your best wisdom. You expected bread, and you have got a stone; break your teeth on it, and don't shriek because the nerves are martyrized: do not doubt that your mental stomach—if you have such a thing—is strong as an ostrich's—the stone will digest. You held out your hand for an egg, and fate put into it a scorpion. Show no consternation: close your fingers firmly upon the gift; let it sting through your palm. Never mind: in time, after your hand and arm have swelled and quivered long with torture, the squeezed scorpion will die, and you will have learned the great lesson how to endure without a sob. For the whole remnant of your life, if you survive the test—some, it is said, die under it—you will be stronger, wiser, less sensitive. This you are not aware of, perhaps, at the time, and so cannot borrow courage of that hope. Nature, however, as has been intimated, is an excellent friend in such cases; sealing the lips, interdicting utterance, commanding a placid dissimulation: a dissimu- lation often wearing an easy and gay mien at first, settling down to sorrow and paleness in time, then passing away and leaving a convenient stoicism, not the less fortifying because it is half-bitter. (I, 7, 117–18)

This passage about dissimulation itself dissimulates, especially in relation to whether Caroline's decision to say nothing is natural or conventional. The idea that nature would brand any demonstration of feeling "a rebel- lion against" a woman's "instincts" suggests the former, but the passage as a whole is alive with the contradictory insight. For example, it speaks of "a lover masculine" and "a lover feminine," phrases that suggest cultural constructs and locate imposed classifications. The essential feminist insight is that the confusion between what is natural and what is conventional sustains patriarchal oppression, which "consists of imposing certain social standards of femininity on all biological women, in order precisely to make us believe that the chosen standards for 'femininity' are *natural*."[19] Com- menting on this passage, Gilbert and Gubar argue that "the assurance that 'the stone will digest' or 'the squeezed scorpion will die' is contradicted not only by the images themselves but by the grotesque transubstantiation from bread to stone, from egg to scorpion, which is prescribed as a suitable punishment for someone 'guilty' of loving."[20] The inverted commas around "guilty" mark their resistance to the narrative "voice of repression," but Brontë asserts that a woman who protests her situation feels shame, not guilt, thereby recognizing that her aim is not to avoid doing wrong but to avoid being blamed. The essential element in shame, Darwin writes, is self-attention in relation to the opinion of others. "It is not the consciousness of guilt, but the thought that others think or know us to be guilty which crimsons the face."[21]

Stanley Cavell writes eloquently about the nexus of self-attention and social awareness in shame:

> Shame itself is exactly arbitrary and inflexible, and extreme in its effect. It is familiar to find that what mortifies one person seems wholly unimportant to another. Think of being ashamed of one's origins, one's accent, one's ignorance, one's skin, one's clothes, one's legs or teeth. . . . It is the most isolating of feelings, the most comprehensible perhaps as an idea, but the most incomprehensible or incommunicable in fact. Shame, I've said, is the most primitive, most private, of emotions; but it is also the most primitive of *social* responses. With the discovery of the individual, whether in Paradise or in the Renaissance, there is the simultaneous discovery of the isolation of the individual; his presence to himself, but simultaneously to *others*. Moreover, shame is felt not only toward one's own actions and one's own being, but toward the actions and the being of those with whom one is identified—fathers, daughters, wives . . . the beings whose self-revelations reveal oneself. Families, any objects of one's love and commitment, ought to be the places where shame is overcome (hence happy families are all alike); but they are also the place of its deepest manufacture, and one is then hostage to that power, or fugitive.[22]

Shame, the emotion that feels most private, is also "the most primitive of *social* responses." The individual's discovery of her isolation is simultaneously a discovery of her presence for others and the possibility of her association with them. A woman who characterizes herself as "a lover feminine" is acknowledging her own shame in relation to the actions and being of other women. *Shirley*'s narrator shows how Caroline naturalizes social conventions by internalizing blame and shows that women are active as well as passive, agents as well as victims, in the generation of gender. They have a lot to gain by becoming complicitous in patriarchal oppression. By speaking of "inward remorse," "self-treachery," and "self-contempt," they can attribute vindictiveness to an impersonal force like nature rather than to the men and women who are the "objects of one's love and commitment."

In a later passage on the condition of old maids, *Shirley*'s narrator argues that women dissimulate to avoid scorn, that scorn masks responsibility, and that responsibility begins in the family:

. . . to such grievances as society cannot readily cure, it usually forbids utterance, on pain of its scorn: this scorn being only a sort of tinselled cloak to its
deformed weakness. People hate to be reminded of ills they are unable or
unwilling to remedy: such reminder, in forcing on them a sense of their own
incapacity, or a more painful sense of an obligation to make some unpleasant
effort, troubles their ease and shakes their self-complacency. Old maids, like
the houseless and unemployed poor, should not ask for a place and an occupation in the world: the demand disturbs the happy and rich: it disturbs
parents. (II, 11, 441)

On the one hand, there are "such grievances as society cannot readily
cure"; old maids, the houseless, and the unemployed poor tell us what
these are. On the other, there are people who "hate to be reminded of ills
they are unable or unwilling to remedy," the happy, the rich, and parents.
Like the houseless, old maids are out of place, and like the unemployed
poor, they lack an occupation. What is required is that all these relations
of domination be hidden. Shame in these instances attaches itself to the
wrong objects, to the silent who are dispossessed and required not to utter
a reproach, rather than to those who collude in their dispossession and
require their silence.

Mrs. Yorke's insistence that her daughter Rose not be "too forward to
talk" provides a further commentary on Caroline's analysis of her situation.
According to Mrs. Yorke, "it becomes all children, especially girls, to be
silent in the presence of their elders." "And why especially girls, mother?"
Rose asks. Because "discretion and reserve is a girl's best wisdom" (I, 9, 173).
The echo of the narrator's own words—"ask no questions; utter no remonstrances; it is your best wisdom"—suggests the difficulty of firmly
settling the tone of either passage and brings Mrs. Yorke's repressive injunctions into relation with both the fable of the scorpion, the "lesson" of
which is "how to endure without a sob," and Caroline's understanding
that the demands of women are prohibited because they disturb parents.
In the familiar passages from Matthew and Luke to which the passage
about Caroline's anguish alludes, a father's receptivity to his son's demands
is the model for God's responsiveness to human prayer:

Ask, and it will be given you; seek and you will find; knock, and it will be
opened to you. For every one who asks receives, and he who seeks finds, and
to him who knocks it will be opened. Or what man of you, if his son asks
him for bread, will give him a stone? [23]

For every one who asks receives, and he who seeks finds, and to him who
knocks it will be opened. What father among you, if his son asks for a fish,

will instead of a fish give him a serpent; or if he asks for an egg, will give him a scorpion?[24]

But a woman's hope—"you expected bread"—and desire—"you held out your hand for an egg"—are punishable by torture. Moreover, a woman's hunger is not merely denied. The response to it is its negative inversion, an act of force-feeding that would get the (mental) stomach to digest what not only does not nourish but breaks the teeth and martyrizes the nerves. The verb "digest" is intransitive here, an action performed by the food rather than the body: "the stone will digest." The scorpion also is active, causing the hand and arm to swell in a grotesque parody of repletion.

Three verses of an old Scotch ballad, "Puir Mary Lee," the story of a woman who is "ill-used," follow Caroline's pledge of silence. Mary is uncomplaining, yet she is "deeply-feeling" and "strongly-resentful," and she curses Robin-a-Ree. The point of quoting the ballad would seem to be to claim Caroline's kinship with other betrayed women, but the narrator denies any connection between the poor peasant-girl and the parson's niece:

> But what has been said in the last page or two is not germane to Caroline Helstone's feelings, or to the state of things between her and Robert Moore. Robert had done her no wrong: he had told her no lie; it was she that was to blame, if any one was: what bitterness her mind distilled should and would be poured on her own head. She had loved without being asked to love,—a natural, sometimes an inevitable chance, but big with misery. (I, 7, 119)

Speaking for rather than to Caroline, the narrator does not instruct her in how to perceive her relationship with Robert but represents Caroline's own view of it, that of a woman more civilized—less close to her own nature—than Mary Lee. But Brontë's metaphor exposes Caroline's defense of Robert as disingenuous and her own self-accusations as a reflex of social scorn. Loving without being asked to love is as natural and inevitable a chance as pregnancy itself. "She had loved without being asked to love,—a natural, sometimes an inevitable chance, but big with misery." Her metaphor assimilates the shame of loving and the shame of resenting to the shame—not guilt—of the unwed mother.

Caroline's self-respect depends on her capacity to digest, or to suffer digestion, and denies the usual equation of submission and weakness along with that of femininity and a delicate stomach. As John Kucich argues, Brontë sees such self-conflict as both harrowing and heroic.[25] But " half-bitter" refers to the unpleasant taste in Caroline's mouth as she stomachs her stone and to her resentment, that is, to how it feels to stomach a stone. She both acknowledges and justifies the deflection of this resentment away from Robert and toward herself: "what bitterness her mind distilled should and would be poured on her own head." The negative reward for her silence is obvious—she cannot be an object of scorn or (like Mary Lee) pity. The positive reward is no less important: her silence preserves both her anger and her idealized image of Robert Moore.

In *Villette*, Brontë represents such a state of mind even more fully than she does in *Shirley*. There, all "marvelous fiction" belongs to a narrative outside of and prior to that of the novel itself and admitted to it only by way of occasional references to "past days" when Lucy "*could* feel. About the present, it was better to be stoical; about the future—such a future as mine—to be dead. And in catalepsy and a dead trance, I studiously held the quick of my nature" (I, 12, 151–52). Freud calls this melancholia, and his differentiation of it from mourning might have been generated out of Brontë's study of Caroline Helstone. "In mourning," Freud writes, "it is the world which has become poor and empty; in melancholia it is the ego itself." According to Freud, the melancholiac's loss of self-esteem is the result of a perverse "identification of the ego with the abandoned object," so that the object-loss is transformed into an ego-loss.[26] The hostility against the object can now be expressed as hostility against the self, and inhibition can be safely exchanged for exhibition, always an aspect of these wasting illnesses.

Shirley finds Caroline reciting "The Castaway" to herself, and Cowper beautifully catches the melancholy despair of the abandoned and self-blaming (but not self-pitying) sufferer. "I hear in it," Caroline says, "no sob or sorrow, only the cry of despair; but, that cry uttered, I believe the deadly spasm passed from his heart; that he wept abundantly, and was comforted" (II, 1, 253–54). The cry gives relief, yet it is a relief that Brontë regularly denies to women. Mary Taylor, Brontë's feminist friend, is the biographical model for Rose Yorke, who refuses to idealize Caroline's stoicism:

> I am resolved that my life shall be a life: not a black trance like the toad's, buried in marble; nor a long, slow death like yours in Briarfield Rectory. . . . Might you not as well be tediously dying, as forever shut up in that glebe-house—a place that, when I pass it, always reminds me of a windowed grave?" (II, 12, 451)

Like Mary Taylor, Rose Yorke chooses emigration to another hemisphere, one of Carlyle's two practical solutions to the conditions of the working classes in *Chartism* and a solution that William Farren and Robert Moore also consider. Caroline's silence cannot be such a solution to the condition of women, as Rose Yorke perceives, for her life is too much like death. Nature's excellent friendship to women in "sealing the lips, interdicting utterance," and "commanding a placid dissimulation" provides the plot of Mary Cave's life: she *is* the dissimulation that is imagined as wearing "an easy and gay mien at first, settling down to sorrow and paleness in time, then passing away and leaving a convenient stoicism." Rose Yorke's image of the black trance of the toad buried in marble revises the novel's earlier image of this "girl of living marble," and explicitly identifies Caroline's story as a re-telling of Mary Cave's. "Better to try all things and find all empty," she tells her, "than to try nothing and leave your life a blank" (II, 12, 452).

When Mrs. Yorke reminds her daughter that "solid satisfaction is only to be realized by doing one's duty," Rose turns her mother's words against her in a brilliant, feminist reading of the parable of the talents, which concludes with the words of which Cowper's poem is "a narrative expansion," "cast the unprofitable servant into outer darkness": [27]

> Right, mother! And if my Master has given me ten talents, my duty is to trade with them, and make them ten talents more. Not in the dust of household drawers shall the coin be interred. I will *not* deposit it in a broken-spouted tea-pot, and shut it up in a china-closet among tea-things. I will *not* commit it to your work-table to be smothered in piles of woollen hose. I will *not* prison it in the linen-press to find shrouds among the sheets: and least of all, mother—(she got up from the floor)—least of all will I hide it in a tureen of cold potatoes, to be ranged with bread, butter, pasty, and ham on the shelves of the larder. (II, 12, 452)

Gilbert and Gubar observe that the pun on "talents" connects "the financial dependence of women and the destruction of their creative potential,"[28] but what is more remarkable about Rose Yorke's reading of the Christian parable is the sense that making money is itself the creative activity at issue. These talents are literal coins, specifically capital to be used rather than saved. Women's work is distinguished from men's work both because men's work is paid work and because it generates goods and money while women's work—the daily, repetitive chores performed by women in the passage—only preserves and repairs what men acquire and require. Mary Taylor's report after opening her shop in New Zealand suggests how accurately Brontë represented her friend's dissatisfaction with the work traditionally assigned to women: "The best of it [the shop] is that your labour has some return and you are not forced to work on hopelessly without result."[29] Caroline asks her uncle's permission to seek work as a governess, but her fantasy, revealed to Robert early on in the novel, is to learn the cloth-trade and make money by it. Confined to the home, she also resents having to darn stockings or give tea to the curates when she would rather be reading. In Rose's dark view, the home is tediously deathly and deadening, no longer a refuge from the outside world, a productive unit, or the place where children are nurtured and reared. Her passionate defense of capitalist enterprise subsumes a Marxist analysis of the alienation of women from the carceral spaces and tools associated with their labor (household drawers, china-closets, linen presses, larders, tureens, and teapots) and from their very selves, divided by contradictory duties and imperatives.

Despite the power of this analysis, however, *Shirley* backs away from its largest implications by making work outside the home an issue only for unmarried women. Mary Taylor sharply criticized Brontë for this in the same letter in which she reported having opened her shop in New Zealand:

> I have seen some extracts from 'Shirley' in which you talk of women working. And this first duty, this great necessity you seem to think that some women may indulge in—if they give up marriage and don't make themselves too disagreeable to the other sex. You are a coward and a traitor. A woman who works is by that alone better than one who does not and a woman who does not happen to be rich and who *still* earns no money and does not wish to do so, is guilty of a great fault—almost a crime—a dereliction of duty which leads rapidly and almost certainly to all manner of degradation. It is very wrong of you to *plead* for toleration for workers on the ground of their being in peculiar circumstances and few in number or singular in disposition. Work or degradation is the lot of all except the very small number born to wealth.[30]

Taylor's criticism is unanswerable, given its once revolutionary and still simplifying premise: "A woman who works [outside the home] is by that alone better than one who does not." Better, Taylor argues, because financial independence is her only sure protection against degradation. Brontë doesn't accept this premise, because her knowledge that the exclusion of women from work outside the home makes their lives intolerable conflicts with her belief that the happiest of women are those who are happily married. She is unable or unwilling to relinquish her faith in love as a solvent despite all the evidence in *Shirley* that marriage is not just regularly unhappy but suicidal, as in the story of Mary Cave, and degrading, as in the story of Mrs. Pryor.

Of the two loveless old maids Caroline visits, Miss Mann is the more interesting because the less amiable. Neither a saint like Miss Ainley nor a comedy spinster like Jane Austen's Miss Bates, she practices a self-burial like the toad's in marble:

> She herself sat primly and somewhat grimly tidy in a cushioned rocking-chair, her hands busied with some knitting: this was her favourite work, as it required the least exertion. She scarcely rose as Caroline entered; to avoid excitement was one of Miss Mann's aims in life: she had been composing herself ever since she came down in the morning, and had just attained a certain lethargic state of tranquillity when the visitor's knock at the door startled her, and undid her day's work. She was scarcely pleased, therefore, to see Miss Helstone: she received her with reserve, bade her be seated with austerity, and when she had got her placed opposite, she fixed her with her eye. (I, 10, 198–99)

At first glance, Miss Mann seems the antithesis of Mary Cave, the marble beauty. She is the entirely undesirable woman, as Brontë indicates by both her name and her eye, which is, Robert Moore says, equal to the Medusa's and capable of changing male flesh into stone. But this difference masks a likeness and a reciprocity. "A woman is for a man both more and less than a person," Adrienne Rich writes,

> she is something terribly necessary and necessarily terrible. She is not simply "more than an exploited worker"; she is not simply the "other"; she is first of all the Mother who has to be possessed, reduced, controlled, lest she swallow him back into her dark caves, or stare him into stone.[31]

Although both Miss Mann and Mary Cave are deadly, Miss Mann is more threatening as well as more vital. In addition to fixing people with her Gorgon eye, she flays them alive, operates on their faults "like some surgeon," and dissects impartially almost everyone (II, 10, 200). Yet she suffers from the affliction all the novel's women share; another "dying tenant of a decaying house," she has "a starved, ghostly longing for appreciation and affection":

> To this extenuated spectre, perhaps, a crumb is not thrown once a year; but when ahungered and athirst to famine—when all humanity has forgotten the dying tenant of a decaying house—Divine Mercy remembers the mourner, and a shower of manna falls for lips that earthly nutriment is to pass no more. (II, 10, 201)

Like emigration, this turn to Christian myth involves dying to an old world in order to be reborn into a new one. It anticipates Caroline's long decline and the recovery that ultimately appeases her own "starved, ghostly longing for appreciation and affection."

I have said that the two powerful fantasies conjoined in Caroline's story are that complete dependence, the entire abnegation of self, will be rewarded by a "shower of manna" and that a regression to infancy in which the child recovers her prior relationship to the world as nourishing mother will really bring that world back into being. In Caroline, the anger that has its source in unappeased hunger is turned inward, where it feeds on her and she feeds on it.[32] Like other heroines of sensibility, Caroline might have been rescued from the silence that has its most likely conclusion in a premature death by Robert Moore's change of heart, but this occurs too late. Instead, she discovers her own long-lost mother in her best friend's governess. This outcome is so important to Brontë that she imposes it on the narrative of Caroline's life despite its manifold improbabilities and awkwardnesses. These include Mrs. Pryor's explanation of her abandonment of Caroline as an infant ("I let you go as a babe, because you were pretty, and I feared your loveliness; deeming it the stamp of perversity"); her reappearance in Caroline's vicinity, where she is unrecognized by her brother-in-law, Caroline's uncle; and everyone's silence about her relation to Robert and Louis Moore, who are her nephews, as well as Caroline's cousins. "But if you *are* my mother," Caroline says, "the world is all changed to me. Surely I can live—I should like to recover—" (III, 1, 487). This speech is Brontë's version of Miranda's, and after she has made it, Caroline not only revives but her world does seem to be braver and newer.

By restoring Mrs. Pryor to Caroline, *Shirley* firmly locates the model for the individual's relationship to the world in the earliest bond of all, that of mother and child. Because the acceptance of food is "the primary acknowledgement of one's dependence on the world,"[33] the refusal of food can constitute an assertion of radical independence. At the same time, however, the model of mother and infant argues that such independence is not only self-defeating but illusory. Human infants are more dependent for longer than the young of other species. Able to demand food, they cannot take it unless it is given. "The power of the mother is, first of all, to give or withhold nourishment and warmth, to give or withhold survival itself."[34] Caroline has no memory of a life with her mother, but she remembers her father as a man who "went out early every morning, and often forgot to return and give her her dinner during the day, and at night, when he came back, was like a madman, furious, terrible; or—still more painful—like an idiot, imbecile, senseless" (I, 7, 115). This memory of a bad father stands in for what is repressed, the memory of a bad mother, for both Caroline and the narrator understand Mrs. Pryor's abandonment of her child as a desperate consequence of her own oppression: "I *have* suffered!" she tells Caroline. "None saw,—none knew; there was no sympathy—no redemption—no redress!" (III, 1, 489). The darkest secret in *Shirley* is the secret of a feminine identity constituted by imprisonment in a house, dependence on a powerful male figure for nourishment, and willingness to turn anger against the self, as Caroline does, or against the daughter who is a part of the self, as Mrs. Pryor does. Caroline's thoughts about sexual difference support such a reading of childhood lessons:

> "Different, indeed," she concluded, "is Robert's mental condition to mine: I think only of him; he has no room, no leisure to think of me. The feeling called love is and has been for two years the predominant emotion of my heart; always there, always awake, always astir: quite other feelings absorb his reflections, and govern his faculties. He is rising now, going to leave the church, for service is over. Will he turn his head towards this pew?—no—not once—he has not one look for me: that is hard: a kind glance would have made me happy till tomorrow: I have not got it; he would not give it; he is gone. Strange that grief should now almost choke me, because another human being's eye has failed to greet mine." (I, 10, 192)

"I have not got it; he would not give it" insists again on the deep reciprocity of nourishment. Caroline cannot eat unless she is fed.

Except in its requirement that she instinctively love her child, Mrs. Pryor, like Mrs. Yorke, the other significant mother in *Shirley*, subscribes to the patriarchal ideology that confirms her powerlessness and guilt even before she abandons her child to a brutal and careless father. In telling the story of Mrs. Pryor's life as a governess before her marriage, Brontë quotes liberally from Rigby's review of *Jane Eyre*, attributing the quotations to Mrs. Pryor's employer and pupil, Mrs. and Miss Hardman. The name figures in a version of Gothic doubling or mirroring: Mrs. Pryor (then Miss Grey) escapes from the house of Hardman only to find herself securely imprisoned by the man named Helstone. So many years later, Mrs. Pryor still defends the system according to which the "crimes" and "imprudencies" of some fathers create governesses for the benefit of the daughters of others. "Implicit submission to authorities, scrupulous deference to our betters (under which term I, of course, include the higher classes of society) are, in my opinion, indispensable to the wellbeing of every community" (II,10, 425). At the same time, she strongly deprecates the illusion of "mutual love": "Two people can never literally be as one . . . let all the single be satisfied with their freedom" (II, 10, 427). Recovering her grown-up daughter, Mrs. Pryor recovers the dream of the fusional relation she failed to find in her marriage and refused to trust in her early relation to that child:

> I say you are *mine*. I have proved it. I thought perhaps you were all his, which would have been a cruel dispensation for me: I find it is *not* so. God permitted me to be the parent of my child's mind: it belongs to me: it is my property—my *right*. (II, 1, 486)

This is fiercely acquisitive and possessive, a passionate love that is also sexually jealous. Indeed, relations between the reunited mother and daughter must be sufficiently like those between lovers for Mrs. Pryor and Robert Moore to stand in for each other in Caroline's story. Moore's abandonment of Caroline reenacts the abandonment of her by Mrs. Pryor, and Mrs. Pryor takes Moore's place as Caroline's rescuer. When Moore finally comes to propose to Caroline, he puts his arm around her and she mistakes his touch for Mrs. Pryor's: "Caroline thought she knew who had drawn near: she received the touch unstartled" (II, 14, 731). The novel does not answer the question of whether Caroline seeks a lover in her mother or a mother in her lover, but it connects a woman's capacity for sexual response to her earliest experience of a nurturing female body and her longing to recover her own infancy when love was not only "the predominant emotion of her heart" but like an infant itself, held close to the heart, and "always there, always awake, always astir."

*   *   *

An image of mother and infant is at the center of *Coriolanus*, the play that Robert and Caroline read together in Chapter 6. This is Volumnia, chastising her daughter-in-law Virgilia for flinching at the thought of Coriolanus's battle wounds:

> . . . The brests of *Hecuba*
> When she did suckle *Hector*, look'd not lovelier
> Then *Hectors* forhead, when it spit forth blood
> At Grecian sword. (I, iii) [35]

So wonderful a compacting of our most primitive impulses, the desire to eat or incorporate and the opposite desire to spit out or expel, deserves the attention Janet Adelman pays it in her powerful psychoanalytic reading of the play. She shows how Volumnia's image functions as a defense against the "vulnerability inherent in taking nourishment when it transforms feeding into spitting out, an aggressive expelling," and the wound as mouth into "an instrument of attack."[36] As Stanley Cavell recognizes, Volumnia's image transforms not only the infant's mouth but the mother's breast into a wound and instrument of attack. The very milk that sustains the infant's life becomes the mother's blood that eagerly spills the man's. Volumnia's allusion recalls her difference from Hecuba, who not only bares her breast to Hector but holds it out to him in a desperate effort to persuade her son not to meet his enemies outside the walls of Troy:

> . . . Hektor, my child, be moved by this,
> and pity me, if ever I unbound
> a quieting breast for you.[37]

Coriolanus is corrosive in its pitiless denial of the possibility of a nourishing organic relationship between mother and child. Virgilia is the play's hostage to pity, a woman equally remarkable for her ineffectuality and her silence.[38]

Reading *Coriolanus* provides an occasion for Caroline to play a commanding role with Moore, for English is his second language, and the reading reverses their usual roles as teacher and pupil. Moreover, because Moore reads the comic scenes badly, Caroline reads them for him. If Brontë has in mind the scenes involving the plebeians, Caroline speaks for them, yet to call these scenes comic is to diminish their serious claim on us. In his remarkable study of the first scene of *Coriolanus*, Bertolt Brecht argues against the practice of making the plebeians "seem ridiculous" in the "normal" or "bourgeois" theater. "If they let themselves be taken in I wouldn't find them comic but tragic. That would be a possible scene, *for such things happen*, but a horrifying one."[39] It is difficult for the plebeians to identify themselves as an oppressed class and even more difficult for them to revolt, revolt being "the unnatural rather than the natural thing." Brontë's later treatment of *Shirley*'s workers subsumes an analysis of popular revolt very like Brecht's, but in the scene of the play's reading, Caroline takes Moore's side, not that of the plebeians. She chooses *Coriolanus* for Moore's reading lesson in order to reveal his resemblance to Shakespeare's hero. Moore shares Coriolanus's pride, his disdain for "his famished fellow-men," and an admiration for a foreign hero (Napoleon) that contrasts

sharply with his scorn for his own countrymen, "these English clowns."
After the reading, Caroline answers Moore's question about Coriolanus's
fault—the cause of the citizens' hatred and his banishment—by quoting
a portion of Aufidius's speech in Act V. Asked to choose among the
traits Aufidius assigns to Coriolanus (pride, "defect of judgment," and
nature—"Not to be other than one thing"), she pedantically elucidates the
play's "moral":

> "It was a spice of all: and you must not be proud to your workpeople; you
> must not neglect chances of soothing them, and you must not be of an in-
> flexible nature, uttering a request as austerely as if it were a command."
> (I, 6, 105)

This interpretation aligns her with Moore rather than with his disaffected
workers, but by putting the novel's industrial conflict in the service of an
exposition of its hero's character, it carries a larger political charge. Like
Coriolanus itself, *Shirley* values individual conflict more than class conflict
and each character's struggle with himself or herself more than the social
struggle in which they are caught up.

Both *Coriolanus* and *Shirley* were written during a period of rising
corn prices, fear of starvation, and popular turmoil, and both involve war,
famine, and civil insurrection. In Shakespeare's time, popular distress was
associated with the Enclosure Acts and the loss of traditional rights to
land, but the "moral problem, or social tension" of the play is, in Kenneth
Burke's reading of it, "simply a kind of discord intrinsic to the distinction
between upper classes and lower class." Shakespeare managed "a certain
'distance,'" Burke writes, "by treating the problem in terms not of contemporary London but of ancient Rome."[40] Brontë's decision to set her novel
in the near past achieves a similar distance, but it also shifts the focus of
class conflict from Chartism to Luddism. The decision to focus on Luddism rather than Chartism is significant apart from the explanation offered
by Gaskell and repeated by Margaret Smith and Jane Jack, that Brontë's
"school-days had been partly spent in the heart of the Luddite country"
and that "she was anxious to write of things she had known and seen."[41]
Rigby's review of *Jane Eyre* suggests how dangerous the Chartist movement still appeared in 1848, near the end of a decade when rising corn
prices, crop failures, and agitation for repeal of the Corn Laws reproduced
the conditions on which Luddism had thrived, but the scale of the response to Luddism was grander. Lacking an effective police force, the
West Riding mill-owners had to depend on themselves or the military.

According to Asa Briggs, the "12,000 troops employed against the Ludd-
ites greatly excelled in size the army which Wellington took into the Pen-
insula in 1808."[42] Luddite attacks on property and life aroused fears of
lawlessness and insurrection more directly than later Chartist demonstrations and assemblies, and Luddism was regularly confused with crime
in general and with food riots, especially since what began as a food riot
might end in an attack on machinery. *Shirley* both ignites these fears and
dampens them: its workers are criminals when they attack Moore's new
frames, his mill, and his life, but they are cowardly, weak criminals. Both
Moore and the faithful workers who bring his new frames to him are
unarmed when they are attacked, and the mill itself is defended not by a
troop of soldiers but by a dozen brave men.

In *Coriolanus*, the plebeians charge that the patricians are hoarding
food. Although *Shirley*'s workers are not asking that food be distributed
but that they be given back the jobs they have lost, the novel responds to
their demands as if their hunger were the only issue. In an excellent summary of the history of Luddism and its relation to *Shirley*, Igor Webb
makes the important point that the manufacturers' assertion of "*their* freedom to do as they like with *their* property . . . abolished, in theory and
fact, the freedom of workers to control their work, and violated the system
of work relationships around which life in the woollen districts—and elsewhere—had been organized for generations."[43] In substituting machinery
for men, Moore treats his men as machines, expressing his own freedom
by making them merely instrumental to his own enterprise, as the plebeians are merely instrumental to that of Coriolanus, who has a war against
the Volsces to prosecute. "I'll make my cloth as I please, and according to
the best lights I have," Moore tells his workers, asserting the aristocrat's
privilege of doing as one likes. "In its manufacture I will employ what
means I choose."

As in *Coriolanus*, the hero is someone whose character magnifies the
tensions within his world and whose actions play them up. Burke's formula for tragic catharsis as exemplified by *Coriolanus* defines the tragic
hero as someone whose excesses force us "to confront the discriminatory
motives intrinsic to society as we know it" and whose functions are at once
"expressive," therapeutic, and ultimately purgative when the issue is his
own downfall and "a promise of general peace."[44] Tragedy also lurks
within Robert Moore's story, but it is subordinated to the sentimental
comedy of Caroline Helstone's story. Assigning the tragic parts of *Coriolanus* to Moore and the comic parts to Caroline has already provided a

model for this gendering of genre. Tragedy is traditionally masculine, but *Shirley*'s feminine comedy proves more exacting. The tragic potential of Moore's confrontation with the workers is diminished to the degree that he is willing to profit from Caroline's instruction. The tragic outcome she foresees, the attempted assassination, occurs and ministers to Moore's re-generation, but it fails to become socially redemptive. Its symbolic value in the novel depends on its contribution to Brontë's analysis of good and bad mothering, an analysis that requires that Moore, like Coriolanus, con-front the mother's power to withhold and destroy.

Brontë was influenced by Shakespeare's tribunes in her representation of *Shirley*'s chief agitators, Moses Barraclough and Noah o' Tim's, and she was also responding to the Chartist, not Luddite, issue of who was to represent the workers. Moore accuses Noah and Moses of "selfish am-bition, as dangerous as it is puerile" (I, 8, 152), but if Brontë's portrait of the agitators makes a strong case against self-representation for the work-ers, her portrait of William Farren does the opposite. Moreover, while *Shirley* fully shares the anxiety of its own age and Shakespeare's about "the mob," it not only undercuts that anxiety by limiting its workers' delegation to twelve orderly supplicants but makes a stronger case than *Coriolanus* for its workers' humanity. They are men with specific skills and particular trades (some are in shirt-sleeves and some wear blue aprons; most of them are cloth-dressers), and they speak in the West Riding dialect that keeps us from forgetting Moore's foreign blood and foreign ways of thinking. William Farren, who argues strongly against Moore's careless disdain for his workers, speaks eloquently about the hunger of his fellow workers and their families:

"I've not much faith i' Moses Barraclough," said he; "and I would speak a word to you myseln, Mr. Moore. It's out o' no ill-will that I'm here, for my part; it's just to mak' a effort to get things straightened, for they're sorely acrooked. Ye see we're ill off,—varry ill off: wer families is poor and pined. We're thrawn out o'work wi' these frames: we can get nought to do: we can earn nought. What is to be done? Mun we say, wisht! and lig us down and dee? Nay: I've no grand words at my tongue's end, Mr. Moore, but I feel that it wad be a low principle for a reasonable man to starve to death like a dumb cratur':—I will n't do't. I'm not for shedding blood: I'd neither kill a man nor hurt a man; and I'm not for pulling down mills and breaking machines: for, as ye say, that way o' going on 'll niver stop invention; but I'll talk,—I'll mak' as big a din as ever I can. Invention may be all right, but I know it isn't right for poor folks to starve. Them that governs us mun find a way to help us: they mun mak' fresh orderations. Ye'll say that's hard to do:—so much

louder mun we shout out then, for so mich slacker will t'Parliament-men be
to set on to a tough job." (I, 8, 153–54)

In *Coriolanus*, as many readers have observed, words substitute for food.
The grim reality is that the plebeians are starving; the grimmer reality, as
Brecht suggests, is that Menenius's fable of the belly may deflect their
attention from the rupture of the organic life of the body politic, a rupture
the fable simultaneously denies and disguises by providing a comprehen-
sible account of the dominance of the patricians that makes that dominance appear not only beneficial but necessary and natural. In the scene in
Shirley, words also substitute for food, but the words are bitter rather than
sweet, hard to digest and swallow. The workers ask for bread, and Moore
gives them a stone. His speech is full of "selfish ambition, as dangerous as
it is puerile":

> "William Farren, neither to your dictation, nor to that of any other, will I
> submit. Talk to me no more about machinery; I will have my own way. I shall
> get new frames in to-morrow:—If you broke these, I would still get more.
> *I'll never give in.*" (I, 8, 154)

In his nobler speech, Farren brilliantly articulates the double bind of
Shirley's workers, and Brontë emphasizes two of his points by putting
them into standard English. He is unwilling to harm either the mill owner
or his machinery ("I'm not for shedding blood: I'd neither kill a man nor
hurt a man . . ."), and he cannot stomach the injustice of his plight ("I
know it isn't right for poor folks to starve . . ."). To accept his distress
passively would be to participate in an act of leveling even more threatening than the destruction of machinery or factories. It would be to accept
death like dumb creatures. This reduction of men to the level of animals
stands in for an instance of leveling more potently insurrectionary, their
reduction to the level of women, for it is women who starve to death
uncomplainingly. Farren insists on his duty to rebel in a conversation with
Caroline and Shirley in which he defines masculinity in opposition to
feminine weakness and dependence:

> Look at t' difference between us: ye're a little, young slender lass, and I'm a
> great strong man: I'm rather more nor twice your age. It is not *my* part then,
> I think, to tak' fro' *ye*—to be under obligations (as they say) to *ye*; and that
> day ye came to our house, and called me to t'door, and offered me five shill-
> ings, which I doubt ye could ill spare,—for ye've no fortin', I know,—that
> day I war fair a rebel—a radical—an insurrectionist; and *ye* made me so.
> (II, 7, 365)

Farren's dilemma suggests the extent to which *Shirley*'s arguments about the silence of women are self-canceling, for the novel simultaneously argues against the silence of women and against the silence of men because they are not women.[45] In their disagreement with Joe Scott, Moore's foreman, immediately after their conversation with Farren, Shirley and Caroline protest the silencing of women with a revisionary reading of the second chapter of St. Paul's first Epistle to Timothy: "Let the woman learn in silence, with all subjection. I suffer not a woman to teach, nor to usurp authority over the man; but to be in silence. For Adam was first formed, then Eve" (II, 7, 370). Caroline speculates that the Greek has been "wrongly translated" and offers a revised text: "Let the woman speak out whenever she sees fit to make an objection." Shirley's feminist myth of the first woman also tells of her right to speak directly to God without Adam's mediation:

> I saw—I now see—a woman-Titan: her robe of blue air spreads to the outskirts of the heath, where yonder flock is grazing. . . . Her forehead has the expanse of a cloud, and is paler than the early moon, risen long before dark gathers: she reclines her bosom on the ridge of Stilbro' Moor; her mighty hands are joined beneath it. So kneeling, face to face she speaks with God. That Eve is Jehovah's daughter, as Adam was his son. (II, 7, 360–61)

Shirley's Eve is both a daughter of Jehovah, equal to his son, and a powerful mother, the mother of gods. Her "mighty hands" are joined beneath a capacious maternal bosom; her willingness to kneel before her father is consonant with her right to address him "face to face."

Lacking the financial resources that enable Rose Yorke's escape to another hemisphere, Farren can only transcend his impossible choice between feminization and radicalization by means of a world-changing fantasy. In a startling reversal of history, the novel relocates him in a pre-industrial world of independent traders who are not producers and of men who cultivate the land. The few natural tears he weeps in his distress are said to be drops "much more like the 'first of a thunder-shower' than those which oozed from the wound of the gladiator" (I, 9, 155). This transformation of tears into rain confirms both his affinity with the natural world and his inability to triumph over the unnatural conditions that bind him. Mr. Hall, the motherly vicar of Nunnely, preserves him from starvation in an action that parallels Mrs. Pryor's rescue of Caroline. He offers to lend Farren five pounds to "begin selling stuff." Soon, at Robert Moore's urging, Hiram Yorke, the fatherly Yorkshire landowner, employs Farren as a gardener on his estate. When Farren makes his final appearance several chapters later, he can assure Shirley that he is very well off.

Brontë's treatment of Farren elicits sympathy for the novel's workers as individuals, not "English clowns," and simultaneously argues against any solution to their difficulties that is not an individualizing one. It denies that their oppression, like that of single women in Mary Taylor's view, is inherent in the warped system of things. In this way, William Farren and Caroline Helstone represent the interests of workers and women, while the relief each is granted fails to address the suffering of the groups to which each belongs. Such relief provides an escape from the anxieties of a present reality but cannot contain or transform those anxieties, which surface dangerously in the attack on Moore's mill at the center of the novel.

Brontë narrates this battle from the point of view of Caroline and Shirley, who are safely hidden behind a wall that partly obscures their vision and forces them to rely on their hearing for information. Their situation marks their own exclusion, as women, from industrial strife. Helstone has entrusted his pistols to Shirley so that she can defend his household in case of intrusion, but he tells her nothing of what is afoot. When Shirley and Caroline sneak off to the scene of the battle, they are careful to maintain their invisibility. As Eagleton points out, the workers in this scene are also "wholly invisible."[46] Hidden by the night, they answer to numbers instead of names when their leaders call the roll. Having spent their articulate force in their earlier meeting with Moore, the inhuman noises of the battle drown their voices. The partial exclusion of the act of violence itself from this scene—Shirley and Caroline hear but don't see what is happening—is a measure of the anxiety that such a rupture arouses, but the main effect of the workers' invisibility as individuals is to make them newly visible as a class:

> Caste stands up, ireful, against Caste; and the indignant, wronged spirit of the Middle Rank bears down in zeal and scorn on the famished and furious mass of the Operative Class. It is difficult to be tolerant—difficult to be just—in such moments. (II, 8, 386)

This new visibility of "the famished and furious mass of the Operative Class" consolidates the interests that oppose the workers, those of the mill owner, the landowner, the warlike parson, and their daughters. The invisibility of the women at this moment of conflict keeps their connection to the workers in view, but their attention to the care and feeding of the wounded after the battle cannot alter their self-contradictory allegiance to those who respond to the demands of the "famished and furious" only with "zeal and scorn."

The attempted assassination of Moore by the mad Antinomian Mike Hartley toward the end of the novel shifts attention away from class issues and back to individual ones. Brontë connects Moore's abandonment of Caroline with the assassination attempt by having it take place just after Moore tells Hiram Yorke the story of his having proposed marriage to Shirley, betraying his love for Caroline and disclosing his base, mercenary motives as Shirley's suitor. Moreover, the most important consequence of the attempted assassination is Moore's moral reformation. Although he had begun to look more closely at "the causes of the present troubles of this country" (III, 7, 616) before the attack, his social education requires a personal experience that replicates Farren's and Caroline's. The shooting transforms him from a "tall, straight shape," a "fine southern head," and a "youth in prime" into another one of the novel's victims, "pallid, lifeless, helpless" (III, 9, 639). Two masculine women, Mrs. Yorke and nurse Horsfall, care for a feminized, infantilized Moore in his illness, dosing him with his own medicine. "Mrs. Horsfall had him at dry-nurse: it was she who was to do for him; and the general conjecture now ran that she did for him accordingly" (III, 9, 643). She "had him at dry-nurse," "doing" for him but not suckling him, a mannish mother whose function is not to nourish her child but to unman him:

> In the commencement of his captivity, Moore used feebly to resist Mrs. Horsfall: he hated the sight of her rough bulk, and dreaded the contact of her hard hands; but she taught him docility in a trice. She made no account whatever of his six feet—his manly thews and sinews: she turned him in his bed as another woman would have turned a babe in its cradle. When he was good, she addressed him as "my dear," and "honey;" and when he was bad, she sometimes shook him. Did he attempt to speak when MacTurk [the surgeon] was there, she lifted her hand and bade him "hush!" like a nurse checking a forward child. (III, 9, 644)

Brontë represents Moore's confinement, passivity, and enforced silence as more distortive than Caroline's, but only by a self-canceling turn like the one according to which the defense of Farren's duty to protest is a defense against his feminization. Caroline's illness, while it removed all adult sexuality from her, confirmed rather than threatened her gender. The implication is that women, unlike men, make good patients because they are naturally docile, and despite Brontë's bitter treatment of Mary Cave's decline, she represents Caroline's dying as like it in being beautifully natural, an expression of her deeply feminine delicacy and dependence: "she wasted like any snow-wreath in thaw; she faded like any flower in drought" (II, 1, 476). Before his illness, Moore had established an identity based on his difference from both workers and women, on his not being dependent like them, unable to take food because food hasn't been given, or dependent on them. After all, his first action in the novel is to superintend the cooking of a mutton chop in his counting-house. "It is my fancy," he tells Malone, "to have every convenience within myself, and not to be dependent on the feminity [*sic*] in the cottage yonder for every mouthful I eat or every drop I drink" (I, 2, 32). His being brought to acknowledge conditions over which he cannot triumph and feelings like Farren's and Caroline's strengthens the claims of the novel's workers and women: "I am hopelessly weak," he tells her, "and the state of my mind is inexpressible—dark, barren, impotent" (III, 10, 663). At the same time, it turns away from them when he picks himself up and leaves his sick-room. Apparently, the male mill owner need not and will not submit like women and workers.

*   *   *

The thesis that redemption follows from a regression into an earlier stage of an individual's or a culture's history is especially problematic in relation to the novel's title character, for Shirley, endowed with a man's name, his fortune, and much of his freedom of action, seems safely exempted from the condition of women. Yet she relinquishes both fortune and freedom when she marries Louis Moore, her cousin's tutor. This marriage is inconsistent with the desire on the part of many modern readers for some affirmation of female power commensurate with Shirley's own myth of the Titan Eve and for some confirmation of the ideal of an equality between men and women commensurate with the novel's own criticism of marriage. But it is, as has often been remarked, consistent with the position Shirley articulates to Caroline during their walk on Nunnely Common. The walk and the plan to visit Nunnwood and its dell, "a deep, hollow cup, lined with turf," with, at its bottom, the ruins of a nunnery, is redolent with the unachieved promise of a separatist intimacy between the two women. They do seriously consider the dreadful hazards of marriage, but Shirley, at least, is enthusiastic about men: "Indisputably, a

great, good, handsome man is the first of created things" (II, 1, 244–45).
To Caroline's ideal of an equality between men and women, Shirley opposes the high appeal of hero worship: "It degrades to stoop—it is glorious to look up. What frets me is, that when I try to esteem, I am baffled:
when religiously inclined, there are but false gods to adore. I disdain to be
a Pagan" (II, 1, 246). Idolatry has many pains, but atheism has no pleasures. Carlyle, a thinker Brontë said she came to like "better and better,"
defines hero worship in a way that makes its religious significance clear.
He calls it "*infinite* admiration": the worshipper can "love his hero or sage
without measure, and idealise, and so, in a sense, idolise him."[47] All that
separates Shirley's idolization of men from other defenses of male privilege
is her insistence on distinguishing only the genuinely superior male nature
as worthy of her homage.

Our view of the distribution of power in the relation of Shirley and
Louis is complicated by the failure of biological and symbolic gender to
coincide in Shirley or Louis as they do in Caroline. *Shirley*'s women have
been defined as economically dependent, and Shirley's possession of the
masculine family name is the sign of her possession of the family property.
Exempted from the woman's duty to earn or marry a living, however, she
is not exempted from the woman's desire for a nourishing relationship that
reproduces mothering. Moreover, Louis Moore, with his "natural right
and power to sustain" Shirley, has as much in common with Jane Eyre or
Lucy Snowe as he does with Rochester, for he is a poor teacher in a great
house, obscure, overlooked, and kept down. In the relation of Louis and
Shirley, Brontë turns from the struggle between workers and masters to
the class struggle that figured in *Jane Eyre*, that between the educated,
penniless offspring of middle-class parents and the gentry. Brontë's decision to use Louis as a first-person narrator reveals the extent of her
identification with him, as her refusal to consider any of the novel's events
from Shirley's point of view reveals her distance from this anomalous,
socially powerful heroine.

In defending Shirley's marriage to Louis against those detractors like
Shirley's uncle, Mr. Sympson, who would base any claim to superiority in
rank, property, and connections, the novel once again appeals to the logic
according to which one instance of leveling can be justified by its avoidance of another more threatening instance. In the case of the workers,
their obligation to assert their identity as men rather than dumb animals
justifies their protest against unemployment. In the case of Louis Moore

and Shirley, a traditional gender hierarchy according to which "Adam was first formed, then Eve" justifies a marriage between an aristocratic land-owner and a poor tutor. But although Shirley and Brontë accede to this relation of priority, which Shirley affirms in her identification of the Titan Eve as Jehovah's daughter, both have so far defended a woman's right to speech. Louis's courtship of Shirley also denies this right, depriving Shirley of a voice in obvious and significant ways. Whereas Caroline chose silence in her relation with Robert Moore, Shirley chooses to reproduce her master's voice.

In *Bearing the Word*, Margaret Homans explores the patrilineal dichotomy between the selfless, feminine act of transmitting a text, often a text in a foreign language, and "male, self-centered criticism and bequest" of texts.[48] We have already seen Caroline and Shirley challenging not only the silencing of women but the translation by men of the Pauline text and presuming to substitute a translation of their own that will legitimate the speech of women. In "Coriolanus," both Robert and Caroline were readers, and when, in the same chapter, Robert elicits Caroline's recitation of Chénier's "La Jeune Captive," she both looks for his praise, "smiling like any happy, docile child," and defends her own stake in the performance: "When I meet with *real* poetry, I cannot rest till I have learned it by heart, and so made it partly mine" (I, 6, 107). Such an act of reading isn't selfless, though it may raise questions about the extent to which Caroline's independent power of speech is limited by her appropriation of another's words. The whole question of a woman's relation to a foreign language, and to the man who teaches it to her, arises again in the chapter called "The First Blue-Stocking," when Louis regains his power over Shirley by making her speak his language. In this chapter, the silence of women involves their repetition of the speech of men.

Louis begins by asking Shirley to read to him in French from St. Pierre's "Fragments de l'Amazone." When her "Anglicized tones" make her falter, she asks him to provide her with a model: "What *he* read, *she* repeated: she caught his accent in three minutes" (III, 4, 547). Louis's praise—"C'est presque le Français rattrapé"—has a larger reference. It reminds us that what is being recovered or rescued is Shirley's past and that Louis's capture of the woman he later calls "tameless" depends on his ability to take Shirley back in time, that is, to undo the coming of age that brought her into her property and make her once again the pupil she was when she lived in her uncle's house. Shirley's reading of "Le Cheval

Dompté," a piece that Louis once made her learn as a punishment for proud, passionate behavior, suggests that the pupil's speech is at best an especially talented kind of mimicry:

> Shirley, by degrees, inclined her ear as he went on. Her face, before turned from him, *re*turned towards him. When he ceased, she took the word up as if from his lips: she took his very tone; she seized his very accent; she delivered the periods as he had delivered them: she reproduced his manner, his pronunciation, his expression. (III, 4, 558)

"Le Songe d'Athalie" follows:

> He said it for her; she took it from him; she found lively excitement in the pleasure of making his language her own: she asked for further indulgence; all the old school-pieces were revived, and with them Shirley's old school-days. (III, 4, 558)

This language lesson takes Shirley and Louis back to their former roles of master and pupil and demonstrates the essential nature of that relationship, as Brontë represents it here. The pupil imitates the master, and her ambition to excel is safely assimilated to a flattering willingness to reproduce his speech and safely detached from any threat of competitive opposition.

The erotic content of this extended scene of instruction relies on Brontë's representation of Shirley's submission as a seduction and on the familiar dynamics of visual pleasure in the teacher/pupil relationship. When a woman performs another's speech in *Shirley*, she loses her self-consciousness as a subject both hidden and silent. Situated as an objectified and inconscient other, she becomes available for voyeuristic appreciation. This dynamic was also at work when Caroline recited "La Jeune Captive" for Robert, who could watch her "without her perceiving where his gaze was fixed" (I, 6, 107). The dynamic of the kiss, an exchange without necessary dominance, partly but only partly cuts across it, for when Shirley takes Louis's word "as if from his lips," Brontë acknowledges her pleasure as well as her agency. In making Shirley once again Louis's pupil, *Shirley* reverses the progress of *Jane Eyre*, and the earlier novel's hegemonic axis, for Jane is Rochester's pupil in the sense of being "the apple of his eye," not only his best object of vision but his vision itself, and vision in the earlier novel is already closely allied to language as object and subject: "He saw nature—he saw books through me; and never did I weary of gazing for his behalf, and of putting into words the effect of field, tree, town, river, cloud, sunbeam—of the landscape before us; of the weather round us—and impressing by sound on his ear what light could no longer stamp on his eye" (3, 12, 577).

In *Shirley*, as in *The Professor*, relations of dominance and submission are reversible, and Louis addresses Shirley as "my pupil, my sovereign" (III, 13, 711) and declares himself "her slave" (III, 6, 599). His willingness to repeat Shirley's tedious devoir, "La Première Femme Savante," which he has improbably memorized, is especially interesting in demonstrating such a reversal, but Louis's submission to Shirley's language on this occasion is made problematic by the likelihood that her exercise in composition is itself an exercise in reproduction performed within the schoolroom, so that in making Shirley's language his own, Louis merely repeats himself. Brontë's awkward relation to this chapter is, I think, suggested by the act of translation she herself performs when she Englishes the title of Shirley's devoir, "La Première Femme Savante," as her chapter title, "The First Blue-Stocking," for a blue-stocking is more pedantic than wise, a warning to women not to claim more learning than is thought appropriate for their sex.

The ruptures of the narrative in the third volume, Shirley's extravagant devoir and the long excerpts from Louis Moore's feverish diary, signal the pressure that the Louis/Shirley relation exerts on the novel. Brontë's delegation of narrative authority to Robert Moore when he tells the story of his proposing to Shirley is the only occasion in the novel when events are seen from Moore's point of view, and Shirley remains the only one of four main characters whose point of view is never attempted. Shirley complicates her friendship with Caroline by refusing to confide either her love for Louis or the fraternal feelings for Robert that prevent her from being a romantic rival. Her unavailability as a point of view partly explains Brontë's decision to present the story of Louis's courtship from his point of view, but only Brontë's deep sympathy with Louis explains her decision to present that point of view by quoting from his diary. This repetition on the narrative level of Shirley's own posture in relation to Louis confirms Brontë's admiration for her tutor: "She took the word up, as if from his lips."

Shirley's devoir and Louis's diary present complementary transfiguring fantasies closely resembling those of the main narrative but degraded by an extravagant sentimentality. The devoir mythologizes Caroline's experience ("But if you *are* my mother, the world is all changed to me"), substituting a bridegroom for Mrs. Pryor, one who can claim to have given "the very flame which lit Eva's being" (III, 4, 552), and conflating the sexual and the maternal:

> The Evening flushed full of hope: the Air panted; the Moon—rising be-
> fore—ascended large, but her light showed no shape.
> "Lean towards me, Eva. Enter my arms; repose thus." (III, 4, 551).

Eva is a "desolate young savage," "bereaved of both parents" and forgotten
by her tribe. "None cares for this child: she is fed sometimes, but oftener
forgotten. . . ." An invisible visitor comes to Eva with "a living draught
from Heaven": "I drink—it is as if sweetest dew visited my lips in a full
current. My arid heart revives: my affliction is lightened: my strait and
struggle are gone. And the night changes! the wood, the hill, the moon,
the wide sky—all change!" This reading of the devoir ignores the interpretive claim it makes for itself as an allegory of the marriage of Genius
and Humanity, but this anagogical reading of the story of Eva matters less
than a literal reading that emphasizes the novel's investment in marriage
as a reproduction of the relation of nourishing mother and nursing infant.

The first excerpt from Louis's diary, his record of "what I dare utter
to nothing living," describes Shirley as a child whom he has "a natural
right and power to sustain" and exults in her faults as "the steps by which
I mount to ascendancy over her." The appeal to natural superiority then
yields to a mawkish daydream in which their social positions are altered,
providing an opportunity for Louis to insist that his appreciation of Shirley does not depend on her social advantages even while enabling him to
show a proper pride about his own social responsibilities:

> If I were a gentleman, and she waited on me as a servant, I could not
> help liking that Shirley. Take from her her education—take her ornaments,
> her sumptuous dress—all extrinsic advantages—take all grace, but such as
> the symmetry of her form renders inevitable; present her to me at a cottage-
> door, in a stuff gown; let her offer me there a draught of water, with that
> smile—with that warm good-will with which she now dispenses manorial
> hospitality—I should like her. I should wish to stay an hour: I should linger
> to talk with that rustic. I should not feel as I *now* do: I should find in her
> nothing divine; but whenever I met the young peasant, it would be with
> pleasure—whenever I left her, it would be with regret. (III, 6, 593–94)

The second excerpt from Louis's diary recounts his encounter with Shirley
in the schoolroom, where he taunts her with a portrait of the bride who
will accompany him to the "western wilds," "some young, penniless,
friendless orphan girl" whom he would teach his "language," his "habits,"
his "principles," and then "reward" with his "love" (III, 13, 702). Though
Shirley has sufficient spirit to remark on Louis's vanity, the marriage he
describes is the one she yearns to achieve.

In marrying Louis, Shirley enacts what Nancy Armstrong refers to as "the cultural formula, the symbolic exchange of masculine power for feminine authority."[49] Writing about this exchange in *Jane Eyre*, Armstrong argues that Jane breaks from Rochester not simply because he is married to Bertha but because she has no economic power to relinquish, for what enables her return to Rochester is not the knowledge that Bertha is dead (knowledge she significantly lacks) but the economic fact of her inheritance. "The novel seems to insist that only when an exchange of economic for emotional power has been fully and freely transacted, can the female achieve her proper dominion over the home." As an aristocratic landowner, the economic power Shirley has to exchange far exceeds Jane's, so that her marriage to the penniless tutor constitutes not just an exchange but a divestiture. Both actions are expressed symbolically when Shirley and Louis finally exchange their vows. Shirley declares that she has lost her household keys and has only a sixpence to give her housekeeper. "Mastering at once the sixpence and the hand that held it," Louis demands: "'Am I to die without you, or am I to live for you?'" Having settled the issue, Shirley asks: "And are we equal then, sir? Are we equal at last?" (III, 13, 710–11). The equality at stake in this scene is social, and it depends on Louis's mastering Shirley's fortune with her hand. His title to her fortune in turn depends on the authority she has over his heart, for the darkest part of Robert Moore's confession to Hiram Yorke of his mercenary proposal to Shirley is his having tried to cheat her into mistaking "my half-coarse, half-cold admiration, for true-throbbing, manly love." When Shirley tells Robert that he "spoke like a brigand who demanded my purse, rather than like a lover who asked my heart" (III, 7, 607), she criticizes the form and substance of his declaration but does not challenge his right as a poor man to lay claim to a woman's fortune. Shirley will only exchange her independence for "true-throbbing, manly love."

The marriages of Caroline and Shirley to Robert and Louis Moore confirm a view of history according to which time in its forward movement is not redemptive, and history is best imagined as the grotesque transubstantiation of bread into stone. Lacking all confidence in the possibility of human progress toward solutions to human problems like those of its women and workers, *Shirley* is committed to the restoration of an earlier state of things. By making both the tutor and the mill-owner into lovers who are avatars of a nourishing mother, Brontë infantilizes her female characters. At the same time, however, she seeks to legitimate their demands by naturalizing them.

Kenneth Burke helpfully describes invective, lamentation, and praise as instances of "a primary 'freedom of speech'":

> Invective is rooted extralinguistically in the helpless rage of an infant that states its attitude by utterances wholly unbridled. In this sense, no mode of expression could be more "radical," unless it be the closely allied motive of sheer *lamentation*, undirected wailing. And perhaps the sounds of contentment which an infant makes, when nursing or when being bedded or fondled, mark the pre-articulate origins of a third basic "freedom," *praise*.[50]

These three utterances delimit *Shirley*'s expressive range. Its curses on invidious curates, cold mill owners, and selfish parents are contained in a sustained lament that yields awkwardly to praise. More profoundly conservative than *Jane Eyre*, *Shirley* is also more radical because of its defense of a "wholly unbridled utterance." In voicing the protest of Jane Eyre's "millions . . . in silent revolt against their lot," *Shirley* has a stronger claim than *Jane Eyre* to be called Brontë's feminist manifesto. By reversing the relation of dominance established by property, Shirley's marriage to Louis suggests "the tone of mind and thought which has overthrown authority . . . and fostered Chartism and Rebellion. . . ." By confirming the relation of dominance established by gender, the same marriage situates its author firmly in the camp of those who resist violent change. Like the other self-canceling reversals in *Shirley*, Shirley's marriage to Louis understands the contradictions that require it but fails to resolve them.

5. The Performing Body: *Villette* After *Wuthering Heights*

"Is Mr. Heathcliff a man? If so, is he mad? And if not, is he a devil?" "Is he a ghoul, or a vampire?" Like the contemporary reviewers of *Wuthering Heights*, Charlotte Brontë takes Isabella's and Nelly's questions to heart in her "Editor's Preface" to the 1850 edition of the novel:

> Heathcliff betrays one solitary human feeling, and that is *not* his love for Catherine; which is a sentiment fierce and inhuman: a passion such as might boil and glow in the bad essence of some evil genius; a fire that might form the tormented center—the ever-suffering soul of a magnate of the infernal world: and by its quenchless and ceaseless ravage effect the execution of the decree which dooms him to carry Hell with him wherever he wanders. No; the single link that connects Heathcliff with humanity is his rudely confessed regard for Hareton Earnshaw—the young man whom he has ruined; and then his half-implied esteem for Nelly Dean. These solitary traits omitted, we should say he was child neither of Lascar nor gypsy, but a man's shape animated by demon life—a Ghoul—an Afreet.[1]

Brontë's defense of her sister as Heathcliff's creator relies on the premise of authorial inconscience: "Having formed these beings, she did not know what she had done." Both the theory of artistic creation set out in the preface (no author can be responsible for the "creative gift") and the history of Emily Brontë's life contained in the "Biographical Notice" (this particular author was "genuinely good and truly great") support this premise. Yet the final paragraph of Brontë's preface confirms her admiration of Heathcliff, for she recreates the novel as a whole in his image, and having done so, not only deprecates its demonism but praises its divinity. A boundary figure, at once human and inhuman, a work of art (half statue) and nature (half rock), he is the image of the novel he dominates and the focus of Brontë's contradictory responses:

> 'Wuthering Heights' was hewn in a wild workshop, with simple tools, out of homely materials. The statuary found a granite block on a solitary moor: gazing thereon, he saw how from the crag might be elicited a head, savage,

swart, sinister; a form moulded with at least one element of grandeur—
power. He wrought with a rude chisel, and from no model but the vision of
his meditations. With time and labour, the crag took human shape; and there
it stands colossal, dark, and frowning, half statue, half rock: in the former
sense, terrible and goblin-like; in the latter, almost beautiful, for its colouring
is of mellow grey, and moorland moss clothes it; and heath, with its blooming bells and balmy fragrance, grows faithfully close to the giant's foot.[2]

This appropriates Cathy's comparison of her love for Heathcliff to "the
eternal rocks beneath" the changing foliage and revises the ending of
Wuthering Heights, with its image of three graves "on the slope next the
moor," "the middle one grey, and half buried in heath—Edgar Linton's
only harmonized by the turf, and moss creeping up its foot—Heathcliff's
still bare." Lockwood's "benign sky" with "moths fluttering among the
heath, and hare-bells" and a "soft wind breathing through the grass" (II,
20, 414) is the most obvious source of Brontë's imagery, but she revises
the ending of her sister's novel when she causes the moorland moss to
clothe Heathcliff and the heath to grow "faithfully close to the giant's
foot." In this way, the 1850 edition of *Wuthering Heights* keeps Brontë's
faith with her sister not just by wiping the dust off her gravestone but by
adorning Heathcliff's.

The familial resemblances between *Villette* and *Wuthering Heights*
that concern me here are the product of Brontë's re-reading of her sister's
novel when she edited it for publication in 1850. Brontë's defense of *Wuthering Heights* in the 1850 edition is inseparable from her defense against it,
and especially against its most threatening element, the character of
Heathcliff. For her, he is both the embodiment of a self in torment and
the agent of spectacles too horrible for settled contemplation. In appropriating his demonic power for one of her own characters, the actress
Vashti, and by extension, for her heroine, Lucy Snowe, Brontë finds a way
to honor it while making it safe for contemplation. While Emily Brontë
locates the forces of disruption in an outsider who is also a socially aggressive, marrying male, Charlotte Brontë locates them in a woman artist who
embodies illegitimate passion and self-destructive suffering.

In what follows, I want to establish not only the Vashti's connection
to Heathcliff but the connection between Brontë's criticism of *Wuthering
Heights* and the role of the theater in *Villette*. The theater provides Brontë
with a familiar context for treating acts of self-representation and with a
familiar model for an investment of the self in others. It had already provided Keats with an understanding of the poetical Character and a philo-

sophical defense of art: "It does no harm from its relish of the dark side of things any more than from its taste for the bright one; because they both end in speculation."[3] Self-division and self-extension are not less spectacular but more speculative in *Villette* than they are in *Wuthering Heights*. Both novels explore "the danger of being haunted by alien versions of the self" and a fascination with the self outside the self, the incarnation of the self as another.[4]

Actual theatrical performances figure only twice in *Villette*, but many episodes wear the aspect of the theater. For example, all of Mme. Beck's pupils perform before an audience of male suitors, who are invited to watch but forbidden to participate in the dancing that follows Lucy's acting in the vaudeville. Lucy acts not only in the vaudeville but also whenever she mounts the raised estrade that sets the teacher off from her pupil-spectators. Specific acts of classroom discipline—tearing a rebellious pupil's composition in two or locking a disruptive pupil in the closet—are public performances that dramatize her authority. Most important of all, the nun who makes five appearances in the novel is a pure piece of theater, a role assumed by Alfred de Hamal to facilitate his trysts with Ginevra Fanshawe. The Pensionnat vaudeville demonstrates Lucy's talents as a performer of other selves, but her account of the Vashti's performance presents the theater as the site of more daunting creative acts. As an exhibition, the Vashti's acting is scandalous in its obliteration of the boundaries between inside and outside and far-reaching in its implications for personality. In her portrait of the Vashti, Brontë confronts both the demonism of the stage and the staginess of her sister's demonic hero.

Villette is the only one of Brontë's novels that includes a professional artist and is seriously concerned with the criticism of art. Lucy Snowe visits art galleries, attends a concert, performs in a play, and sees one. As an art critic, she responds powerfully to the morality of representations, specifically representations of women who are desirable to a male audience at least partly because they are depicted as undesiring. In "La vie d'une femme," a set of four allegorical paintings, the morally reprehensible woman is spiritless. The sentient blankness of the young, unmarried woman in the first painting of the series is covered by the relations established in the paintings that follow, first to marriage, then to motherhood, and finally to widowing. In the "Cleopatra," the morally reprehensible woman is allegorized as gratified appetite. In Lucy's view, she is as sentiently somnolent as the young widow, gluttony conducing to spiritlessness as surely as deprivation.

Brontë's Vashti differs from these represented women in being desiring but not desirable. Like Heathcliff, she is a figure for malevolent passion wasting its own flesh in repeated acts of energetic opposition. More repellent than seductive to male viewers, she stands "locked in struggle, rigid in resistance." And Brontë's representation is notable for the entire absence of a surrounding context of any kind. In contrast to the Cleopatra, whose relation to the material world is signaled by her own bulk and by the array of objects littering the foreground of the canvas, the Vashti is a ravaged spirit, alone on the stage, without props, supporting actors, or even an identifiable play in which to act. Although the biographical model for Vashti, Rachel Félix, acted the title role in Racine's *Esther*,[5] Brontë named her actress for Esther's predecessor, the queen who is banished because she refuses to display herself before her husband's guests. With this name, she marks her artist's distinctive relation to her audience: she is detached from it and unwilling to please it. Lucy's criticism of the Vashti's performance responds to the morality of what is represented on the stage, "Hate and Murder and Madness incarnate," but it also responds to the morality of the act of representation itself. On the one hand, Lucy questions the morality of an art that seeks to give objective form to what has previously only been imagined. On the other, she admires the woman who casts herself as a creator rather than a creation, thereby imposing her will on the world rather than performing its will for her.

Brontë's portrait of the Vashti stands as the affirmation of the woman as artist that is the most obvious omission from her defense of *Wuthering Heights*, for the "Editor's Preface" denies both the author's creative agency (she is only the "nominal artist") and her gender ("He wrought with a rude chisel"). In *Villette*, Vashti's claim to be an artist is to have done what Emily Brontë has done. Each creates a powerful form "from no model but the vision of [her] meditations." Dr. John's criticism of the Vashti—"he judged her as a woman, not an artist: it was a branding judgment" (II, 23, 373)—has its source in G. H. Lewes' review of *Shirley*.

> I will tell you why I was so hurt by that review in the 'Edinburgh'—not because its criticism was keen or its blame sometimes severe; not because its praise was stinted (for, indeed, I think you give me quite as much praise as I deserve), but because after I had said earnestly that I wished critics would judge me as an *author*, not as a woman, you so roughly—I even thought so cruelly—handled the question of sex.[6]

Lewes exhorts women not to think of rivaling men but to write as women, yet he ranks their art as second-rate. To be judged as a woman and not an artist is to be judged as Lewes judges Brontë by quoting Schiller's criticism of Madame de Stael's *Corinne* and applying it to *Shirley*: "This person wants every thing that is graceful in a woman; and, nevertheless, the faults of her book are altogether womanly faults. She steps out of her sex—without elevating herself above it."[7]

Lucy's dramatic criticism is deeply pertinent to her sense of herself and her relation to the world. The claim that the theater creates a new reality is first made when M. Paul responds to Lucy's and Ginevra's acting in the school vaudeville: "'C'est peut-être plus beau que votre modèle,' said he, 'mais ce n'est pas juste'" (I, 14, 196). Together, they create a reality that did not exist in either the script or the world that contains the stage. In the play, two rivals, a fop and an earnest, prosaic lover who is called "Ours" (both bear and hero), contend for the favors of a coquette, and Lucy calls attention to the resemblance between this configuration and that of the narrative the play interrupts. The secret competition between Alfred de Hamal and Dr. John for Ginevra's favors animates Ginevra's and Lucy's acting and exposes each man to himself and the other:

> In the 'Ours,' or sincere lover, I saw Dr. John. Did I pity him, as erst? No, I hardened my heart, rivalled and out-rivalled him. I knew myself but a fop, but where *he* was outcast *I* could please. Now I know I acted as if wishful and resolute to win and conquer. Ginevra seconded me. . . . (I, 14, 196)

Lucy takes her revenge on de Hamal by presenting him as a theatrical construct, essentially insincere apart from his dedication to the role he plays. At the same time, she joins Ginevra in punishing Dr. John. While the vaudeville gives full play to the Ginevra/Dr. John/de Hamal love triangle, it also makes a different love triangle in the novel visible. In this triangle, Lucy is Ginevra's rival for Dr. John. Moreover, these triangles correspond, as Lucy's conversation with Dr. John later that night indicates. When he insists that Lucy and "every woman older than [Ginevra], must feel for such a simple, innocent, girlish fairy, a sort of motherly or elder-sisterly fondness," she responds that he "and every man of a less refined mould" than de Hamal "must feel for him a sort of admiring affection, such as Mars and the coarser deities may be supposed to have borne the young, graceful Apollo" (I, 14, 211).

Lucy's defensiveness in this scene reveals the extent to which she understands that Dr. John's admiration of Ginevra is implicitly a criticism of her, for the very qualities that make Ginevra super-feminine and are supposed to endear her to women as well as men are the ones Lucy most notably lacks. Ginevra's question—"Who *are* you, Miss Snowe?" (II, 27,

440)—sounds throughout *Villette*, and although it has its source in Lucy's mysterious origins and Ginevra's confusion about Lucy's social standing, it also marks the uncertainty that derives from Lucy's deficiency of those identifiably female attributes Ginevra possesses. Lucy's resistance to wearing male clothing in the play, even though she plays a man's part in relation to Ginevra both on and off stage, suggests one danger in acts of impersonation. Her situation reverses the more familiar one in which male actors take the parts of women and recalls the argument against the theater that finds authority in the scriptural injunction against blurring the line that divides the sexes.[8] Wearing a man's clothes is a reminder that a powerful longing for male privilege is part of Lucy's nature and that she establishes her gender in the novel not in community with the women around her but in determined difference from the men. When she leaves her job as Mme. Beck's nursery-governess to become the school's new English teacher, for example, she relinquishes the tools of a female trade, the needle and thimble, in favor of the masculine tools she is only beginning to acquire, a knowledge of French and the authority that will command respect from her unruly female pupils. She can accept this translation only by mentally asserting her own womanliness in opposition to Mme. Beck's manliness: "At that instant she did not wear a woman's aspect, but rather a man's. Power of a particular kind strongly limned itself in all her traits, and that power was not *my* kind of power. . . . It seemed as if a challenge of strengths between opposing gifts was given . . ." (I, 8, 107).

In designing her own costume, Lucy both wryly accommodates herself to Paul's insistence that she have "something . . . to announce you as of the nobler sex" (I, 14, 194) and resists the invitation to appear in a costume that would cause the audience to mistake her for a man or perhaps imagine she wishes to be seen as a man.

> Retaining my woman's garb without the slightest retrenchment, I merely assumed in addition, a little vest, a collar, and cravat, and a paletot of small dimensions; the whole being the costume of a brother of one of the pupils. Having loosened my hair out of its braids, made up the long back hair close, and brushed the front hair to one side, I took my hat and gloves in my hand and came out. M. Paul was waiting and so were the others. He looked at me. "That may pass in a Pensionnat," he pronounced. Then added, not unkindly, "Courage, mon ami! Un peu de sang froid—un peu d'aplomb, M. Lucien, et tout ira bien." (I, 14, 194)

This description of Lucy's costume is reminiscent of Brontë's account of how she came to call herself Currer Bell, "the ambiguous choice being dictated by a sort of conscientious scruple at assuming Christian names positively masculine, while we did not like to declare ourselves women, because—without at that time suspecting that our mode of writing and thinking was not what is called 'feminine'—we had a vague impression that authoresses are liable to be looked on with prejudice."⁹ The costume, like the *nom de plume*, responds to the double bind according to which a woman can expect to be condemned (as in Lewes' review) both for not being a man and for acting too much like one. Brontë's ambiguous pseudonym defends against both the prejudice against women writers and the prejudice against a woman's impersonating a man. Although the prejudice against women writers is given no more substance than that which accrues to a "vague impression," the word *authoress* in itself argues that a woman writer is "liable to be looked on with prejudice," for it suggests that her agency is not just different from a man's but derivative.

The effect of Lucy's costume for the vaudeville is more complicated than that of Brontë's pen name, for actual performances of gender are never simply male or female or even simply ambiguous. The masculine or male-identified woman, Lucy with her hair pulled back and the boy's garments added to her ordinary female ones, does not look like a fop, the figure in whom femininity is isolated, abstracted, and fetishized. It does no good to describe both of these representations as androgynous, for the effect of each is different and can best be understood in terms of the kind of desire it arouses, a matter of some significance in relation to the novel's presentation of Alfred de Hamal. Describing him, Lucy notes not only the deficiency of male features that distinguishes him from Dr. John— "*His* features were not delicate, not slight like those of a woman" (I, 15, 208)—but the excess of feminine ones that establishes his resemblance to Ginevra:

> He was a straight-nosed, very correct-featured, little dandy. I say *little* dandy, though he was not beneath the middle standard in stature; but his lineaments were small, and so were his hands and feet; and he was pretty and smooth, and as trim as a doll: so nicely dressed, so nicely curled, so booted and gloved and cravated—he was charming indeed. . . . I observed, too, with a deep rapture of approbation, that the colonel's hands were scarce larger than Miss Fanshawe's own, and suggested that this circumstance might be convenient, as he could wear her gloves at a pinch. (I, 14, 204)

In this account, the fop arouses Dr. John's (and perhaps Lucy's) homophobia and the female desire Freud called narcissistic, for Ginevra's attachment to Alfred de Hamal is an extension of her attachment to herself and a rejection of the object love that Freud valued more highly. Freud's idea that the birth of a child is nature's way of tricking women into object love inevitably suggests its inverse, that the same birth is nature's way of enabling women to move away from object love and toward the love of a being who is first known as a part of one's own body and may be known after in a configuration that reproduces one's own mothering.[10] Emily Brontë's Cathy does not survive the birth of her daughter and namesake, and Ginevra lives to bear a son who combines his father's with his mother's name. By supplanting the father in her affections, Alfred Fanshawe de Bassompierre de Hamal enables Ginevra to reconcentrate her powerful self-love.

A remark Ginevra makes repeats one of Cathy's in *Wuthering Heights* and substantiates their relation. In a scene just before the vaudeville, Lucy stands alongside Ginevra in front of a dressing-room mirror, letting her "self-love have its feast and triumph," and Ginevra tells her, "I would not be you for a kingdom" (I, 14, 202). Cathy makes the same remark to Isabella, when she warns her against her infatuation with Heathcliff:

> "I wouldn't be you for a kingdom, then!" Catherine declared emphatically—and she seemed to speak sincerely. (I, 10, 126)

She goes on to explain Heathcliff to Isabella in a way that confirms Emily Brontë's understanding of Cathy's narcissism. For Cathy's warning against romantic delusions—"He's not a rough diamond—a pearl containing oyster of a rustic; he's a fierce, pitiless wolfish man"—produces her extraordinary account of Heathcliff's desire as an extension, or repetition, of her own:

> I never say to him "let this or that enemy alone, because it would be ungenerous or cruel to harm them," I say, "let them alone, because *I* should hate them to be wronged". . . .[11]

Heathcliff's effort to act on a desire contrary to Cathy's by marrying Isabella produces the train of events that culminates in Cathy's death and then in his obsessive and sadistic violence, an effort to bring the self that has been so depleted by the loss of Cathy back into being. The extraordinary circularity of the plot of *Wuthering Heights* marks his failure. His monumental exertions to gain control over the Grange and the Heights come to nothing, and his death returns both properties to Hareton, who is Hindley Earnshawe's heir and whose name was inscribed over the door of the Heights long before Heathcliff's appearance there.

M. Paul makes the theme of self-love and its connection to women

explicit when he presses Lucy to accept the part of the fop in the vaudeville. No pupil in the school will take the role, he says, because "their vile
amour-propre—that base quality of which women have so much—would
revolt from it" (I, 14, 186). Later Lucy revises M. Paul's formation by iden-
tifying self-love as the ruling passion of both Dr. John, the most conventionally male character in the novel, and M. Paul himself. In M. Paul's
attack on women, *amour-propre* might best be translated as vanity rather
than narcissism, but this in itself reveals a resistance to what narcissism in
women portends. Sarah Kofman persuasively argues for a distinction between vanity or coquetry and narcissism when she analyzes Freud's "On
Narcissism" and Girard's account of coquetry. According to Girard, "coquetry is a very unstable mediation, skin-deep, and constantly in need of
being renewed by fresh desires." Devoting herself to "a secret disdain
which is too intense for the lover's desire to be able to counterbalance,"
the lover's desire lessens the lover in the coquette's opinion. He "is relegated to the realm of the banal, the insipid, and the sordid where dwell
objects who *let themselves be possessed.*"[12] This is useful in explaining Ginevra's indifference to Dr. John's suffering, part of the motivation for her
brilliant performance in the vaudeville, and her compact with Lucy to hu-
miliate the "Ours" character, but Kofman's protest against the idea that
narcissism is a mere strategy or that a woman's self-sufficiency is only a
pretense to attract her lover's desire deepens our sense of Ginevra's genuine
power in the novel:

> Linking Freud to Nietzsche, as we have done, is a way of emphasizing that
> in this text ["On Narcissism"] Freud thinks of woman precisely *as being dif-
> ferent from the coquette*: if he does not see her as assertive or Dionysian, ex-
> actly, at least he sees her as escaping resentment, penis envy, and hysteria, as
> not needing man's desire in order to please and desire herself. As a woman
> needing neither lies nor coquettish strategies to charm man: the enigma of
> woman, for once, can be contemplated without the categories of appearance,
> veil, fetishism, and castration, to which Girard's description unwittingly but
> inevitably brings it back. The coquette is in no way frightening or enigmatic,
> since it is very easy—Freud did not fail to do it—to reduce her desire to the
> envy of the penis of the man she is seeking to seduce. What is frightening is
> woman's indifference to man's desire, her self-sufficiency (even if it is based
> on a fantasy, which is not the same thing as a strategy or a lie): whether this
> self-sufficiency is real or only supposed to be real, it is what makes women
> enigmatic, inaccessible, impenetrable.[13]

According to Freud, the narcissistic woman's beauty and indifference are
fascinating to men because she represents "the lost part of their own narcissism, projected outward."[14] *Pace* Freud, women are also subject to this

fascination. Ginevra figures in Lucy's fantasies as well as Dr. John's, and it is Lucy who dreams of her as a "heroine" during the long vacation when her own self-love is most depleted.

By dressing de Hamal in the nun's costume for his trysts with Ginevra, Brontë economically reverses the relationship of actor to role established in the vaudeville, for just as the fop resembles de Hamal, the nun resembles Lucy. Père Silas's judgment that Lucy can find happiness only as a nun makes her poverty, chastity, and self-suppression oracular, and all the other characters except M. Paul perceive her as nunnishly buried alive. De Hamal sends Ginevra a billet-doux that characterizes Lucy as "une véritable bégueule Brittanique" and "espèce de monstre, brusque et rude comme un vieux caporal de grenadiers, et revêche comme une religieuse" (I, 12, 155). To Mrs. Bretton and Mr. Home, she is "steady little Lucy," "grave" and "sensible," "so little moved, yet so content." For Dr. John, she is at worst eyeless and brainless, at best quiet and "inoffensive as a shadow."

The idea that the nun is Lucy's double, and that she attacks a version of herself in attacking it, has by now been widely accepted,[15] but the nun's threat as double has as much to do with Lucy's persuasive performance of this identity as with the imposition of it on her by others. She castigates Dr. John for his misapprehension of her—"He did not at all guess what I felt: he did not read my eyes, or face, or gestures; though, I doubt not, all spoke" (II, 27, 455)—yet she explains her own refusal to reveal herself to him as his god-sister in terms that make clear the rewards of a disguise:

> . . . I had preferred to keep the matter to myself. I liked entering his presence covered with a cloud he had not seen through, while he stood before me under a ray of special illumination, which shone all partial over his head, trembled about his feet, and cast light no farther. (II, 16, 250)

Lucy herself recognizes a special affinity to the legendary nun by making the "allée défendue" where the nun is supposed to have been buried her own place, and by choosing the burial site itself as the grave in which to lodge the evidence of her own murdered love for Dr. John, his letters to her. A psychological reading of Lucy's destruction of the nun (actually the nun's costume) might focus on the nun as what Erik Erikson calls a "negative identity"; Lucy's attack on the nun would figure, then, as an archetypal instance of distantiation, "the readiness to repudiate, isolate, and, if necessary, destroy those forces and people whose essence seems dangerous to one's own" that is, along with intimacy, a necessary aspect and conse-

quence of the formation of an identity.[16] This reading is not incompatible
with the idea of the nun as the repressed that seeks to return ("a thing
which has not been understood inevitably reappears; like an unlaid ghost,
it cannot rest until the mystery has been solved and the spell broken"[17]),
but it is complicated by the actual solution to the mystery of the nun's
identity and by the nun's relation to a thematics of theatrical representation in the novel.

The nun's habit, designed to disguise de Hamal's maleness, is also
designed to hide precisely those parts of the body that are coded for femaleness; the same ones are accentuated by the clothing of the fop. As an
image, the nun is resolutely female, figuring both sexual vacancy and, by
way of a familiar reversal, female sexual power. This is especially the case
in *Villette*, since the repression and denial of sexuality in Mme. Beck's
school quickens it and since the novel's two actual nuns, the nun of legend
and the nun of history, are both punished for their sexual desires. Yet this
nun's habit is informed by a male spirit and is, in one scene, provided with
the novel's most important phallic prop, the cigar. When Lucy accompanies Dr. John to the concert, they each win lottery prizes, he a lady's head-
dress and she a gentleman's cigar-case. Dr. John is "excessively anxious to
make an exchange," but Lucy "could not be brought to hear reason" (II,
20, 317). She is perversely determined to keep the male object, and perhaps
just as perversely determined to insist that her companion accept the female one. The cigar is always also the sign of M. Paul's absent presence.
Lucy describes him as a "freakish, friendly, cigar-loving phantom" (II, 29,
496), and the smell of his smoke evidences his violations of her female
objects, her work-basket and her desk ("that hand of M. Emanuel's was
on intimate terms with my desk").

When the nun's habit is removed, then, so as to reveal that it hides a
male rather than a female body in a remarkable scene that makes a point
of the absence of the body, the Gothic can be said, in Robert Heilman's
words, to yield to farce.[18] Christina Crosby has argued that "Male or female, self and other are confused when characters perform striking reversals, repeating one another in a production of simulacra that confuse
identities,"[19] but the nun instead emphasizes the difference that necessarily
inheres in resemblances, which are not identities. Lucy resists both Dr.
John's hypothesis that the nun is a double in the sense of being an emission
of her nerve-worn imagination and the idea that her meetings with the
nun are merely coincidental and impersonal. "Who are you?" Lucy asks
the nun, echoing Ginevra's question to her, "and why do you come to

me?" (II, 26, 426). When she attacks the nun's habit left by Ginevra and Alfred in her dormitory bed the nun is at once her double, her bedfellow, her oppressor (the nightmare incubus), and her rival for M. Paul's love (both the first Justine Marie, dead of an excess of febrility but continually revived in memory by the Catholic machinery of Villette, and the second, her niece and namesake). The threatening vitality of the empty nun is the residue of meaning that remains after the mystery of the nun's several appearances in the novel is solved.

Lucy's violence in destroying the nun's habit is more shocking and effective as ritual purgation than is the act of violence at the end of *The Professor* because it is Lucy's only act of violence, because the novel has so largely figured the identification of Lucy with the nun, and because her destruction of the nun coincides with other expulsions—the elopement of Ginevra and Alfred de Hamal from the Pensionnat; the living Justine Marie's apparent displacement of the dead nun in M. Paul's heart; and Lucy's expression of her jealousy. As mystery, the nun is connected both to Lucy's visit to the confessional, where Père Silas told her she could find "repose" only "in the bosom of retreat, and the punctual practice of piety" (I, 15, 227), and to the "crisis and the revelation" (III, 39, 672) just narrated, her sight of M. Paul's ward, the blooming Justine Marie, who makes her debut at the midnight Carnival. Lucy does not yet know that Paul's ward is the namesake of the woman he would have married, the "sainted nun who would have been her aunt had she lived" (III, 39, 673), and she connects her first sight of the second Justine Marie to her encounters with the ghostly nun:

> "La voilà!" suddenly cried one of the gentlemen, "violà Justine Marie qui arrive!"
>
> This moment was for me peculiar. I called up to memory the pictured nun on the panel; present to my mind was the sad love-story; I saw in thought the vision of the garret, the apparition of the alley, the strange birth of the berceau: I underwent a presentiment of discovery, a strong conviction of coming disclosure. Ah! when imagination once runs riot where do we stop . . . ?
>
> With solemn force pressed on my heart the expectation of mystery breaking up: hitherto I had seen this spectre through a glass darkly; now was I to behold it face to face. I leaned forward: I looked. "She comes!" cried Josef Emanuel. (III, 39, 671)

By assuming that M. Paul will marry his ward, who thus replaces his first love, Lucy provides yet another explanation for the ghostly nun. She becomes "the true bearing of the oracle, I had thought she muttered of vision when, in truth, her prediction touched reality" (III, 39, 676).

Lucy's discovery of the nun's habit in her bed is immediately preceded by her acknowledgment that affection, which can be won, can also be lost, and this acknowledgment is the occasion for a horribly punishing act of adaptation and repression:

> I extended my grasp and took it all in. I gathered it to me with a sort of rage of haste, and folded it round me as the soldier struck on the field folds his colours about his breast. I invoked Conviction to nail upon me the certainty, abhorred while embraced, to fix it with the strongest spikes her strongest strokes could drive; and when the iron had entered well my soul, I stood up, as I thought, renovated. . . .
>
> Nothing remained now but to take my freedom to my chamber, to carry it with me to my bed and see what I could make of it. (III, 39, 676–77)

But it is also the occasion for a reversion of feeling and an equivalent punishment:

> And then—something tore me so cruelly under my shawl, something so dug into my side, a vulture so strong in beak and talon, I must be alone to grapple with it. I think I never felt jealousy till now. (III, 39, 677)

Lucy's images of lonely martyrdom, the dying soldier's, Christ's, or Prometheus's, give way to images of aggressive destructiveness when she attacks the nun's habit. Conviction, the giant abstraction that is the source of Lucy's pain in the first passage, becomes concrete as the vulture with its horrible weapons.

Lucy's confrontation with the nun continues this process according to which she embodies her own emotion, abstract and internal, as an enemy, concrete and external, so that she can grapple with it. Ostensibly, the passage that represents her violence against the nun describes a contest between a living person and a pile of clothes:

> In a moment, without exclamation, I had rushed on the haunted couch; nothing leaped out, or sprung, or stirred; all the movement was mine, so was all the life, the reality, the substance, the force; as my instinct felt. I tore her up—the incubus! I held her on high—the goblin! I shook her loose—the mystery! And down she fell—down all round me—down in shreds and fragments—and I trode upon her. (III, 39, 681)

But the clothes are personified, and the passage actually represents Lucy's destruction of them as an attack on an animate, if inhuman, opponent.

The incantatory triplets exorcise three versions of the nun in three aptly different ways. Lucy tears up the incubus, a "feigned evil spirit or demon (originating in personified representations of the nightmare) supposed to descend upon persons in their sleep, as of some heavy weight on the chest and stomach" (OED); she holds up the goblin, only a "mischievous and ugly demon," in a gesture of disdain and mastery; and she shakes loose the mystery, destroying the nun as the embodiment of the religion inimical to Lucy's love for Paul.

The model for this exorcism of Lucy's feeling and her attack on it as a living being is the Vashti's acting, which Lucy describes in language that anticipates her account of her conflict with the ghostly nun:

> I have said that she does not *resent* her grief. No; the weakness of that would make it a lie. To her, what hurts becomes immediately embodied: she looks on it as a thing that can be attacked, worried down, torn in shreds. Scarcely a substance herself, she grapples to conflict with abstractions. (II, 23, 370)

In describing resentment as a sign of weakness and an essential insincerity, Lucy makes explicit the moral ground of her objection to mere defensiveness, however defiant. At the same time, this passage expresses the logic of Heathcliff's sadistic acts after Cathy's death, acts that he refers to as "moral teething." This puzzling phrase suggests that his violence is as natural (and justifiable) as an infant's need to relieve the gnawing pain of cutting teeth, a pain self-born, inevitable, and, for a time, unremitting; to Heathcliff, his victims are less like sentient beings than like a carpet to a puppy or a chewing toy to a baby. In both *Wuthering Heights* and *Villette*, the sufferer finds relief only when an agony is expelled from the sufferer's body and re-embodied as an object with an existence apart from the sufferer's own. Even the language Brontë uses to describe the Vashti's performance of her grief recalls Heathcliff's "moral teething" as well as Lucy's battle with the nun: pain is "a thing that can be attacked, worried down, torn in shreds." The Vashti's and Lucy's enactment of their agony differs from Heathcliff's not in being less savage but in being more speculative. The Vashti's importance in *Villette* is not simply a matter of her explosive violence, her identity as a woman who acts on her feelings rather than containing them, or even her authority as a professional artist. It has also to do with Brontë's effort to do justice to the grandeurs and horrors of her sister's novel by acknowledging its most compelling creative achievement. It will be useful to distinguish the separate strands of Lucy's response to the Vashti and to make the connection between her response and Brontë's responses to both the historical Rachel Félix and *Wuthering Heights*. These responses not only constitute important sources for *Villette* but are closely related to each other.

In creating her actress, Brontë drew on the two performances by Rachel she attended in 1851, *Camilla* (Corneille's *Les Horaces*) and *Adrienne Lecouvreur*, the latter the story of an actress who dies young, written specifically for Rachel, who by the time Brontë saw her, was already dying from consumption. Three aspects of Rachel that figure repeatedly in contemporary accounts would have made a powerful impression on Brontë: her deathliness; the sharp contrast between the weakness of her physical frame and the sheer force of her presence on the stage; and the fairly narrow range of feelings that she excelled in representing.[20] Lucy's first description of the Vashti is intimate with death: she is a "star" verging "already on its judgment-day . . . a chaos—hollow, half-consumed: an orb perished or perishing—half lava, half glow" (II, 23, 368). Fanny Kemble's report on Rachel, after having seen her some ten years earlier, is eloquent:

> Her appearance is very striking: she is of very good height; too thin for beauty, but not for dignity or grace; her want of chest and breadth indeed almost suggest a tendency to pulmonary disease, coupled with her pallor and her youth (she is only just twenty). Her voice is the most remarkable of her natural qualifications for her vocation, being the deepest and most sonorous voice I ever heard from a woman's lips: it wants brilliancy, variety, and tenderness; but it is like a fine, deep-toned bell, and expresses admirably the passions in the delineation of which she excels—scorn, hatred, revenge, vitriolic irony, concentrated rage, seething jealousy, and a fierce love which seems in its excess allied to all the evil which sometimes springs from that bittersweet root.[21]

Brontë recorded her own powerful response to Rachel in two letters, the first of them written to Sydney Dobell soon after she saw her:

> . . . she will come to me in sleepless nights again and yet again. Fiends can hate, scorn, rave, wreathe, and *agonize* as she does, not mere men and women. I neither love, esteem, nor admire this strange being, but (if I could bear the high mental stimulus so long), I would go every night for three months to watch and study its manifestations.[22]

Her response to her sister's reading of *Wuthering Heights* is remarkably similar:

> If the auditor of her work, when read in manuscript, shuddered under the grinding influence of natures so relentless and implacable, of spirits so lost

and fallen; if it was complained that the mere hearing of certain vivid and fearful scenes banished sleep by night, and disturbed mental peace by day, Ellis Bell would wonder what was meant, and suspect the complainant of affectation.[23]

Like both Rachel and Heathcliff, the Vashti offers an escape from the temperateness of ordinary experience, and the demands of self-control:

> The strong magnetism of genius drew my heart out of its wonted orbit; the sunflower turned from the south to a fierce light not solar—a rushing, red, cometary light—hot on vision and to sensation. (III, 23, 371)

And in Rachel Brontë would have discovered a woman who expressed on the stage the passions with which both her sister's demonic hero and her own quiet heroine contend, Heathcliff with a lack of concern for other living beings that Brontë felt compelled to censure. This is how Lucy describes these passions:

> Before calamity she is a tigress; she rends her woes, shivers them in convulsed abhorrence. Pain, for her, has no result in good; tears water no harvest of wisdom: on sickness, on death itself, she looks with the eye of a rebel. Wicked, perhaps, she is, but also she is strong; and her strength has conquered Beauty, has overcome Grace, and bound both at her side, captives peerlessly fair, and docile as fair. Even in the uttermost frenzy of energy is each maenad movement royally, imperially, incedingly upbourne. Her hair, flung loose in revel or war, is still an angel's hair, and glorious under a halo. Fallen, insurgent, banished, she remembers the heaven where she rebelled. Heaven's light, following her exile, pierces its confines, and discloses their forlorn remoteness. (II, 23, 370)

The reference to hair that is "flung loose in revel or war" negotiates the slide from crazed Maenads to fallen angels. Mary Jacobus points out that the Vashti is "a female version of the central Romantic protagonist, the satanic rebel and fallen angel whose damnation is a function of divine tyranny (Blake's Urizen, Byron's Jehovah of sacrifices, Shelley's Jupiter)."[24] In this way too, she is what Cathy never becomes, a female version of Heathcliff, in Brontë's words, a "magnate of the infernal world."

In a letter written to James Taylor five months after she saw Rachel, Brontë more fully confronts the moral influence of such performances on the audience that watches them. Violent spectacles, she argues, are exciting but immoral because they conduce to violence and brutality. "Rachel's acting," she writes, transfixed me with wonder, enchained me with interest, and thrilled me with horror. The tremendous force with which she expresses the very worst passions in their strongest essence forms an exhibition as exciting as the bull-fights of Spain and the gladiatorial combats of old Rome, and (it seemed to me) not one whit more moral than these poisoned stimulants to popular ferocity. It is scarcely human nature that she shows you; it is something wilder and worse; the feelings and fury of a fiend. The great gift of genius she undoubtedly has; but, I fear, she rather abuses it than turns it to good account.[25]

This response is closely related to a passage in *Villette* that also compares the violence of the Vashti's performance to other violent public spectacles but stops short of condemning them as "stimulants to popular ferocity":

Swordsmen thrust through, and dying in their blood on the arena sand; bulls goring horses disembowelled, make a meeker vision for the public eye—a milder condiment for a people's palate—than Vashti torn by seven devils: devils which cried sore and rent the tenement they haunted, but still refused to be exorcised. (II, 23, 369)

Both passages have a close relation to one line of thought expressed in the reviews of *Wuthering Heights*. It is best expressed in Peter Bayne's review of the 1850 edition of the novel:

At the foot of the gallows, touches of nature's tenderness may be marked: in the pallid face of the criminal you may note workings of emotion not to be seen elsewhere. . . . But it admits not of question, that the general effect of such spectacles is brutalizing, and we would therefore without hesitation terminate their publicity. On exactly the same grounds, would we bid our readers avoid works of distempered excitement. Even when such are of the highest excellence in their class, as those of Ellis Bell and Edgar Poe, we would deliberately sentence them to oblivion. Their general effect is to produce a mental state alien to the calm energy and quiet homely feelings of real life; to make the soul the slave of stimulants, and those of the fiercest kind; and, whatever morbid irritability may for a time be fostered, to shrivel and dry up those sympathies which are the most tender, delicate, and precious. Works like those of Edgar Poe and this *Wuthering Heights* must be plainly declared to blunt, to brutalize, and to enervate the mind.[26]

Brontë's own response to Rachel's acting had been very different: "I neither love, esteem, nor admire this strange being, but (if I could bear the high mental stimulus so long), I would go every night for three months to watch and study its manifestations."

But this is not all that is fascinating and dangerous about the Vashti, for what *Villette* captures, that neither the reviewers of *Wuthering Heights* nor Brontë herself, writing about Rachel in her letters, quite acknowledges, is the perfect achievement of her art. Fanny Kemble, a fellow actress, thought Rachel

> the greatest dramatic genius, except Kean, who was not greater, and the most incomparable dramatic artist I ever saw. The qualities I have mentioned as predominating in her performances still appear to me to have been their most striking ones; but her expressions of tenderness, though rare, were perfect.[27]

What Brontë represents in the Vashti is the possibility of an entirely adequate representation of feeling, a possibility that is dangerous not just as spectacle but as metaphysical truth.[28]

Like the Gothic brand, the Vashti's acting obliterates the boundary between what is inside and what is outside, between what cannot be seen and what can.[29] It brings what has so far remained hidden below the threshold of the visible and the expressible into the light. Lucy identifies this achievement as the highest kind of creative act:

> I had seen acting before, but never anything like this: never anything which astonished Hope and hushed Desire; which outstripped Impulse and paled Conception; which, instead of merely irritating imagination with the thought of what *might* be done, at the same time fevering the nerves because it was *not* done, disclosed power like a deep, swollen, winter river, thundering in cataract, and bearing the soul, like a leaf, on the steep and steely sweep of its descent. (II, 23, 371)

This is Charlotte Brontë's finest tribute to *Wuthering Heights* as well as to Rachel, and it suggests her own enlarged understanding of the creative ambition that animates *Villette*. In her last novel, her own perfect achievement is to alter the structure of the visible and expressible. None of her novels is as concerned with the discourses of observation, diagnosis, and report that formulate what can be seen and expressed. None complicates it own discourse by so carefully attending to competing discourses and the institutions that authorize them. In *Villette*, reports about the individual are as contradictory and divisive as Lucy's and Graham Bretton's reports about the Vashti. The event to which the novel recurs is the examination itself, an institutionally regulated activity performed by teachers, doctors, and priests, and, of course, by Lucy herself, the novel's pupil, patient, and supplicant as well as its self-examining narrator.

6. Masking the Self: Voice and Visibility in *Villette*

> What then are the situations, from the representation of which, though accurate, no poetical enjoyment can be derived? They are those in which the suffering finds no vent in action; in which a continuous state of mental distress is prolonged, unrelieved by incident, hope, or resistance; in which there is everything to be endured, nothing to be done. In such situations there is inevitably something morbid. In the description of them something monotonous. When they occur in actual life, they are painful, not tragic; the representation of them in poetry is painful also.
> —Matthew Arnold, Preface to the First Edition of *Poems* (1853)

> You say that [Lucy Snowe] may be thought morbid and weak, unless the history of her life be more fully given. I consider that she *is* both morbid and weak at times; her character sets up no pretensions to unmixed strength, and anybody living her life would necessarily become morbid. It was no impetus of healthy feeling which urged her to the confessional, for instance; it was the semi-delirium of solitary grief and sickness. If, however, the book does not express all this, there must be a great fault somewhere.
> —Charlotte Brontë, letter to W. S. Williams, November 6, 1852

Matthew Arnold might have been describing *Villette* instead of *Empedocles on Etna* when he posited the incompatibility of poetical enjoyment with the representation of a situation "in which a continuous state of mental suffering is prolonged" and "in which there is everything to be endured, nothing to be done." Writing on "Haworth Churchyard," Arnold's elegy for Brontë, Kathleen Tillotson connects his finding *Villette* so repellent to his disowning his own poem.[1] His assertion that Brontë's mind contained nothing but hunger, rebellion, and rage is far better known than his colder criticism of Brontë in a letter to Arthur Hugh Clough:

> Miss Brontë has written a hideous undelightful convulsed constricted novel—what does Thackeray say to it. It is one of the most utterly disagree-

able books I ever read—and having seen her makes it more so. She is so entirely—what Margaret Fuller was partially—a fire without aliment—one of the most distressing barren sights one can witness. Religion or devotion or whatever it is to be called may be impossible for such people now: but they have at any rate not found a substitute for it and it was better for the world when they comforted themselves with it.[2]

Writing about Margaret Fuller, "that partly brazen female," later in the same letter, Arnold reveals why "it was better for the world" when religion could still provide consolation. His "spiritual" response to Fuller is indistinguishable from an aesthetic one:

I incline to think that the meeting with her would have made me return all the contents of my spiritual stomach but through the screen of a book I willingly look at her and allow her exquisite intelligence and fineness of aperçus.

Why does having seen Brontë make *Villette* more disagreeable? Like Dr. John confronting the Vashti, Arnold judges Brontë "as a woman" and finds her "utterly disagreeable." Like his own spiritual stomach, her novel is "hideous undelightful convulsed constricted." Brontë's death provided a screen through which Arnold could differently view her achievement. "Haworth Churchyard" does not deprecate painful situations but finds comfort in the fuller hours and richer life that suffering affords those who die young. It opposes "the sweet / Of a tranquil life in the shade" to the life of passionate feeling Brontë knew and represented in *Villette*. Still, Arnold could more easily grant a privileged susceptibility to pain without loss of charm to men than to women. Thus, the elegy has "Give him emotion, though pain! / Let him live, let him feel, *I have liv'd.*"[3] Although Brontë is the subject of these lines, Arnold's masculine pronouns universalize the experience of dying young and famous. Like Arnold's distaste for his own *Empedocles*, they reveal a sympathy with Brontë that contends against his condescending reference to "such people" in the letter to Clough.

Charlotte Brontë's letter to W. S. Williams, who had read the first two volumes of *Villette* in manuscript, admits his charge against her heroine without acknowledging its implications. Like the novel, the letter attempts a realistic balance between external and internal threats by offering both constitutional and circumstantial explanations for Lucy's state of mind: "her character sets up no pretensions to unmixed strength, and anybody living her life would necessarily become morbid." At the same time, it ignores Williams's hint that morbidity is an unacceptable attribute in a heroine, and one likely to forfeit the sympathy of Brontë's readers. Patrick Brontë felt something like Williams's concern and Arnold's distress when he read *Villette*. In the *Life*, Gaskell records his expressed dislike of "novels which left a melancholy impression upon the mind" and his wish that his daughter would "make her hero and heroine (like the heroes and heroines in fairy-tales) 'marry, and live very happily ever after.'" The well-known consequence of this criticism was that Brontë, who refused to allow Paul Emanuel to survive the voyage from Antigua and marry Lucy, "veil[s] the fate in oracular words."[4]

Brontë assiduous gratification of her father's wishes is consistent with her relationship to him, but it is also consistent with *Villette*'s preference for concealing, evasive, and self-effacing gestures. Lucy's scrupulous account of the outcome of each character's story at the novel's close calls attention to the curtailment of her own history in prospect, but Brontë's letter to Williams ignores his suggestion that Lucy's "history" is incompletely realized in the novel, even while instancing one episode in which it is flagrantly elided. Lucy's visit to the confessional occurs at the novel's center, after her solitude during the long vacation, when she gives her mental condition the clinical designation of hypochondria. In doing so, she implicitly rejects a diagnosis of hysteria, the affliction of which hypochondria was, at least until the end of the nineteenth century, the masculine form.[5] In *Villette*, hypochondria is a regal illness that Lucy suffers along with Labassecour's king. It is inseparable from the circumstances of her life, yet Lucy offers her readers no access to the narrative of these circumstances in her confession to Père Silas, which might have provided the opportunity for her to vindicate her heroine by giving the more complete history of her life Williams wanted.

Acts of withholding or concealment are characteristic of *Villette*, and the most satisfying recent discussions of the novel have noted and regularly connected them to the heroine's morbid pathology. "The novel's real oddity," Mary Jacobus writes, "lies in perversely withholding its true subject, Lucy Snowe, by an act of repression which mimics hers." Lucy's "deliberate ruses, omissions, and falsifications break the unwritten contract of first-person narrative (the confidence between reader and 'I') and unsettle our faith in the reliability of the text."[6] "To see beyond the supposedly imperturbable, opaque surface of Lucy's story is the reader's most challenging responsibility," Janice Carlisle writes. She argues that the third volume of *Villette* is one of Brontë's finest achievements: "For once the characters, not the attitudes of the 'morbid' narrator, dominate and determine the action."[7]

To assume the unproblematic availability of a "true subject," a self that is free, responsible, and the agent of its own actions, is to obscure Brontë's ambitious representation of the self as otherwise subject in *Villette*, subject in specific to coercive definition and regulation. To describe *Villette*'s narrative withholdings as perverse or pathological is to subscribe to a set of normative prescriptions for both narrative and its agent, as if conscious good health and wellness were being substituted for the conscious virtue that shields so many eighteenth- and nineteenth-century heroines. Moreover, such readings unwittingly collude with the very forces that help to produce Lucy's identity as subject and structure her experience in Villette. With *Villette*, Brontë doesn't only "unsettle our faith in the reliability of the text." She unsettles our faith in the availability of a "true subject" and calls attention to the implications of our seeking to "see beyond the supposedly imperturbable, opaque surface of Lucy's story."

Lucy's voice is everywhere audible as the agency of the narrative, but in her dual role as narrated and narrating self, she is silent at crucial moments. She refuses to speak her own name when she recognizes Dr. John as her godbrother, provides the priest with only an "outline" of her story when she confesses, and withholds Dr. John's full name for several chapters. She excludes not only her confession to Père Silas but her letters to Dr. John from the narrative, admitting only that she writes two of them in response to his first letter, one of which she destroys. She buries his letters to her, letters that are also excluded from the narrative. In the academic examination arranged by M. Paul to display her knowledge, Lucy first refuses to speak or write, and in one of the novel's culminating episodes she remains silent when M. Paul arrives at the Pensionnat to bid his pupils farewell. *Villette* is everywhere alive to the difficulties and dangers of self-disclosure.

This chapter is concerned with Lucy's exposure as a character and as the novel's narrator. Both Brontë's letter to Williams and Arnold's words about *Villette* point to what is most original about *Villette*: a heroine who is marked as deviant because she is foreign, heretic, and unhealthy (morbid, hypochondriacal, or neuropathic); a setting that registers more powerfully than that of any other nineteenth-century English novel what Michel Foucault calls the emergence of modern disciplinary power; and an autobiographical narrative that continually enacts Lucy's and her readers' resistance to and complicity with the institutions that seek to establish and proscribe her deviance.

* * *

Most readers of *Villette* are alert to its biographical backgrounds in Brontë's unrequited love for her Belgian schoolmaster, Constantin Héger, the model for Paul Emanuel, and her romantic attraction to her publisher, George Smith, the model for John Graham Bretton, but not to the experience that fundamentally alters Brontë's sense of her own identity just before she began *Villette*. The publication of *Jane Eyre* had vastly extended her relations with other human beings, yet because her identity as Currer Bell was known only within her family, that act of publication confirmed rather than disrupted the absolute division between the family and the world on which Brontë's sense of identity depended. In the spring of 1848, she was still vehemently denying her identity as Currer Bell to Ellen Nussey, her closest friend outside the family:

> I have given *no one* a right either to affirm, or hint, in the most distant manner, that I am 'publishing'—(humbug!) Whoever has said it—if any one has, which I doubt—is no friend of mine. Though twenty books were ascribed to me, I should own none. I scout the idea utterly. Whoever, after I have distinctly rejected the charge, urges it upon me, will do an unkind and an ill-bred thing. The most profound obscurity is infinitely preferable to vulgar notoriety; and that notoriety I neither seek nor will have. If then any Birstallian or Gomersallian should presume to bore you on the subject,—to ask you what 'novel' Miss Brontë has been 'publishing,'—you can just say, with the distinct firmness of which you are perfect mistress, when you choose, that you are authorized by Miss Brontë to say, that she repels and disowns every accusation of the kind. You may add, if you please, that if any one has her confidence, you believe you have, and she has made no drivelling confessions to you on the subject.[8]

So extreme an anxiety about discovery, and a warning against speech that comes close to being a withering curse ("Whosever has said it . . . is no friend of mine. . . . Whoever . . . urges it upon me, will do an unkind and an ill-bred thing.") reveal the dangers Brontë apprehended in the publicity of authorship. Authorship is the operative term here, for Brontë had long conceived of herself as a writer. What she denies is that she is "publishing." Her authority as "Miss Brontë" displaces her authority as Currer Bell, and in her proper, private capacity, "Miss Brontë" authorizes her friend to "repel" and "disown" the published and publishing name. To authorize

Ellen is at once to delegate authority to her and, in this context, to exercise it: Brontë creates Ellen as if she were one of her fictional characters.

The letter to Ellen suggests what it cost Brontë to reveal her identity to her publisher the following July, after Thomas Newby had falsely claimed that the author of *Jane Eyre* was also the author of *Wuthering Heights* and *Agnes Grey*. Her visit to London together with Anne, a first visit for the sister who had not gone to Brussels, and their stay at the Chapter Coffee House, contribute at least as much to *Villette*'s account of Lucy's visit as Brontë's earlier stay there with her father on her way to Brussels. "It was a place solely frequented by men," Gaskell writes, with "but one female servant in the house," and "a strange desolate place for the Miss Brontës to have gone to, from its purely business and masculine aspect." The trip included a first visit to both the Opera and the National Gallery, but in all their encounters with those outside the immediate Smith and Williams families, the Brontës escaped unwelcome scrutiny as the "Miss Browns."[9] More than a year later, in September 1849, Brontë could still tell Williams she was "obliged" to him "for preserving my secret, being at least as anxious as ever (*more* anxious I cannot well be) to keep quiet."[10] Williams had asked whether Brontë thought her secret would survive the publication of *Shirley*. It did not. In November, an article in a Liverpool paper made her known as the new novel's author. Toward the end of the month, she again traveled to London, met Thackeray and Harriet Martineau as Currer Bell, and dined at the Smiths' with seven gentlemen of whom five were critics.[11]

These biographical facts precisely date Brontë's visibility as an author outside her family and suggest a demarcation between private and public identities psychologically and socially more powerful than that which structures Gaskell's *Life*, the publication of *Jane Eyre*. We may agree with Alexander Welsh that "all persons whose primary relations with their fellow beings depend on the written word multiplied in print, and whose material and emotional well-being comes to depend on this relation, are already pseudonymous individuals in that their names appear in print rather than on the lips of persons meeting face to face,"[12] and still acknowledge that Brontë's sense of her identity was radically altered only when her *nom de plume* lost its power to conceal. Brontë's extreme anxiety about public exposure animates Lucy Snowe's elaborate devices to defend against it. George Eliot, who shared Brontë's anxiety about the invasive curiosity of her readers, protested against the identification of living persons with the characters in *Adam Bede*. In a letter to Charles Bray, she locates one of Brontë's motives in writing *Villette*:

> I only wish I could write something that would contribute to heighten men's reverence before the secrets of each other's souls, that there might be less assumption of entire knowingness, as a datum from which inferences are to be drawn.[13]

Two competing vocabularies meet in this sharp response to curiosity, a religious one that enjoins "reverence before the secrets of each other's souls" and a newer secular and scientific one that reconceives experience as "a datum from which inferences are to be drawn."

According to Michel Foucault, one vocabulary displaced the other in a historical rupture that substituted the "calculable" for the "memorable" man, thereby producing the self as the object of scientific analysis and control. In *Discipline and Punish*, Foucault argues that the advent of a mode of social regulation that coerces by means of observation and normalizing judgment and is masked by other "nobler or simply blander intentionalities (to educate, to cure, to produce, to defend),"[14] marks a historical reversal of "the poetical axis of individualization." The disciplinary mechanisms that define individuality in order to master it in modern Western culture are turned towards the child, the patient, the madman, and the delinquent, who are more individualized than the healthy, normal, non-delinquent adult.

> The moment that saw the transition from historico-ritual mechanisms for the formation of individuality to the scientifico-disciplinary mechanisms, when the normal took over from the ancestral, and measurement from status, thus substituting for the individuality of the memorable man that of the calculable man, that moment when the sciences of man became possible is the moment when a new technology of power and a new anatomy of the body were implemented.[15]

Villette is not just situated within this history, for Brontë takes account of Lucy Snowe's individuality in specific relation to the powerful forces that seek to know and control it. The chapters preceding Lucy's departure from England show how an individualized self emerges when it is divided from the world by an experience of alienation and defined as an observer of other selves, a particularized perspective or way of seeing. This division of the self from other selves is, in Brontë's view, always incomplete, leaving the possibility of the doublings and hauntings that figure so largely throughout the novel. Once in Villette, Lucy continues to operate as an observer, but she figures newly as the object of the view of others, someone examined as well as examining. "Surveillance" and "espionnage" are terms native to the language Lucy learns in Villette. They identify the new disciplinary practices that will circumscribe her life and structure her individuality. Villette's presiding spirit is Mme. Beck "in her strongest character—that of a first-rate surveillante" (I, 15, 200). Like Lucy, Mme. Beck is self-effacing, but Brontë connects Mme. Beck's invisibility to the constant watchfulness that secures and sustains her power over others— her children, her pupils, and her employees. Père Silas, Paul Emanuel, and Graham Bretton also observe Lucy, and each is associated with one of the novel's three main institutions, the school, the church, and the medical profession.

Lucy Snowe establishes her individuality by acknowledging her functional implication in the disciplinary practices of each of these institutions, her dual role as both object and agent of an active social restraint. Always under surveillance, she is herself what she calls Mme. Beck, a first-rate surveillante. But unlike the perfectly disciplined selves that figure in Foucault's account of modern institutional life, the self in *Villette* is not only constantly visible to others: it sees these others and is visible to itself. As an observer of observing others, Lucy challenges their power by making them visible. As an observer of the self, she subverts the agencies of discipline by insisting on her capacity for self-determination.

But to limit the "heretic" impulse of Lucy's narrative to resistance is to invoke the negative view of power that Foucault so persuasively opposes. In a late confrontation with Mme. Beck, Lucy feels

> that the whole woman was in my power, because in some moods, such as the present—in some stimulated states of perception, like that of this instant— her habitual disguise, her mask and her domino, were to me a mere network reticulated with holes; and I saw underneath a being heartless, self-indulgent, and ignoble. (III, 38, 647)

For Brontë, knowledge empowers, and Lucy comes to resemble the disciplinary agencies she opposes not only in her acts of self-discipline but in her relentless pursuit of what George Eliot calls "entire knowingness." As an observer of Lucy, the reader of *Villette* is oddly situated, both privileged like the readers of *Jane Eyre* and not—that is, aligned at once with Lucy in her opposition to the coercive forces within the novel and with those forces in their determination to know and judge her. Lucy's uneasy relation to observing others carries over to and informs an uneasy relation to her readers. Paradoxically, the novel is at once a place of refuge where Lucy can express and exhibit herself, a place unlike the world of *Villette*, and another disciplinary site.

*   *   *

Explaining his choice of the word "discipline" to translate "surveiller" in the title of *Discipline and Punish*, Foucault's English translator Alan Sheridan notes that the noun "'surveillance' has an altogether restricted and technical use" in English and that he found other English words equally unsatisfactory as translations of Foucault's French:

> Jeremy Bentham used the term "inspect"—which Foucault translates as "*surveiller*"—but the range of connotations does not correspond. "Supervise" is perhaps closest of all, but again the word has different associations. "Observe" is rather too neutral, though Foucault is aware of the aggression involved in any one-sided observation.[16]

As my earlier chapters have argued, Brontë is similarly aware of and able to mobilize the aggression involved in one-sided observations. In *Villette* she establishes a range of connotations for "surveillance" that closely corresponds to that of its French cognate, associating it both with the high "administrative powers" required "for managing and regulating" a "mass of machinery" and with prime ministerial and superintending roles. In *Villette* surveillance is all that Foucault has imagined and more: "faithless; secret, crafty, passionless; watchful and inscrutable; acute and insensate—withal perfectly decorous. . . ." In a world where rules are "easy, liberal, salutary, and [above all] rational," surveillance keeps those who are surveilled "in distrustful restraint" and "blind ignorance" (I, 8, 100).[17]

By the time the novel manages to formulate so good an understanding of "surveillance," Lucy has been twice inspected, once by M. Paul on the night of her arrival at Mme. Beck's Pensionnat and once by Mme. Beck herself, while she sleeps. These gazes being orderly, unlike those of the two men who dog her steps while she unsuccessfully hunts her inn, seem to Lucy to be authorized, even legitimate, yet they confirm the "paranoid perception that the social world is not a place to exhibit the inner self."[18] Mme. Beck's careful observation of Lucy is not less threatening because it results in a genuine benefit, Lucy's advancement from the nursery "watchtower" to the classroom: ". . . I found myself an object of study: she held me under her eye, she seemed turning me round in her thoughts—measuring my fitness for a purpose, weighing my value in a plan" (I, 8, 104). As a teacher, Lucy becomes one of Mme. Beck's agents, a "lieutenant" who takes her place in "every annoying crisis" (I, 9, 115), yet she never ceases to be the object of a surveillance that tightens when she dares to warn her pupils against lying and when her contacts with Dr. John and M. Paul become more frequent.

The differences between *The Professor* and *Villette* have even more to do with a changed perception of power and its instrumentalities than within the substitution of a female for a male protagonist. To be known in Crimsworth's Brussels is to be vulnerable, an instrument in the hands of others whose power derives from their knowledge and operates vindictively, but in Lucy's Villette, power is no longer vested in individuals like Mdlle. Reuter but in institutions. Despite their shared isolation as English Protestants, Lucy differs from Crimsworth in conceiving of her isolation as an incarceration. "Those who live in retirement," she writes, "whose lives have fallen amid the seclusion of schools or other walled-in and guarded dwellings, are liable to be suddenly and for a long time dropped out of the memory of their friends, the denizens of a freer world" (II, 24, 381). In *Jane Eyre*, Brontë had already described a penal institution wearing the aspect of a school. At Lowood, a regimen of deprivation combines with the threat of public humiliation to enforce outward compliance even when there is inward revolt. Outward non-compliance results in a display of force enacted on the body of the delinquent, Helen Burns, who is singled out for a spectacular punishment. The shift from the school to the family as the central institution in *Shirley* is also a shift from punishment to discipline, as Foucault uses these words. In *Shirley*, the family carries out regulatory functions no less important than those of Lowood, but its dedication to its members' welfare masks its investment in normalizing proscriptions.

With *Villette*, Brontë imagines a school that is disciplinary like the family in *Shirley*. In Mme. Beck's Pensionnat des Demoiselles, social coercion is no less potent than it was in Lowood, but it is less visible, and non-compliance can seem perverse rather than heroic:

> Here was a great houseful of healthy, lively girls, all well-dressed and many of them handsome, gaining knowledge by a marvelously easy method, without painful exertion or useless waste of spirits; not, perhaps, making very rapid progress in anything; taking it easy, but still always employed, and never oppressed. Here was a corps of teachers and masters more stringently tasked, as all the real head-labour was to be done by them, in order to save the pupils, yet having their duties so arranged that they relieved each other in quick succession whenever the work was severe; here, in short, was a foreign school, of which the life, movement, and variety made it a complete and most charming contrast to many English institutions of the same kind. (I, 8, 102–3)

The word "corps" helps to establish this educational establishment's resemblance to a military one. The double sense of "charming" requires two tones of voice, an ironic one in terms of which an appearance belies a reality, and a straight one that recognizes the beguiling effect of such procedures. "Corps" also suggests something of Brontë's linguistic preoccupations in *Villette*, which is not just full of French, like *Shirley*, but full of words that passed from French into English at a late date. According to the OED, "corps" was probably originally pronounced like the English "corpse," but before the end of the eighteenth century, a French pronunciation "generally prevailed," and an English spelling and pronunciation signaled a different sense of the word.

Villette is especially sensitive to the cultural differences linguistic differences mark. With *Villette*, Brontë defends herself against G. H. Lewes's charge of affectation when he pointed out that Brontë's speaking of a "grandmother" as "*une grand'mère*" in *Shirley* was a use of French "little better than that of the 'fashionable' novelists."[19]

> "Let me hear you say, in the voice natural to you, and not in that alien tone, 'Mon ami, je vous pardonne.'"
> He made me smile. Who could help smiling at his wistfulness, his simplicity, his earnestness?
> "Bon!" he cried; "Voilà que le jour va poindre! Dites donc, mon ami."
> "Monsieur Paul, je vous pardonne,"
> "I will have no monsieur: speak the other word, or I shall not believe you sincere: another effort—*mon ami*, or else in English,—my friend'" (II, 27, 460)

Lucy's rencounter with M. Paul ends comfortably, but only because he offers her the option of speaking the English phrase, "my friend," rather than the French one, "mon ami." Less sensitive to the subtle differences between French and English than Lucy, M. Paul is pleased by an offer of friendship that stops short of promising amity by just the degree to which the phrase "my friend" avoids the inflection of "domestic and intimate affection" that attaches to "mon ami," words Lucy will not speak.

Such discriminating attention to translation from one language into another is not just characteristic of *Villette* but crucial to Lucy's adjustment to Villette's foreign culture, its "alien tone," and to Brontë's representation of a continental disciplinary world. Brontë positions a foreign school at the center of this world and "a very great and a very capable woman" at its head. Mme. Beck's "perfect disciplinary gaze" takes in "everything constantly" while she remains invisible:[20]

> In her own single person, she could have comprised the duties of a first minister and a superintendent of police. Wise, firm, faithless; secret, crafty, pas-

sionless; watchful and inscrutable; acute and insensate—withal perfectly decorous—what more could be desired? (I, 8, 102)

Lucy identifies Mme. Beck as "a first-rate surveillante," but Brontë uses "surveillance" before Lucy's arrival in *Villette* to mark the wonder she and Ginevra excite by traveling unsupervised:

> As for the "jeunes Miss," by some their intrepidity is pronounced masculine and "inconvenant," others regard them as the passive victims of an educational and theological system which wantonly dispenses with proper "surveillance." (I, 6, 72)

Shortly after her arrival in Villette, Lucy uses the word "surveillance" in a description of Mme. Beck's school, where there are more than one hundred day pupils, twenty boarders, and several teachers, masters, and servants:

> It is true that madame had her own system for managing and regulating this mass of machinery; and a very pretty system it was: the reader has seen a specimen of it, in that small affair of turning my pocket inside out, and reading my private memoranda. "Surveillance," "espionage,"—these were her watch-words. (I, 8, 99)

In both these instances Brontë assigns "surveillance" a special linguistic status by placing the word within quotation marks, but in the first, its close companionship with other French words and phrases confirms its foreignness, while in the second, the presence of "espionage," spelled in the English way, suggests the naturalization of these French words and practices. A few pages later, Lucy completes the process when she refers to Mme. Beck's ruling "by espionage" and according to a system of "keeping girls in distrustful restraint, in blind ignorance, and under a surveillance that left them no moment and no corner for retirement . . ."(I, 8, 100).

The entries for "espionage" and "surveillance" in the OED confirm their related histories. First used by English writers in the last decade of the eighteenth century, they are felt to be foreign well into the nineteenth century and regularly italicized. Jeremy Bentham, Foucault's most demonic disciplinarian, is the first writer to use "espionage" comfortably in a sentence that remarks on how discomfited the English are by it: "To the word espionage a stigma is attached" (1825). The citations for "surveillance" in the OED indicate that the word usually appears in the nineteenth century in a French context. Because the OED does not cite *Villette*, it assigns the first comfortable English use of the word to J. C. Morison in a biography of Macaulay published in 1882: "No Puritanic surveillance directed his choice of books." But by mid-century, Brontë had already used the word in a letter to Ellen Nussey about her second visit with George Smith:

> Mrs. Smith is rather stern, but she has sense and discrimination; she watched me very narrowly when surrounded by gentlemen, she never took her eye from me. I liked the surveillance, both when it kept guard over me amongst many, or only with her cherished one. She soon, I am convinced, saw in what light I received all, Thackeray included. Her 'George' is a very fine specimen of a young English man-of-business; so I regard him, and I am proud to be one of his props.[21]

The different occasions for maternal surveillance suggest the distance between "she never took her eye from me" and "I liked the surveillance." On the one hand, Mrs. Smith chaperones Brontë's exchanges with the gentlemen invited to meet her, protecting her against incursive demonstrations; on the other, she supervises Brontë's exchanges with her son, warily watching for signs of romantic interest. Brontë does not tell Ellen how George Smith "regards" her, but her definition of him as "a young English man-of-business" produces a complementary and uncomplimentary view of her: she is "one of his props."

In *Villette*, surveillance is more sinister and regularly issues in episodes of examination, according to Foucault, the means by which power holds its subjects "in a mechanism of objectification."[22] I have already referred to Mme. Beck's examination of Lucy on the night of her arrival in Villette without making clear its nature. Mme. Beck, who is directly responsible for the only appearance of a policeman in the novel (she calls one to expel Mrs. Sweeney), is the character whose actions most closely approximate theirs. While Lucy feigns sleep, she examines both her and her belongings. In addition to counting Lucy's money, reading her memorandum-book, and discovering a plaited lock of grey hair, Mme. Beck completes her duties as a competent police-detective by making a wax impression of the keys to Lucy's trunk, desk, and work-box in preparation for a later inspection.

This scene of inspection establishes Lucy's hidden belongings as an important register of Lucy's hidden selfhood, for Lucy's things express her as fully as Mrs. Sweeney's "wardrobe of rather suspicious splendour" expresses her. Moreover, in invading Lucy's privacy, Mme. Beck acts as the reader's agent, for "the wish to form from the garments a judgment respecting the wearer" is the reader's as well as hers. The reader profits from Mme. Beck's detecting, for Lucy has not told us that she counts a lock of Miss Marchmont's hair among her treasured possessions. This scene is reenacted several chapters later, after Lucy intercepts a billet-doux intended for Ginevra and is seen in close conversation with Dr. John. Escaping from the daily "lecture pieuse" to the dormitory, she surprises Mme. Beck meticulously inspecting the contents of her drawers and work-box and finding, among other things, an item with a significance like that of the plaited lock of Miss Marchmont's hair, "a certain little bunch of white violets that had once been silently presented to me by a stranger" who is only later identified as M. Paul. "Had she creased one solitary article," Lucy assures us, "I own I should have felt much greater difficulty in forgiving her; but finding all straight and orderly, I said, 'Let bygones be bygones. I am unharmed: why should I bear malice?'" (I, 13, 166). Lucy's point here is not only that Madame's inspection is respectable but that her end has not been achieved: "I am unharmed." She does not interrupt Mme. Beck for two reasons: first, she has the pathetic consolation of knowing that Mme. Beck's scrutiny cannot discover what she most wishes to know:

> as to her system: it did me no harm: she might work me with it to her heart's content: nothing would come of the operation. Loverless and inexpectant of love, I was as safe from spies in my heart-poverty, as the beggar from thieves in his destitution of purse. (I, 13, 165)

Second, she wants to avoid the "thorough knowledge of each other" that would result from a confrontation in which Lucy would have to admit to seeing, and knowing, her inspector—"I should have looked into her eyes, and *she* into mine" (I, 13, 165).

Lucy reacts powerfully and ambivalently to her discovery of Mme. Beck's activities. On the other hand, she is amused by the "spectacle of a suspicious nature so far misled by its own inventions" as to conceive of a romance between Lucy and Dr. John; on the other, she is mortified by her own "heart-poverty": "a kind of wrath smote me, and then bitterness followed: it was the rock struck, and Meribah's waters gushing out" (I, 8, 166). Mme. Beck's inspection also exposes Lucy's deviance: in a school filled with blooming young women, Lucy's only tokens of emotional experience are a lock of steel-grey hair and a bunch of withered violets. At the same time, it suggests how the prohibition against sexual experience functions as an incitement to it. The white beds in the pupils' dormitory are called "lits d'ange" (I, 13, 164), the pensionnat is "a demi-convent," and the pupils don white dresses with sashes of blue, the Virgin's colors, for the ball that celebrates Mme. Beck's fête. Yet the most important feature of the ball is a "small, forlorn band" of young men who are admitted as "spectators" but prohibited from joining in the dancing. Lucy's analysis of Mme. Beck's success in mounting this spectacle concentrates on her originality in giving entrance to the young men:

> In the first place, the parents were made accomplices to the deed, for it was only through their meditation that it was brought about. Secondly: the admission of these rattle-snakes, so fascinating and so dangerous, served to draw out madame precisely in her strongest character—that of a first-rate *surveillante*. Thirdly: their presence furnished a most piquant ingredient to the entertainment: the pupils knew it, and saw it, and the view of such golden apples shining afar off, animated them with a spirit no other circumstance could have kindled. (I, 14, 200)

Mme. Beck's surveillance produces the heated atmosphere in which sex is an animating preoccupation. When Ginevra Fanshawe has her clandestine meetings with Alfred de Hamal, she also successfully resists the power of Mme. Beck's constraining surveillance while confirming the normality that consists of not being "loverless and inexpectant of love," thereby doubly earning Lucy's admiration as a heroine.

＊   ＊   ＊

The ritual of confession mediates between Mme. Beck's examination of Lucy in the first volume of the novel and Dr. John's examination of her in the second. The real danger of Mme. Beck's inspection of Lucy's belongings is that she will cease to be an object of surveillance. In a sense, she passes Mme. Beck's examination by failing to arouse her interest, but the consequences of her failure are postponed until the long vacation. "My spirits had long been gradually sinking; now that the prop of employment was withdrawn, they went down fast" (I, 15, 218). During the vacation, Lucy not only lacks employment but becomes virtually invisible, for she is seen by no one except the cretin—"her brain, her eyes, her ears, her heart slept content"—and Goton, a servant occupying a "far distant attic." Lucy's visit to the confessional reestablishes her visibility. The confessional is designed to protect the invisibility of the one who speaks, and, according to Lucy, the priest "never turned his eyes to regard me" but "only quietly inclined his ear to my lips." Yet she forces him to look at her when she admits she is Protestant. At the end of her confession, she hears reassuring news: "On no account would I lose sight of you" (II, 15, 227).

In the confessional, Lucy experiences the concentrated relief that comes from telling her story, yet she resists the priest's authority. She does this with a counter-exercise of her own power: when he turns to look at her, she examines him, and when he tells her his address, she withholds hers. But Lucy defends herself from not only this priest but also her readers. In a counter-exercise of her narrative power, she withholds from us the substance of her confession. We cannot know whether Lucy engages in an act of repression. All we know is that she engages in an act of suppression by excluding her confession from the narrative. "As to what I said," Lucy later tells Dr. John, "it was no confidence, no narrative. I have done nothing wrong: my life has not been active enough for any dark deed, either of romance or reality: all I poured out was a dreary, desperate complaint" (II, 17, 264).

For the priest, Lucy's confession is a sign of divine power, and her "impressions" are "messengers from God to bring you back to the true church" (I, 15, 227). Religion's counter-message is not merely Arnold's consolation; it is salvation. But for the doctor, Lucy's confession is evidence of a nervous illness requiring medical treatment. The plot of the novel follows that of history by making the doctor the priest's successor, for when Lucy collapses on the steps of a church, Père Silas, who has followed her from the confessional, consigns her to Dr. John's care. This transfer of responsibility for Lucy makes the rejection of superstition and the priest's authority all but coincident with the establishment of the doctor's, and the first appearance of the haunting nun confirms his role as Lucy's partner in the medical examination, a secular ritual that *Villette* both likens and opposes to confession.

The difference between Père Silas and Dr. John as examiners is not just a difference in aim, the priest compelling Lucy's narrative in the name of salvation, the doctor compelling it in the service of health. It is also a difference in technique. For the priest, the voice in confession is disembodied, but for the doctor, what Lucy tells is only one element in a cluster of physiological signs. When he "regards her scientifically as a patient" (II, 23, 364), these signs become symptoms:

> "Tell *me*," said Dr. Bretton; "I will hear it in my professional character: I look on you now from a professional point of view, and I read, perhaps, all you would conceal—in your eye, which is curiously vivid and restless; in your cheek, which the blood has forsaken; in your hand, which you cannot steady. Come, Lucy, speak and tell me." (II, 22, 355)

The priest's nun is as much outside Lucy as the impulse that drives her to the confessional; the doctor's emanates from Lucy's disturbed mind. Yet to look on Lucy from a professional point of view, whether the priest's or the doctor's, is to see "all you would conceal." Later, Dr. John will controvert Lucy's denial that she has seen the nun a second time by decrying "the old symptoms" (II, 23, 368). Without Lucy's corroboration, these symptoms make visible what was previously hidden from view.

Lucy is more vulnerable to the doctor's judgment than to the priest's partly because she admits to hypochondria and partly because she connects her sight of the nun to her reading of Dr. John's first letter to her. When she thinks that she has lost it, she becomes a "grovelling, groping monomaniac" (II, 22, 353). The spectre of madness haunts hypochondria, but monomania refers specifically to an obvious psychic rupture. "Unlike delirium or mania it could be revealed in a single bizarre act disrupting a superficially ordinary life."[23] Having given only a "vague" account of what she has seen, Lucy resists Dr. John's pressing inquiry: "I never will tell exactly what I saw . . . unless some one else sees it too, and then I will give corroborative testimony; but otherwise, I shall be discredited and accused of dreaming." Writing of Johnson's hypochondria, Boswell insisted on the distinction between "a disorder which affects only the imagination" and "a disorder by which the judgement itself is impaired":

> This distinction was made to me by the late Professor Gaubius of Leyden, physician to the Prince of Orange, in a conversation which I had with him several years ago, and he expanded it thus: "If (said he) a man tells me that he is grievously disturbed, for that he *imagines* he sees a ruffian coming against him with a drawn sword, though at the same time he is *conscious* it is a delusion, I pronounce him to have a disordered imagination; but if a man tells me that he *sees* this, and in consternation calls me to look at it, I pronounce him to be *mad*."[24]

Alert to such distinctions; Lucy has an "avenging dream" she knows to be a dream during the long vacation, even as she knows that the transformation of the "ghostly white beds" in the dormitory into "spectres" is a delusion (I, 15, 222–24). Her insistence on "corroborative testimony" as a precondition for admitting that she has seen something like a nun expresses her conviction that her judgment is sound while acknowledging the unavoidable appearance of madness. As in the ritual of confession, the patient corroborates the truth of her experience by overcoming her own resistance to speaking about it. In part, she can do so because the condition of confidentiality pertains to the sick-room as much as to the confessional. "You may trust me as implicitly as you did Père Silas. Indeed, the doctor is perhaps the safer confessor of the two, though he has not gray hair" (II, 22, 357).

Dr. John's diagnosis is that Lucy has "a case of spectral illusion: I fear, following on and resulting from a long-continued mental conflict," and his advice is to "cultivate" happiness and "a cheerful mind."

> No mockery in this world ever sounds to me so hollow as that of being told to *cultivate* happiness. What does such advice mean? Happiness is not a potato, to be planted in mould, and tilled with manure. Happiness is a glory shining far down upon us out of Heaven. (II, 22, 358)

The prescription was standard. Johnson had similar advice for Boswell, when he complained of melancholy, though Johnson's happiness is, like Lucy's, a glory and not a potato: "Fix your thoughts upon your business, fill your intervals with company, and sunshine will again break in upon your mind."[25] Dr. John's subsequent letters to Lucy and her weekly visits to La Terrasse are part of "a course of cordial and attentive treatment": "Dr. Bretton failed not to tell me *why* he was so kind: 'To keep away the nun,' he said; 'he was determined to dispute with her her prey'" (II, 23, 364). This turn of affairs, though it gains Lucy some attention, cannot satisfy, for she is alert to the insult implied by Dr. John's assurance that she is "safer" in the hands of a handsome, young, and romantically inclined doctor than she was in those of the gray-haired priest. Lucy weeps when Dr. John's letters to her pass "their examination" by Mme. Beck. After M. Paul opens and reads them, she consigns them to the grave. She connects her impulse and mood in the burial scene to those that brought her to the confessional. In both episodes, she prepares a morbid spectacle and entombs a grief. In both, the narrative container, bottle or priest's ear, is "sealed hermetically." In both, Lucy reveals and conceals, giving each narrative, her own and Dr. John's, the distinction of a mourning ritual while making a secret of its substance.

Lucy's relationship with Dr. John is complicated not only by the romantic attraction to him she denies but by her carefully thought out response to him as a doctor. For *Villette* is as alert to what remains invisible, outside the scope of scientific apprehension, as it is to the increased visibility the individual gains by coming under the doctor's eye. In the Vashti chapter, Brontë represents the scene on the stage as another scene of examination, for Dr. John, who observes that Vashti "not with wonder, nor worship, nor yet dismay, but simply with intense curiosity" (II, 23, 372), observes her "as a patient." The reader who identifies with Dr. John's point of view remains detached and analytical, yet at the same time, somewhat repelled, for the Vashti falls short of the ideal of feminine health embodied in the "mighty brawn, the muscle, the abounding blood, the full-fed flesh" of the painted Cleopatra. A dying woman, she is torn by passion, afflicted by grief, and maddened by calamity. The reader who identifies with Lucy is drawn by "the strong magnetism of genius" "to a fierce light, not solar—a rushing, red, cometary light—hot on vision and to sensation"(II, 23, 371). Sensation is immediate and absorbing, agitating and exciting, and Lucy is never more removed from Dr. John than she is when she recognizes his immunity to the pain of the Vashti's agony, the thrill of her morbid vitality.

Lucy's opposition to Dr. John's point of view cannot be disinterested. Speaking of her case, she has already deplored its limitations: "doctors are so self-opinionated, so immovable in their dry, materialistic views" (II, 23, 368). But if Dr. John is too detached to be "impressible," he is also insufficiently detached in a different sense: "he judged her as a woman, not an artist: it was a branding judgment" (II, 23, 373). The judgment is "branding" because it invokes a different normative ideal, a femininity to which sensation, passion, and nervous excitability are alien. In this way too, Dr. John's confrontation with the Vashti reenacts his confrontation with Lucy, who elicits his sympathy but cannot excite his admiration. Only Polly manages to appeal to Dr. John as a woman while engaging his attention as a patient, and she does so by masking the likeness she bears to Lucy. From the beginning, Lucy insists on Polly's susceptibilities. "These sudden, dangerous natures—*sensitive* as they are called—offer many a curious spectacle to those whom a cooler temperament has secured from participation in their angular vagaries" (I, 2, 16). Later, she conjectures that "under harshness, or neglect" neither Polly's outward nor her inward self

> would have ripened to what they now are. Much pain, much fear, much struggle would have troubled the very lines of your features, broken their regularity, would have harassed your nerves into the fever of habitual irritation: you would have lost in health and cheerfulness, in grace and sweetness. (III, 32, 545)

This suggests that Polly might have become Lucy under the influence of different circumstances. When she replaces Lucy as Dr. John's patient, there are no more letters for Lucy and no more visits to La Terrasse.

But if Polly takes Lucy's place as Dr. John's patient, Lucy also takes

Dr. John's place when she ministers to the injured patient. She narrates her own examination of Polly more fully than Dr. John's:

> The chamber was a room shadowy with pale-blue hangings, vaporous with curtainings and veilings of muslin; the bed seemed to me like snow-drift and mist—spotless, soft, and gauzy. Making the women stand apart, I undressed their mistress, without their well-meaning but clumsy aid. I was not in a sufficiently collected mood to note with separate distinctness every detail of the attire I removed, but I received a general impression of refinement, delicacy, and perfect personal cultivation; which, in a period of after thought, offered in my reflections a singular contrast to notes retained of Miss Ginevra Fanshawe's appointments. (II, 23, 378)

The romantic appeal of the setting, the erotic coloring of Lucy's examination of Polly, and her own agitation are in susceptible tension with Lucy's clinical and sanitary observations. In comparing Polly to Ginevra, she anticipates Dr. John's transfer of his affections from the one to the other, but her description of Polly and Polly's chamber, with its bed "like snow-drift and mist," also sustains Polly's connection to Lucy. If further corroboration of Lucy's identification with Polly is required, it is provided when Polly examines Dr. John "with a repetition of the serious, direct gaze I thought peculiar in its gravity and intensity." Her gaze repeats Lucy's as well as her own, for Polly recognizes Graham Bretton in Dr. John just as Lucy had earlier recognized him, and like Lucy, she keeps this discovery to herself. In this scene, Lucy enjoys two vicarious pleasures, that of the examining medical man and that of the examined patient, for she is both Dr. John's eyes and what those "impressionable" eyes see. At the same time, she suffers the inevitable pain of acknowledging once again that Dr. John's interest in her is merely professional.

This discrimination between a professional and a personal gaze, together with an insight into their possible intersection, is deeply embedded in *Villette*'s plot and in the crucial configurations of Brontë's life: not only in her two most significant professional relations with her teacher and her publisher, but also in her relations with the readers and critics who, like G. H. Lewes, judge her "as a woman, not an artist." On the one hand, the female patient longs to be appreciated as a woman. On the other, the female artist suffers from her identification as a woman. Whether the gaze is too professional or not professional enough, Brontë resists a prescriptive diagnosis.

*   *   *

M. Paul's examination of Lucy, which has its inception on the night of her arrival in Villette, is continuous with Mme. Beck's and Dr. John's. Like Mme. Beck, he carries out policing functions, reading Lucy's letters, listening to her through keyholes, examining the contents of her desk, and observing her, sometimes through a glass, during her solitary walks in the *allée défendue*. Later, he will act as Père Silas's agent in trying to convert her to Catholicism. And he is the only one, apart from Dr. John, who knows Lucy has seen the nun and can corroborate her vision, sustaining her claim to sanity. Yet he differs from these others in his clumsiness as spy and his willingness to be discovered. If Lucy disrupts and subverts the disciplinary practices of the school, the church, and the medical profession by subjecting its agents to counter-examination, M. Paul's surveillance disrupts by being so visible: "Never was a more undisguised schemer, a franker, looser intriguer. He would analyze his own machinations: elaborately contrive plots, and forthwith indulge in explanatory boasts of their skill" (II, 27, 433).

But M. Paul differs most importantly from Lucy's other examiners in finding something worth examining. His fullest expression of what it is destroys Lucy's composure one evening at the Hotel Crécy:

> "Petite chatte, doucerette, coquette!" sibillated the sudden boa-constrictor; "vous avez l'air bien triste, soumise, rêveuse, mais vous ne l'êtes pas; c'est moi qui vous le dis: Sauvage! la flamme a l'âme, l'éclair aux yeux!" (II, 27, 456)

Perhaps M. Paul is here a boa-constrictor because Lucy associates him with the spectators at Mme. Beck's ball, the young men who are at once serpents and "golden apples," tempters of and tempted by, the young women who perform for them. Lucy's deviance, her difference from the others in the pensionnat, has so far been constituted primarily as sexual unattractiveness. Under M. Paul's examination, this deviance will be reconstituted as spiritual and intellectual distinction. Lucy is morally opposed to M. Paul's acts of surveillance: "To study the human heart thus," she primly tells him, "is to banquet secretly and sacrilegiously on Eve's apples" (III, 31, 530). Her metaphor is appropriate not just to the setting, Mme. Beck's enclosed garden with its ancient pear tree, but to the acts M. Paul witnesses there, the confessions of sexual knowledge, its articulation by word, attitude, or gesture. But these acts of surveillance are insufficient in themselves and require another kind of objectifying observation, one that takes place repeatedly and ritually within the classroom.

The academic examination is an anomaly in Mme. Beck's school, where the pupils gain knowledge "by a marvelously easy method, without painful exertion or useless waste of spirits" and where no noteworthy intellectual accomplishment is expected of them. As public display, the ball is more effective, and within the school, Mme. Beck and M. Paul rule over separate spheres. The academic examination only begins to function as a disciplinary technique in the third volume of the novel, after M. Paul has undertaken Lucy's tuition:

> In M. Emanuel's soul rankled a chronic suspicion that I knew both Greek and Latin. As monkeys are said to have the power of speech if they would but use it, and are reported to conceal this faculty in fear of its being turned to their detriment, so to me was ascribed a fund of knowledge which I was supposed criminally and craftily to conceal. The privileges of a "classical education," it was insinuated, had been mine; on flowers of Hymettus I had revelled; a golden store, hived in memory, now silently sustained my efforts, and privily nurtured my wits. (III, 30. 511)

As pupil, Lucy is delinquent because she conceals her knowledge "criminally and craftily." Worse than not knowing is not admitting what one knows. The examining teacher seeks to wrest the pupil's knowledge from her, a project animated by his determination to know her thoroughly and justified by his need to know her if he is to direct her course of study. In trying to discover which authors and texts Lucy has read, M. Paul seeks to classify and document her knowledge, to objectify knowledge by locating it within the field of the examination, in this case, the classics, not within the examined subject.

Although Lucy longs to surprise M. Paul with her learning, longs indeed for the "privileges of [the] 'classical education'" she lacks, she is also proud of what she knows. Asked patronizingly whether she feels herself to be "an ignoramus," she has a ready answer:

> Not exactly. I am ignorant, monsieur, in the knowledge you ascribe to me, but I *sometimes*, not *always*, feel a knowledge of my own. (III, 30, 514)

"'What did I mean?' he inquired, sharply." Lucy's account of herself subverts M. Paul's efforts to classify her knowledge by establishing the knowledge proper to an individual as a separate category. In Lucy's view, knowledge has its value as something to be felt, irregularly and without warning, not as a pre-existent something that can be "ascribed" to someone as a possession or attribute.[26] Refusing M. Paul's demand that she improvise a composition in French with the other pupils on the next public examination day, Lucy describes herself as "by nature a cypher" (III, 30, 515). She is a cipher not only because she effaces herself but because she remains incalculable, safely outside the field of her examiner's knowledge.

M. Paul's efforts to examine Lucy culminate in the academic "show-trial" he arranges to clear himself of the charge that he has signed Lucy's name to his own essays. His two colleagues examine Lucy in classics, French history, and "various 'ologies." At first, she knows no answers; then, she has ideas but lacks words. "I either *could* not, or *would* not speak—I am not sure which: partly, I think my nerves had gone wrong, and partly my humour was crossed" (III, 35, 580). "Est-elle donc idiote?" one whispers to the other. Although Lucy's examiners insist on their higher aims—"Nous agissons dans l'intérêt de la vérité. Nous ne voulons pas vous blesser"—their examination is punishing. Finally, asked to improvise a theme on "Human Justice," Lucy prepares to resist absolutely when suddenly she recognizes her examiners as the very men who

> had half frightened me to death on the night of my desolate arrival in Villette. These, I felt morally certain, were the very heroes who had driven a friendless foreigner beyond her reckoning and her strength, chased her breathless over a whole quarter of the town. (III, 35)

Most readers will pause at this unlikely coincidence. Why is it so much worse for Lucy to identify her examiners as her pursuers than it would be for her to acknowledge the resemblance of one act of harassment to another? Because such coincidences are the stuff of persecution fantasies. They sustain a paranoid perception of the world as a place in which everything hangs together. In the very different world of *Jane Eyre*, differences ground resemblances: St. John Rivers is like John Reed or the Reverend Mr. Brocklehurst because he is neither the one nor the other. But in *Villette* differences are unstable and resemblances regularly collapse into identities. Thus, Dr. John turns out to be Graham Bretton, the Countess de Bassompierre turns out to be Polly Home, and the Messieurs Boissec (Dry Wood) and Rochemorte (Dead Rock) turn out to be "two faces looking out of the forest of long hair, moustache, and whisker—those two cold yet bold, trustless yet presumptuous visages . . . projected in full gaslight from behind the pillars of a portico" (III, 35, 582).

A paranoid view of the world enlarges the self, which finds new security in vindicating its defensive postures. According to Paul Smith, paranoia "creates a fictional universe which is threatening to its creator: it is full of the bad things against which he or she must clearly defend. For the 'subject' here the obviousness of the need for defence has its correlate in the fixity and obstinacy of the outside world."[27] Brontë doesn't ask us to question Lucy's identification of her examiners as the men who harassed her on the night of her arrival in Villette, anymore than we question her identification of Dr. John as the one who gave her directions to the Rue Fossette on the same occasion. Instead, she asks us to believe in the objective anxieties against which her heroine defends herself. By insisting that the "fixity and obstinacy of the outside world" is actual rather than delusory, as in her demystification of the haunting attic nun, Brontë represents a response that looks paranoid but is justified by actual circumstances. The coherence of the world of *Villette* confirms the coherence of the self constrained to live in it.

As in her earlier encounter with her examiners. Lucy perseveres in taking her own direction. In an act of opposition and resistance more moving than silence, she finds words and produces a narrative:

> An idea once seized, I fell to work. "Human Justice" rushed before me in novel guise, a red, random beldame with arms akimbo. I saw her in her house, the den of confusion: servants called to her for orders or help which she did not give; beggars stood at her door waiting and starving unnoticed; a swarm of children, sick and quarrelsome, crawled round her feet and yelled in her ears appeals for notice, sympathy, cure, redress. The honest woman cared for none of these things. She had a warm seat of her own by the fire, she had her own solace in a short black pipe, and a bottle of Mrs. Sweeney's soothing syrup; she smoked and she sipped and she enjoyed her paradise, and whenever a cry of the suffering souls about her pierced her ears too keenly—my jolly dame seized the poker or the hearth-brush: if the offender was weak, wronged, and sickly, she effectually settled him; if he was strong, lively, and violent, she only menaced, then plunged her hand in her deep pouch, and flung a liberal shower of sugar-plums. (III, 35, 582–83)

To recall the episode of examination in which the six masked Brontë children provided the answers their father expected of them is to understand how radically disruptive Lucy's narrative is simply by being a response her examiners cannot have expected and cannot evaluate. And Lucy's refusal to speak at all is telling. Accused of having signed her name to M. Paul's writing, she claims her own voice in an act of writing. The quiet pun lurking in "novel guise," both "new" and "novelistic," suggests the close relation Brontë saw between her art as a novelist and "a knowledge of [her] own." Exhibited as an object of curiosity and study, Brontë's heroine presents "a dead blank." Challenged to improvise a theme, she creates a paranoid fantasy that cynically refracts the social world of *Villette*. This world resembles that of *Wuthering Heights* more closely than that of any other novel by Charlotte Brontë. In it, the weak and sickly are punished, while those who are strong, lively, and violent are rewarded.

*   *   *

Villette's most striking coincidence occurs at its center, when Lucy wakes up in La Terrasse after her collapse outside the confessional, and we discover that the Pensionnat's Dr. John is John Graham Bretton, Lucy's godbrother and the hero of the early chapters of the novel. At this point, Lucy reveals that she "first recognized him on that occasion, noted several chapters back, when my unguardedly-fixed attention had drawn on me the mortification of an implied rebuke":

> To *say* anything on the subject, to *hint* at my discovery, had not suited my habits of thought, or assimilated with my system of feeling. On the contrary, I had preferred to keep the matter to myself. I liked entering his presence covered with a cloud he had not seen through, while he stood before me under a ray of special illumination, which shone all partial over his head, trembled about his feet, and cast light no farther.
> Well I knew that to him it could make little difference, were I to come forward and announce, "This is Lucy Snowe!" So I kept back in my teacher's place; and as he never asked my name, so I never gave it. He heard me called "Miss," and "Miss Lucy;" he never heard the surname, "Snowe." As to spontaneous recognition—though I, perhaps, was still less changed than he—the idea never approached his mind, and why should I suggest it? (II, 16, 249–50)

Lucy has at least two motives for keeping her identity a secret from Dr. John. First, she fully acknowledges her pleasure in the power over him that comes from seeing and knowing him while she remains unseen and unknown to him. Then, she complicates this explanation by insisting, not wrongly, on his indifference to her, her lack of the power to attract his attention. With her silence, then, Lucy seeks the satisfactions of power over Dr. John and also seeks to avoid the dissatisfactions of feeling her own powerlessness for him. In our usual thinking, self-effacement is at odds with self-concern, but Lucy's silence is at once self-concerned and self-effacing. Her self-effacement makes her unavailable for recognition, or rather unavailable for the misrecognition that accompanies judgment.

As other readers have noticed, Lucy's keeping her name a secret from Dr. John is different from the narrator's keeping Dr. John's identity as Graham Bretton a secret from the reader. The only hint to the reader that

Lucy has discovered his identity is the "direct, inquiring gaze" that elicits
Dr. John's blank stare and rebuke (I, 10, 136). I take the narrator's motives
for silence to be like the character's, in a situation that establishes Brontë's
identification of her reader with Dr. John, each operating in his or her
professional character:

> "Tell *me* . . . I will hear it in my professional character: I look on you now
> from a professional point of view, and I read, perhaps, all you would
> conceal. . . . Come, Lucy, speak and tell me." (II, 22, 355)

The narrator's charge that Dr. John "did not at all guess what I felt: he did
not read my eyes, or face, or gestures; though, I doubt not, all spoke" (II,
27, 455) makes him the object of her readers' criticism, but instead of placing her readers at a comfortable distance from this medical man, she insists
on their seeing themselves in him. Through Dr. John, Brontë exposes the
aggressions involved in our attempt to read Lucy.

   Even *Villette*'s title is an effacement, perhaps a concealment. Like the
title of *Wuthering Heights* and unlike the titles of Charlotte Brontë's other
novels, it holds the name of its heroine in reserve. And Lucy is so periph-
eral to the action of the novel's first three chapters that many readers have
been misled by them into thinking of Polly as the novel's heroine. Self-
effacement is, of course, the foundation of a moral program especially
enjoined on nineteenth-century women, whose concern for others was
supposed not only to take precedence over self-concern but to disable it.
In her role as Polly's counselor, Lucy recommends self-effacement when
she cautions her not to grieve because Graham (who calls Polly "little
Mousie" rather than "Missy") cares less for her than she cares for him:
"Don't fret, and don't expect too much of him, or else he will feel you to
be troublesome, and then it is all over"(I, 3, 43). From one point of view,
feminine morbidity, the nervous and physical ailments afflicting Lucy and
other nineteenth-century women, are the required evidence of a selfless
dedication to others even at the expense of self; from another, they are a
sure sign of dedication to self. In hypochondria as in paranoia, the self
reveals its heightened importance for itself.

   Some blend of self-effacement and self-concern characterizes Lucy's
defensive conduct in all her engagements with Dr. John and her readers.
These are attempts to manage others as well as acts of self-management.
As one woman's story, *Villette* is remarkable because the institutional diagnosis of the heroine as heretic, ill, or idiot, that is, as someone in need
of the care of others, not only foment resistance but also issue in a re-

sponsive and responsible determination on her part to care for herself. Even more remarkably, *Villette* connects its heroine's capacity to defend herself against the institutions that would mask their control over her as concern—the Church, the medical profession, and the academic establishment—with its narrator's capacity to defend herself against conventions of reading that also prescribe self-revelation and self-exposure.

These are the usual conditions for readerly concern, but Brontë makes her own conditions in *Villette*. "Trouble no quiet, kind heart," the narrator writes at the close of the novel, after hinting at the wreck of the ship bringing M. Paul back to Lucy:

> leave sunny imaginations hope. Let it be theirs to conceive the delight of joy born again fresh out of great terror, the rapture of rescue from peril, the wondrous reprieve from dread, the fruition of return. Let them picture union and a happy succeeding life. (III, 42, 715)

The temptation to go beyond the undecidability of *Villette*'s ending is very great, and few readers would want to ignore Gaskell's account of how Brontë altered it to comply with her father's wish for a normative conclusion to Lucy's life, an ending in which the hero and heroine would "marry and live happily ever after." But *Villette* avoids closure both by effacing Lucy's grim fate and by undermining its reader's expectation of ever fully knowing it.

Lucy's last word to her readers, after she has deflected their attention from the uncertainty of Lucy's future to the certainty of the ends of the other characters, is "farewell":

> Mme. Beck prospered all the days of her life; so did Père Silas; Madam Walravens fulfilled her ninetieth year before she died. Farewell. (III, 42, 715)

This implicitly contrasts Lucy's outcome with the outcomes of the other characters and explicitly contrasts the extents to which we may know them. Such a "farewell" ceremonially acknowledges the physical separation of reader from book that is about to occur and at the same time insists on the moral and psychological separation of reader from narrator that has all along been the condition of this narrative. Its imagined reader is, after all, a "quiet, kind heart," a "sunny imagination," someone who is like Dr. John and the other characters in *Villette* and unlike Lucy precisely in being destined to fare well.

Like the mask in the childhood episode of interrogation with which I began, *Villette*'s first-person narrative promises to reveal a self ordinarily hidden from view but instead exposes the cultural conditions that seek to define this self for itself. By repeatedly enacting disclosures that are also foreclosures, the novel resists the autobiographical imperative of total and continuous visibility and gives salience to the spaces where a self in hiding escapes an empowered knowledge. But Lucy doesn't just exercise her own power in defending against her readers' power over her. She insists that these readers recognize their implication in the expectations and practices that subject her to suspicion, surveillance, and normalizing discipline.

In her Preface to the 1850 edition of *Wuthering Heights*, Charlotte Brontë had deprecated her sister's failure "to defend her own most manifest rights." In *Villette*, she creates a character as alert to her own most manifest rights as she is to the manifest wrongs she contends against. These are embodied as external anxieties rather than internalized as the creations of a morbid fancy, even though Lucy "*is* both morbid and weak at times."

> To her, what hurts becomes immediately embodied: she looks on it as a thing that can be attacked, worried down,, torn in shreds. Scarcely a substance herself, she grapples to conflict with abstractions. (II, 23, 370)

There is more rigid resistance to social constraints and less accommodation to sunny imaginations unclouded by any perception of them in *Villette* than in any of Brontë's other novels. In her last novel Charlotte Brontë bends only as her powers tend and arrives at her darkest vision of the circumstances that require her heroine's defensive conduct and her own.

Notes

Chapter 1

1. E. C. Gaskell, *The Life of Charlotte Brontë*, ed. Alan Shelston (Harmondsworth: Penguin, 1975), 94–95. Patrick Brontë does not date this episode, although he gives Maria's age as about ten and Anne's as about four. It probably occurred shortly before Maria and Elizabeth went away to school in July of 1824.

2. The phrase appears in Felicity A. Nussbaum's *The Autobiographical Subject: Gender and Ideology in Eighteenth-Century England* (Baltimore: Johns Hopkins University Press, 1989), xix.

3. *The Flesh Made Word: Female Figures and Women's Bodies* (New York: Oxford University Press, 1987), 5–6. Michie argues that the female body, so largely present in Victorian sub-genres like pornography and melodrama, is absent from Victorian novels.

4. *The Brontës: Their Lives, Friendships and Correspondence in Four Volumes*, ed. Thomas J. Wise and John Alexander Symington (Oxford: Shakespeare Head Press, 1932), vol. 3, 99.

5. "Playing the Other," in *Nothing to Do with Dionysus? Athenian Drama in its Social Context* (Princeton, N. J.: Princeton University Press, 1990), 74. The phrase "sensibly alive" comes from William James's *The Principles of Psychology*, ed. Frederick H. Burkhardt et al., 3 vols. (Cambridge, Mass.: Harvard University Press, 1981), vol. 2, 1067. For a fuller discussion of James's idea of the body, see below.

6. I review the criticism on both sides of this question in my text, below, and in the notes attached to that portion of the text. In *Repression in Victorian Fiction: Charlotte Brontë, George Eliot, and Charles Dickens* (Berkeley: University of California Press, 1987), John Kucich departs from the tradition of treating repression in Brontë's novels as distortive by treating it as a "particular Brontëan formulation of desire" and one of its "strategies" (38).

7. "The Lesson of Balzac," in *Henry James: Literary Criticism*, ed. Leon Edel, 2 vols. (New York: Viking Press, 1984), vol. 1, 118–19.

8. Charles Dickens, *Little Dorrit*, Book 2, chapter 21.

9. I have the information that "defensive" in its modern sense "appears to have been employed at least since 1965" from one of the editors of the *New Oxford English Dictionary*, who was kind enough to answer an inquiry about it.

10. *London Review of Books*, February 4, 1988, 6.

11. *London Review of Books*, February 18, 1988, 27.

12. *Ariel and the Police: Michel Foucault, William James, Wallace Stevens* (Madison: University of Wisconsin Press, 1988), 136–37.

13. *The Ego and the Mechanisms of Defence*, trans. Cecil Baines (New York: International Universities Press, 1946), 45–46. "Later, this term was abandoned and, as time went on, was replaced by that of 'repression.' The relation between the two notions, however, remained undetermined." Later still, in an appendix to *Inhibitions, Symptoms and Anxiety* (1926), Freud suggested that "defence" should be employed as a general term for "all the techniques which the ego makes use of in conflicts which may lead to neurosis"; repression was only one of these (47).

14. Joseph Sandler with Anna Freud, *The Analysis of Defense: The Ego and the Mechanisms of Defense Revisited* (New York: International Universities Press, 1985), 269–70; 312; 341.

15. Trans. Donald Nicholson-Smith (London: Hogarth Press, 1973), 103–7.

16. *The Diary and Letters of Madame D'Arblay*, ed. Charlotte Barrett, vol. 2 (London: Bickers and Son, n.d.), 339–40.

17. *The Structure of Complex Words* (Ann Arbor: University of Michigan Press, 1967), 43–44.

18. Arnold's words appear in a letter to Mrs. Foster, quoted in *The Brontës: The Critical Heritage*, ed. Miriam Allott (London: Routledge & Kegan Paul, 1974), 201. Kathleen Tillotson's connection between Arnold's powerful response to *Villette* and his recent repudiation of *Empedocles on Etna* because "the suffering finds no vent in action" and the situation is "painful, not tragic" seems exactly right ("'Haworth Churchyard': The Making of Arnold's Elegy," *Brontë Society Transactions* 15, 77 [1967], 117–18). For a fuller discussion of Arnold's response to Brontë, see below, Chapter 6.

19. "When We Dead Awaken," in *On Lies, Secrets, and Silence: Selected Prose 1966–78* (New York: W. W. Norton, 1979), 37.

20. *A Room of One's Own* (New York: Harcourt, Brace and World, 1957), 70–74.

21. *A Literature of Their Own: British Women Novelists from Brontë to Lessing* (Princeton, N. J.: Princeton University Press, 1977), 289. The validity of Showalter's charge against Woolf is difficult to establish both because Woolf's position on anger and protest is in keeping with a Romantic aesthetic that exalted the impersonality of great art, and because it is always too easy to translate an effect—Woolf's evasion of certain kinds of disapproval—into a neurotic cause—Woolf's need to forestall such criticism. Woolf's immense admiration for Jane Austen follows from her sense that the circumstances of a nineteenth-century woman writer were inimical to the impersonality she believed was characteristic of the highest art: "when people compare Shakespeare and Jane Austen, they may mean that the minds of both had consumed all impediments; and for that reason we do not know Jane Austen and we do not know Shakespeare, and for that reason Jane Austen pervades every word that she wrote, and so does Shakespeare." Mary Poovey provides a very full account of these circumstances in *The Proper Lady and the Woman Writer* (Chicago: University of Chicago Press, 1984). See especially her introductory chapter.

22. *Samuel Johnson* (New York: Harcourt Brace Jovanovich, 1977), 489–90.

23. *Keywords: A Vocabulary of Culture and Society* (London: Hogarth Press,

1976); *The English Novel from Dickens to Lawrence* (London: Hogarth Press, 1984), 73–74.

24. "Language and Social Change," in *The State of the Language*, ed. Leonard Michaels and Christopher Ricks (Berkeley: University of California Press, 1980), 566.

25. *Lives, Friendships*, vol. 4, 189.

26. Quoted in *Critical Heritage*, 105–12.

27. *Lives, Friendships*, vol. 4, 207.

28. Gaskell, *Life*, 360.

29. Gaskell, *Life*, 334.

30. *Lives, Friendships*, vol. 4, 222–23.

31. Charles Dickens, *Oliver Twist*, ed. Kathleen Tillotson (Oxford: Oxford University Press, 1982), Author's Preface to the Third Edition, xxv.

32. Quoted in *Critical Heritage*, 89. For an excellent discussion of the double critical standard in the mid-nineteenth century, see Inga-Stina Ewbank, who also quotes this passage in *Their Proper Sphere: A Study of the Brontë Sisters as Early-Victorian Female Novelists* (Cambridge, Mass.: Harvard University Press, 1968), 2.

33. *Lives, Friendships*, vol. 4, 199–200.

34. Gaskell, *Life*, 526.

35. *The Structure of Complex Words*, 412.

36. *The Second Sex*, trans. and ed. H. M. Parshley (New York: Bantam Books, 1961, rpt. 1970), 570–71.

37. J. Hillis Miller is alone in giving importance to this edition, but his emphasis in writing about *Wuthering Heights* in *Fiction and Repetition: Seven English Novels* (Cambridge, Mass.: Harvard University Press, 1982) is entirely different from mine. He argues that Brontë's biographical notice and preface "establish the rhetorical stance" and "with their multiple interpretations, each based on some aspect of the actual text of [the novel], establish a program for all the hundreds of essays and books on *Wuthering Heights* which were to follow" (47–49). Philip Drew, in "Charlotte Brontë as Critic of *Wuthering Heights*" (in *The Brontës: A Collection of Critical Essays*, ed. Ian Gregor [Englewood Cliffs, N. J.: Prentice-Hall, 1970], 44–58) reviews Brontë's criticism of *Wuthering Heights* admiringly, noting the difference between her view of the novel's morality and that of modern critics. For a fuller account of Brontë's relation to her sister's novel, see below, Chapter 5.

38. Emily Brontë, *Wuthering Heights*, ed. Hilda Marsden and Ian Jack (Oxford: Clarendon Press, 1976), 435.

39. *Wuthering Heights*, 436. In a letter to W. S. Williams, Brontë speaks of having been "sternly rated at first for having taken an unwarrantable liberty" when she confessed to her discovery of the poems (*Lives, Friendships*, vol. 2, 256).

40. *Wuthering Heights*, 438.

41. *Lives, Friendships*, vol. 3, 15–16.

42. *Wuthering Heights*, 441.

43. *The Complete Poems of Emily Jane Brontë*, ed. C. W. Hatfield (New York: Columbia University Press, 1941), 255–56. The *of* in line 3 is ambiguously either genitive or objective, so that lines 3 and 4 say either that one stops chasing wealth

and learning in order to turn to "idle dreams of things which cannot be" or that one quits the chase by wealth and learning for such idle dreams. The first reading makes somewhat more sense, for even if wealth and learning are associated with "idle dreams" rather than practical achievements, it is difficult to imagine them chasing after the same dreams. In contrast to the present progressive participles of the first stanza, the future tense verb of the second stanza makes a distinction between the kind of quest that has so often provided an escape and the quest that will this day be undertaken. In this reading, the poem sounds vaguely autobiographical, recalling the worlds of both Gondal and Angria but recalling even more strongly the language in which Charlotte Brontë describes the visions that produced her own early tales. Phrases like "shadowy region" and "unreal world" are familiar to us from the "Roe Head Journal," where she most explicitly contrasts the ordinary world to the visionary world that nourished her imagination.

44. *Lives, Friendships*, vol. 3, 23.

45. "'Often Rebuked . . .'": Emily's After All?" *Brontë Society Transactions* 18, 93 (1983), 222–26. See also Flora Katherine Willett, "Which Brontë Was 'Often Rebuked'? A Note Favouring Anne," *Brontë Society Transactions* 18, 92 (1982), 143–48.

46. This is Brontë's word in the "Biographical Notice": "An interpreter ought always to have stood between her and the world" (440). The editors of the Clarendon *Wuthering Heights* conclude that there is no evidence that Brontë referred to any "knowledge of her sister's intentions and preferences" in preparing the 1850 edition of *Wuthering Heights* in which she made changes in paragraphing, punctuation, and the representation of dialect speech. According to Derek Roper, she altered 18 percent of the lines in poems she selected for the 1850 printing, dropping twenty and writing nine herself. See Hilda Marsden and Ian Jack, *Wuthering Heights*, xiii–xxxii, and Derek Roper, "The Revision of Emily Brontë's Poems of 1846," *The Library* Sixth Series 6 (1984), 153–67.

47. Gaskell, *Life*, 397.

48. G. H. Lewes, unsigned review in the *Edinburgh Review*, January 1850. Reprinted in *Critical Heritage*, 160–69.

49. *Lives, Friendships*, vol. 3, 66.

50. Gaskell had Brontë's letters to Lewes from him and prints them together with an excerpt from his letter to her about them in the *Life*, 397–98. Brontë's letters are also printed in *Lives, Friendships*, vol. 3, 67–68. The first letter is undated, but the second is dated January 19th, 1850.

51. *Thinking About Women* (New York: Harcourt, Brace and World, 1968), 65–68.

52. *Lives, Friendships*, vol. 3, 99.

53. *Boswell's Life of Johnson*, 6 volumes, ed. George Birkbeck Hill (Oxford: Clarendon Press, 1934, rpt. 1971), vol. 2, 49. In the passage preceding this one, Boswell quotes Johnson's definition of Richardson's "characters of nature" as characters "where a man must dive into the recesses of the human heart."

54. *Writing Degree Zero*, trans. Annette Lavers and Colin Smith (London: Jonathan Cape, 1967), 16–17. Mary Douglas also quotes this passage in *Natural Symbols: Explorations in Cosmology* (New York: Pantheon Books, 1970).

55. *The Expression of the Emotions in Man and Animals*, revised and abridged by C. M. Beadnell (London: Watts and Co., 1948), 118.

56. *The Principles of Psychology*, vol. 2, 1067–68. "*If we fancy some strong emotion, and then try to abstract from our consciousness of it all the feelings of its bodily symptoms, we find we have nothing left behind,* no 'mind-stuff' out of which the emotion can be constituted, and that a cold and neutral state of intellectual perception is all that remains" (emphasis in original).

57. See *Natural Symbols: Explorations in Cosmology*, 65, 70–71.

Chapter 2

1. Kathleen Tillotson argues that *The Professor* is crippled by structural difficulties that result from Brontë's inability to distance herself sufficiently from the themes of her early writings (*The Novels of the Eighteen-Forties* [Oxford: Clarendon Press, 1954], 283–84), while Enid Duthie attributes the novel's problems to her inability to distance herself sufficiently from her unhappy love affair with M. Héger. "She put into *The Professor* all of Brussels which she could, at that time, endure to resuscitate" (*The Foreign Novels of Charlotte Brontë* [New York: Barnes and Noble, 1975], 87). Some of Brontë's critics have agreed with her that *The Professor* lacks romance, for instance, Christine Alexander, for whom the novel is an "over-reaction to the extravagances of her juvenilia" (*The Early Writings of Charlotte Brontë* [Oxford: Basil Blackwell, 1983]) and R. B. Martin (*The Accents of Persuasion: Charlotte Brontë's Novels* [London: Faber and Faber, 1966]), who divides Brontë's four novels into two categories, realistic and unsuccessful (*The Professor* and *Shirley*) and romantic and successful (*Jane Eyre* and *Villette*). Others, like John Maynard, have denied the preface's suggestion that *The Professor* is "an unfortunate attempt at cold-blooded slice-of-life writing." Maynard emphasizes the novel's "rather happy ending" and its focus "on the process of desire finding fulfillment" (*Charlotte Brontë and Sexuality* [Cambridge: Cambridge University Press, 1984], 73).

2. In "The Value of Vindictiveness," Karen Horney explores the relation between vindictiveness and vindication, arguing that in neurosis "vindictiveness can become a character trait; it can amount to a vindictive attitude toward life; it can become a way of life." At the same time, she sees this neurotic experience as an exaggeration of the psychological conflicts that are typical in a given culture (*American Journal of Psychoanalysis* 8 [1948], 3–12). See also Marcia Westkott, *The Feminist Legacy of Karen Horney* (New Haven, Conn.: Yale University Press, 1986), 12–13.

3. As Michael McKeon writes, "That the piety and fervor of Protestant reformation should have aided in the development of an ideology in which human self-sufficiency renders God strictly superfluous is only the most strikingly paradoxical instance of the general truth that once set in motion, absolutist reform reforms absolutely" (*The Origins of the English Novel, 1600–1740* [Baltimore: Johns Hopkins University Press, 1987], 200).

4. *The Brontës: Their Lives, Friendships and Correspondence in Four Volumes*, ed. Thomas J. Wise and John Alexander Symington (Oxford: Shakespeare Head Press, 1932), vol. 2, 13. Brontë's letter is, of course, in French. The translation is the editors'.

5. Southey's letters are given in *Lives, Friendships*, vol. 1, 156–58.

6. E.C. Gaskell, *The Life of Charlotte Brontë*, ed. Alan Shelston (Harmondsworth: Penguin, 1975), 173–74.

7. *Lives, Friendships*, vol. 1, 158.

8. Ms. in the Brontë Parsonage Museum Library, seven pages, beginning "My Compliments to the weather. I wonder what it would be at" and known as part of the "Roe Head Journal." Quoted in Fannie Elizabeth Ratchford, *The Brontës' Web of Childhood* (New York: Columbia University Press, 1941), 107. Christine Alexander dates it c. March 1837. Brontë wrote two long narratives, *Julia* and *Four Years Ago*, shortly after her letter to Southey. See Christine Alexander, *The Early Writings of Charlotte Brontë* (Oxford: Basil Blackwell, 1983), 158.

9. Ms. in pencil and Brontë's ordinary script in the Brontë Parsonage Museum, 2 pages. Alexander does not date this manuscript, but it is likely that it was written soon after the publication of *Jane Eyre* when Brontë first considered revising *The Professor* and resubmitting it to Smith, Elder. The editors of the Clarendon edition of *The Professor* print this draft preface in an appendix (295–96) and suggest a date of November or December 1847. There is a discrepancy between Brontë's reference to seven chapters that can be omitted in a revised version of the novel and the six chapters that actually contain Crimsworth's experience before arriving in Belgium in the novel we have.

10. *Lives, Friendships*, vol. 2, 161–62.

11. *Novels of the Eighteen-Forties*, 283–84.

12. Gaskell, *Life*, 305. The seventh publisher to whom Brontë sent the manuscript of *The Professor* was Smith, Elder, and the first comment by a publisher's reader on it was made by W. S. Williams, who indicated interest in a three-volume work.

13. "Gender, Relation, and Difference in Psychoanalytic Perspective," in *The Future of Difference*, ed. Hester Eisenstein and Alice Jardine (New Brunswick, N. J.: Rutgers University Press, 1985), 3–19. Chodorow takes issue with the Freudian premise that "males are 'not females' in earliest development" and that females define themselves as not males when they perceive their lack of a penis. Her point about the difference between the early childhood development of boys and that of girls is also made by others, including Coppèlia Kahn: "While the boy's sense of *self* begins in union with the feminine, his sense of *masculinity* arises against it" (quoted in Eve Sedgwick, *Between Men: English Literature and Male Homosocial Desire* [New York: Columbia University Press, 1985], 24–25).

14. Ms. of *The Professor*, in the Pierpont Morgan Library. See M. M. Brammer, "The Manuscript of *The Professor*," *Review of English Studies* New Series 2 (1960), 161.

15. Ms. of *The Professor*, quoted in the Clarendon edition (22, 200). M. M. Brammer comments on it, 159.

16. "Class, Power and Charlotte Brontë," *Critical Quarterly* 14 (1972), 229.

17. Sally Shuttleworth, *George Eliot and Nineteenth-Century Science* (Cambridge: Cambridge University Press, 1984), 123.

18. *The Mismeasure of Man* (New York: W. W. Norton, 1981), 28.

19. O. S. and L. N. Fowler, *New Illustrated Self-Instruction in Phrenology and Physiology* (London: W. Tweedie, n.d.), 58.

20. Gould, *Mismeasure of Man*, 28.

21. Crimsworth's racial and religious bigotry clearly exceeds any that might be attributed to Brontë, but in a letter to Ellen Nussey, she uses the same logic that he does to derive the "national character of the Belgians" from the attributes of the Belgians she has met in her school:

> If the national character of the Belgians is to be measured by the character of most of the girls in the school, it is a character singularly cold, selfish, animal and inferior—They are besides very mutinous and difficult for the teachers to manage—and their principles are rotten to the core—we avoid them—which is not difficult to do—as we have the brand of Protestantism and Anglicism upon us.

Brontë's last sentence suggests an explanation for her vindictiveness in a sense of prior insult or injury: "we have the brand of Protestantism and Anglicism upon us." In the same letter, she reminds Ellen that there are "some Catholics—who are as good as any Christians can be to whom the bible is a sealed book and much better than scores of Protestants" (*Lives, Friendships*, vol. 1, 267). Of course, events in her own life while she was a pupil-teacher in Brussels suggest more threateningly divisive feelings, at least about Catholicism. Only two months after her letter to Ellen, she wrote Emily about making her confession to the priest in Ste. Gudule, "only a freak" that Emily had better not report to their father (*Lives, Friendships*, vol. 1, 303–4). It is significant that this openness to Catholicism finds a place in *Villette* but not in *The Professor*.

22. John Maynard, for instance, says nothing about Crimsworth's attitudes toward Catholicism or his relations with his male pupils and offers a sympathetic account of his treatment of the "girls": "Faced with ordinary problems of discipline and of forcing some English through their thick Belgian skulls, Crimsworth abandons his idea of most girls as angels or even fledgling angels" (*Charlotte Brontë and Sexuality*, 81). In *Myths of Power: A Marxist Study of the Brontës*, Terry Eagleton notes that Crimsworth "gains faintly sadistic pleasure from the effects of his own self-defensive impenetrability" (London: Macmillan, 1975), 229.

23. Quoted in *The Brontës: The Critical Heritage*, ed. Miriam Allott (London: Routledge & Kegan Paul, 1974), 174.

24. *The Religion of the Heart: Anglican Evangelicalism in the Nineteenth-Century Novel* (Oxford: Clarendon Press, 1979), 55.

25. *Middlemarch*, ed. W. J. Harvey (Harmondsworth: Penguin, 1965), Book 1, Chapter 10.

26. Maynard, *Brontë and Sexuality*, 6, 84.

27. *Deceit, Desire, & the Novel: Self and Other in Literary Structure* (Baltimore: Johns Hopkins University Press, 1965), 111. See also Sedgwick, *Between Men*, 21–27. Sedgwick writes persuasively about romantic and erotic triangles in several Victorian works as figures for disguising the bond between male rivals, who use women as "exchangeable, perhaps symbolic, property for the primary purpose of cementing the bonds of men with men." The "triadic" structures Eagleton identifies as the recurrent form of the political and social ideology of Brontë's novels are not related to Girard's triangles. Eagleton's triads describe a thematics of political compromise by situating each protagonist between a Romantic radical and an autocratic conservative. Despite his assertion that these "roles are fluid and permeable," important characters in the novels are simply excluded from his account of them. Thus his discussion of *The Professor* focuses on a triangle that situates Crimsworth in relation to his brother Edward and Hunsden Yorke Hunsden but largely neglects Crimsworth's relations with both Frances Henri and Mdlle. Reuter. In Eagleton's reading, *The Professor* is "essentially a more dishonest and idealised version of *Jane Eyre* and *Villette*" because its use of a male protagonist produces a concern with the "victory rather than the vulnerability of the solitary social aspirant" (*Myths of Power*, 74, 34). Eagleton's idea that there is in Brontë's novels a kind of repetition that depends on a scheme, rather than on a story or a subject matter, and that economic goals are as important as erotic ones does, however, have something in common with my own view.

28. Helene Moglen suggests that such relations have their source in Brontë's own "masochistic personality" (*Charlotte Brontë: The Self Conceived* [New York: Norton, 1976], 59), and Eagleton points out their connection with other capitalist power relations (*Myths of Power*, 29–30). Dianne Sadoff combines psychoanalytic method with feminist theory to interpret masochism in the novels as "stories about the female fantasy in a patriarchal and phallocentric culture," a fantasy she traces back to Freud's account of the pattern of desire and punishment articulated in the daughter's fantasy that is the subject of "A Child is Being Beaten" (*Monsters of Affection: Dickens, Brontë, and Eliot on Fatherhood* [Baltimore: Johns Hopkins University Press, 1982], 123–25).

29. Quoted in *Critical Heritage*, 355–56.

30. Victor A. Neufeldt, ed., *The Poems of Charlotte Brontë: A New Text and Commentary* (New York: Garland Publishing, 1985). These stanzas do not appear in a closely related later poem, which Tom Winnifrith discusses together with "Rochester's Song to Jane Eyre" in *Brontë Facts and Brontë Problems* (London: Macmillan, 1983), 1–13. Winnifrith argues that since the later poem does not reflect the dramatic situation of any character in any Brontë novel, it must reflect Brontë's situation. This he takes to be an "unlawful" love for M. Héger: "Mr Rochester certainly and Charlotte Brontë probably on the evidence of the Berg manuscript contemplated adultery" (12)! But the later poem cannot require a basis in the actual facts of Brontë's experience, or make clear anything but the intensity of its own dramatized passion. The later poem tells the story of an implacable rivalry that is a dark undercurrent in *The Professor* and surfaces later in *Villette*:

> Cold as a statue's grew his eye,
> Hard as a rock his brow,

Cold hard to me—but tenderly
He kissed my rival now.

31. "Passionate Reserve and Reserved Passion in Brontë," *English Literary History* 52 (1985), 934. This argument is extended by John Kucich in *Repression in Victorian Fiction: Charlotte Brontë, George Eliot, and Charles Dickens* (Berkeley: University of California Press, 1987).

32. Girard, *Deceit, Desire*, 181.

33. In *The Madwoman in the Attic: The Woman Writer and the Nineteenth-Century Literary Imagination* (New Haven, Conn.: Yale University Press, 1979), Gilbert and Gubar interpret the shooting of the dog differently: "If the incident does not advance the story, it does clarify Brontë's symbolism: Crimsworth is anxious not only to kill the dog but to kill what the dog represents. Now fully a patriarch and professor, he sees Yorke Hunsden, as well as the dog Yorke, as a diseased, rabid element in his life." Thus Crimsworth's shooting of the dog is "an attack on Hunsden's radicalism and his own attraction to it" rather than a more fundamental act of self-murder (334–35).

34. For "dog," see William Empson, *The Structure of Complex Words* (1957; rpt. Ann Arbor: University of Michigan Press, 1967), 158–74.

35. See note 9.

36. *Lives, Friendships*, vol. 2, 161–62.

37. *Lives, Friendships*, vol. 4, 52–53.

Chapter 3

1. E. C. Gaskell, *The Life of Charlotte Brontë*, ed. Alan Shelston (Harmondsworth: Penguin, 1975), 305.

2. J. L. Austin, *Sense and Sensibilia*, ed. G. J. Warnock (Oxford: Clarendon Press, 1962), 3.

3. *The Brontës: Their Lives, Friendships and Correspondence in Four Volumes*, ed. Thomas J. Wise and John Alexander Symington (Oxford: Shakespeare Head Press, 1932), vol. 2, 13.

4. Miniature autograph manuscript diary fragment, 2 pages, beginning "I'm just going to write because I cannot help it," and known as part of the "Roe Head Journal," in the Brontë Parsonage Museum (Bonnell 98[7]).

5. Gaskell, *Life*, 129, 307.

6. "Fire and Eyre: Charlotte Brontë's War of Earthly Elements," in *Language of Fiction: Essays in Criticism and Verbal Analysis of the English Novel* (New York: Columbia University Press, 1966).

7. The evidence for the pronunciation of the name of the man who was made Lieutenant Governor of New Zealand in 1846 is mixed. I have been told that there is a square in Edinburgh that bears the name Eyre and is pronounced "Ire." There is today, in Haworth, among the many shops named after the Brontës and their creations, a beauty parlor that bears the name "Jane Ayre" on its sign, as if to disambiguate the pronunciation of Jane's surname.

8. *Christian Remembrancer* (April 1848), rpt. in *The Brontës: The Critical Heritage*, ed. Miriam Allott (London: Routledge and Kegan Paul, 1974), 88–92.

Cf. Virginia Woolf's still cogent remarks in *"Jane Eyre* and *Wuthering Heights"*: Charlotte Brontë "does not attempt to solve the problems of human life; she is even unaware that such problems exist; all her force, and it is the more tremendous for being constricted, goes into the assertion, 'I love', 'I hate', 'I suffer'" (*"Jane Eyre* and *Wuthering Heights,"* in *Collected Essays*, 4 vols. [New York: Harcourt, Brace and World, 1967], vol. 1, 187). In her account of Brontë's arrival at Roe Head, Mary Taylor also remarks on her strong Irish accent.

9. *Collected Essays*, vol. 1, 186. G. Armour Craig also makes Woolf's point: "The power of the 'I' in this novel is secret, undisclosable, absolute. There are no terms to explain its dominance, because no terms can appear which are not under its dominance" ("Private Vision and Social Order," in *Jane Eyre: An Authoritative Text, Backgrounds, Criticism*, ed. Richard J. Dunn [New York: W. W. Norton, 1971], 478). See also Janet H. Freeman, "Speech and Silence in *Jane Eyre,"* *Studies in English Literature* 24 (1984), 683–700.

10. See F. R. Leavis, *The Great Tradition* (London: Chatto & Windus, 1948), and Raymond Williams, *The English Novel: From Dickens to Lawrence* (London: Hogarth Press, 1984), on the novel's eccentricity. See Gayatri Spivak on the novel's centrality for Anglo-American feminism ("Three Women's Texts and a Critique of Imperialism," *Critical Inquiry* 12 [1985], 243–61).

11. Spivak, "Three Women's Texts," 246.

12. *"Vanity Fair*—and *Jane Eyre,"* *Quarterly Review* (Dec. 1848), 176. (This portion of the review is not reprinted in *Critical Heritage*.)

13. Sylvia Plath, *Collected Poems*, ed. Ted Hughes (New York: Harper and Row, 1981).

14. I take this phrase from Merleau-Ponty's "Eye and Mind," in *The Primacy of Perception, and Other Essays on Phenomenological Psychology, the Philosophy of Art, History, and Politics*, ed. James M. Edie (Evanston, Ill.: Northwestern University Press, 1964).

15. Deuteronomy 6:8, 11:18.

16. *From Copyright to Copperfield: The Identity of Dickens* (Cambridge, Mass.: Harvard University Press, 1987), 160.

17. Merleau-Ponty, *The Primacy of Perception*, 163.

18. *Honey-Mad Women: Emancipatory Strategies in Women's Writing* (New York: Columbia University Press, 1988), 37.

19. But the pupils of male subjects also dilated to slides of political leaders they preferred and constricted to other politicians. See Michael Argyle and Mark Cook, *Gaze and Mutual Gaze* (Cambridge: Cambridge University Press, 1976), 62–63. Research into visual communication began in the 1960s and attempted to describe patterns associated with looking, which was defined as gaze at the eyes, and eye-contact, which was defined as mutual looking. But according to D. R. Rutter (*Looking and Seeing: The Role of Visual Communication in Social Interaction* [New York: John Wiley, 1984]), "eye-contact was exposed as a chance event" in the mid-1970s. Evidence showed "that the duration of eye-contact in a whole range of encounters was almost precisely what chance would predict. All that eye-contact could communicate was a piece of information: I am looking at you, you are looking at me, and we have each other's attention. Emotion was irrelevant." Seeing, now defined as "visual access to the whole person," became the focus of research (xi–xii).

20. "The sex which is not one," in *New French Feminisms: An Anthology*, ed. Elaine Marks and Isabelle de Courtivron (Amherst: University of Massachusetts Press, 1980), 101. See also Laura Mulvey's analysis of the dominant scopic economy of traditional narrative film in "Visual Pleasure and Narrative Cinema," *Screen* 16 (1975), rpt. in *Visual and Other Pleasures* (Bloomington: Indiana University Press, 1989), 14–26; and E. Ann Kaplan, "Is the Gaze Male?" in *Women and Film: Both Sides of the Camera* (New York: Methuen, 1984), especially 23–25.

21. *Alice Doesn't: Feminism, Semiotics, Cinema* (Bloomington: Indiana University Press, 1984), 68–69. See also 58–67:

> In a sense, then, narrative and visual pleasure constitute the frame of reference of cinema, one which provides the measure of desire. I believe this statement must apply to women as it does to men. The difference is, quite literally, that it is men who have defined the "visible things" of cinema, who have defined the object and modalities of vision, pleasure, and meaning on the basis of perceptual and conceptual schemata provided by patriarchal ideological and social formations. In the frame of reference of men's cinema, narrative, and visual theories, the male is the measure of desire, quite as the phallic is its signifier and the standard of visibility in psychoanalysis.

22. The phrase is John Jones's, and his account of Keats's lovers in *The Eve of St. Agnes* sharply contrasts the situation of Brontë's lovers. *John Keats's Dream of Truth* (London: Chatto and Windus, 1969), 29.

23. London: Longman, 1985, 203–5.

24. Robert Baldwin provides a useful bibliography of books and articles on this literary tradition in "'Gates Pure and Shining and Serene': Mutual Gazing as an Amatory Motif in Western Literature and Art," *Renaissance and Reformation* 10 (1986), 23–48. According to Baldwin, the gaze of lovers is traditionally not mutual but "one way, either a dart-like glance from the beloved which penetrates the lover's eyes and wounds his heart, or an equally devastating glance of the lover at the physical beauty of the beloved."

25. C. Ruth Sabol and Todd K. Randar, *A Concordance to Brontë's Jane Eyre* (New York: Garland Publishing, 1981).

26. Quoted in Stephen Greenblatt, *Renaissance Self-Fashioning: From More to Shakespeare* (Chicago: University of Chicago Press, 1980), 248.

27. *Natural Supernaturalism: Tradition and Revolution in Romantic Literature* (New York: Norton, 1971), 48; see also 35–37.

28. "'Jane Eyre' and the 'Warped System of Things,'" in *Reading the Victorian Novel*, ed. Ian Gregor (New York: Barnes and Noble, 1980), 136.

29. *Bearing the Word: Language and Female Experience in Nineteenth-Century Women's Writing* (Chicago: University of Chicago Press, 1986), 16, 88.

30. *Charlotte Brontë: Style in the Novel* (Madison: University of Wisconsin Press, 1973), 56–57.

31. Carlyle's definition of a miracle is in the chapter of *Sartor Resartus* titled "Natural Supernaturalism" (New York: Harper and Brothers, 1848), 201.

32. Quoted in *Critical Heritage*, 421.

33. Nancy Armstrong argues persuasively that Jane's inheritance, not the

death of Bertha Rochester, is the enabling event in the plot. According to Armstrong, the proof that Jane's alliance with Rochester was not "disallowed" simply because he was married is that she returns to him while believing that he is still married. "The novel seems to insist that only when an exchange of economic for emotional power has been fully and freely transacted, can the female achieve her proper dominion over the home" ("The Rise of Feminine Authority in the Novel," *Novel* [1982], 137).

34. *Phoenix II: Uncollected, Unpublished, and Other Prose Works*, ed. Warren Roberts and Harry T. Moore (New York: Viking Press, 1968), 174–75.

35. *The Standard Edition of the Complete Psychological Works of Sigmund Freud*, 24 vols., trans. James Strachey et al. (London: Hogarth Press and the Institute of Psycho-Analysis, 1953), vol. 17, 231.

36. "The Brontës: a Centennial Observance," *Kenyon Review* 9 (1947), 487–506. Dianne Sadoff's psychoanalytical reading of the novel follows Chase's line of interpretation in seeing Rochester's punishment as "a 'symbolic castration' . . . that does not signify 'equality' but rather a fear of sexual difference and masculine power" (*Monsters of Affection: Dickens, Brontë, and Eliot on Fatherhood* [Baltimore: Johns Hopkins University Press, 1982], 184).

37. C. S. Lewis, *A Preface to Paradise Lost* (New York: Oxford University Press, 1966), 134.

38. Sandra M. Gilbert and Susan Gubar, *The Madwoman in the Attic: The Woman Writer and the Nineteenth-Century Literary Imagination* (New Haven, Conn.: Yale University Press, 1979), 368; *Toward a Recognition of Androgyny* (New York: Knopf, 1973), 59; *Charlotte Brontë: The Self Conceived* (New York: Norton, 1976), 142. Gilbert's and Gubar's reading of the novel has helped to shape the ongoing investigation by feminist critics of the culturally authorized connections between female sexuality and madness. They shift our attention from Jane's relation with Rochester to her relation with Bertha, Jane's "truest and darkest double," the "ferocious secret self Jane has been trying to repress ever since her days at Gateshead" (360). In a more radical unraveling of the relationship between Jane and Bertha and of the culturally authorized connections it manifests, Gayatri Spivak argues that the "emergent perspective of feminist criticism reproduces the axioms of imperialism" by treating the "native female" as an element in "the psychobiography of the militant female subject." Spivak's quarrel isn't with feminist criticism only. While not seeking "to undermine the excellence of the individual artist," she hopes to "incite a degree of rage against the imperialist narrativization of history, that it should produce so abject a script for her" (243–61).

39. "Private Vision and Social Order," 477.

40. Lewis, *Preface*, 134.

41. *Madwoman in the Attic*, 369.

42. *Charlotte Brontë and Sexuality* (Cambridge: Cambridge University Press, 1984), 138–39.

43. I am quoting Fredric Jameson's account of the attack on Freud in *The Anti-Oedipus* in *The Political Unconscious: Narrative as a Socially Symbolic Act* (Ithaca, N. Y.: Cornell University Press, 1981), 22.

44. *Jane Eyre*, 602. The confusion about hands is not properly a confusion.

On the symbolism of the right hand, the side that is "sacred, noble and precious," and the left hand, the "profane and common" side, see R. Hertz's "The Hands" (in *Rules and Meanings: The Anthropology of Everyday Knowledge*, ed. Mary Douglas [Harmondsworth: Penguin, 1973], 118–24) and my discussion of literal and figurative senses below.

45. *The Christian Remembrancer*, quoted in *Critical Heritage*, 91. Elizabeth Rigby was firmer in declaring the novel "pre-eminently an anti-Christian composition," but she locates its blasphemy in a "murmuring against the comforts of the rich and against the privations of the poor, which, so far as the individual is concerned, is a murmuring against God's appointment" (*Critical Heritage*, 109).

46. *Times Literary Supplement* (August 11, 1927), review of C. H. Haskins.

47. Luke 2:19.

48. I am quoting R. B. Martin, who sees Jane and Rochester as "a microcosm of man's striving for Christian reward" in *The Accents of Persuasion: Charlotte Brontë's Novels* (London: Faber and Faber, 1966), 81–83.

49. *Bearing the Word*, 30.

50. Homans, whose chapter on *Jane Eyre* is titled "Dreaming of Children: Literalization in *Jane Eyre*," neglects to mention the child who is actually born to Jane.

Chapter 4

1. G. H. Lewes was one of the first to make this complaint about *Shirley* in the review that drew Brontë's fire: "But in *Shirley* all unity, in consequence of defective art, is wanting. There is no passionate link; nor is there any artistic fusion, or intergrowth, by which one part evolves itself from another" (quoted in *The Brontës: The Critical Heritage*, ed. Miriam Allott [London: Routledge and Kegan Paul, 1974], 164).

2. *Disowning Knowledge in Six Plays of Shakespeare* (Cambridge: Cambridge University Press, 1987). I have quoted this passage from Cavell's essay on *Coriolanus*.

3. Raymond Williams, *Culture and Society 1780–1950* (New York: Harper and Row, 1958); Catherine Gallagher, *The Industrial Reformation of English Fiction: Social Discourse and Narrative Form, 1832–1867* (Chicago: University of Chicago Press, 1985), 269. The idea that *Shirley* is "not, of course, a social novel which falls into the same category as Mrs. Gaskell's *Mary Barton* or *North and South*," put this way by Asa Briggs in an address before the Brontë Society (*Brontë Society Transactions* 13, 68 [1958], 206), has been repeatedly expressed.

4. Sandra M. Gilbert and Susan Gubar, *The Madwoman in the Attic: Women Writers and the Nineteenth-Century Literary Imagination* (New Haven, Conn: Yale University Press, 1979), 374.

5. "Three Women's Texts and a Critique of Imperialism," *Critical Inquiry* 12 (1985), 243–48.

6. December 1848, lxxxiv, 153–85, partly rpt. in *Critical Heritage*, 105–12. Excerpts from this review are also printed in the Clarendon *Shirley*, along with

Brontë's intended preface, 797–804. I have quoted the review from the preface, giving Brontë's punctuation and capitalization. The preface itself (dated August 29, 1849), was presented to the Brontë Society by Mrs. Seton Gordon in 1974 and first published in *Brontë Society Transactions* in 1975.

7. I have taken this definition of the family from Catherine Gallagher, who is here summarizing works by Sarah Ellis and Arthur Helps. In her excellent chapter on "Family and Society: the Rhetoric of Reconciliation in the Debate over Industrialism," she makes the point that the family in industrial novels regularly functions metonymically or metaphorically.

8. The fragment "John Henry," which Brontë probably wrote just before she began *Shirley*, perhaps as part of her effort to revise *The Professor*, focuses on marital misery less extravagant than that of Rochester and Bertha but more common.

9. See Sigmund Freud, *Beyond the Pleasure Principle*, trans. and ed. James Strachey (New York: Norton, 1961). It is in relation to this powerful resistance to the present and future that the deaths of Branwell, Emily, and Anne Brontë, which occurred after Brontë had written most of the second volume of the novel and before she completed it, have their main influence. In his brief discussion of *Shirley* in *The Providential Aesthetic in Victorian Fiction* (Charlottesville: University of Virginia Press, 1985), Thomas Vargish notes but does not explain a related impression: "The novel's thematic structure is formed throughout by a peculiar rhythmic fluctuation between suffering and happiness, weakness and strength, sickness and health" (69).

10. The sex of *Shirley*'s narrator is difficult to determine, but Brontë's preface to *Shirley* represents a male narrator and so helps to establish her own sense of the novel's voice.

11. *The Political Unconscious: Narrative as a Socially Symbolic Act* (Ithaca, N. Y.: Cornell University Press, 1981), 78–79.

12. *The Brontës: Their Lives, Friendships and Correspondence in Four Volumes*, ed. Thomas J. Wise and John Alexander Symington (Oxford: Shakespeare Head Press, 1932), vol. 2, 152.

13. These variants are recorded in the Clarendon edition of the novel.

14. Cf. Gilbert and Gubar: "Even the noblest patriarchs are obsessed with delusive and contradictory images of women, Brontë implies, images pernicious enough to cause Mary Cave's death. She is therefore an emblem, a warning that the fate of women inhabiting a male-controlled society involves suicidal self-renunciation" (*Madwoman in the Attic*, 376).

15. See Freud's "Mourning and Melancholia," in *The Standard Edition of the Complete Psychological Works of Sigmund Freud*, 24 vols., trans. James Strachey et al. (London: Hogarth Press and the Institute of Psycho-Analysis, 1953), vol. 14, 239–58.

16. *The Enigma of Woman: Woman in Freud's Writings*, trans. Catherine Porter (Ithaca, N. Y.: Cornell University Press, 1985), 43.

17. *Critical Heritage*, 149.

18. Sally Shuttleworth, *George Eliot and Nineteenth-Century Science* (Cambridge: Cambridge University Press, 1984), 135.

19. See Toril Moi, *Sexual/Textual Politics: Feminist Literary Theory* (London: Methuen, 1985), 65.

20. Gilbert and Gubar, *Madwoman in the Attic*, 377–78.

21. *The Expression of the Emotions in Man and Animals*, revised and abridged by C. M. Beadnell (London: Watts and Co., 1948), 153–62.

22. Cavell, *Disowning Knowledge*, 58.

23. Matthew 7:7–10.

24. Luke 11:10–12.

25. *Repression in Victorian Fiction: Charlotte Brontë, George Eliot, and Charles Dickens* (Berkeley: University of California Press, 1987), 60.

26. See Freud, "Mourning and Melancholia," vol. 14, 237–58.

27. The words are in Matthew 30. The phrase "narrative expansion" comes from Fredric V. Bogel, *Literature and Insubstantiality in Later Eighteenth-Century England* (Princeton, N.J.: Princeton University Press, 1984), 210–13.

28. Gilbert and Gubar, *Madwoman in the Attic*, 390.

29. *Lives, Friendships*, vol. 3, 104.

30. *Lives, Friendships*, vol. 3, 104–5.

31. *Of Woman Born: Motherhood as Experience and Institution* (New York: Norton, 1976), 112.

32. Gilbert and Gubar describe Caroline as anorexic and anorexia as "a theme in women's literature" (390), but her illness during the long period when she refuses ordinary food is different from anorexia in being characterized by a loss of appetite rather than by an unwillingness or inability to eat or digest. Because anorexia is a woman's disorder and one associated with a denial of adulthood as a consequence (specifically, amenorrhoea) and perhaps as a cause, however, it does bear on the pattern I am tracing in *Shirley*.

33. I have taken the quoted phrases from Janet Adelman's fine essay on *Coriolanus*, "'Anger's My Meat': Feeding, Dependency, and Aggression in *Coriolanus*," in Murray M. Schwartz and Coppèlia Kahn, eds., *Representing Shakespeare: New Psychoanalytic Essays* (Baltimore: Johns Hopkins University Press, 1980), 129–49.

34. Adrienne Rich, in *Of Woman Born*, 67.

35. Quotations from Shakespeare are from the Nonesuch Press edition of *The Complete Works of William Shakespeare* (New York: Random House Inc., 1939).

36. Adelman, "Anger," 131.

37. *The Iliad*, Book XXII, trans. Robert Fitzgerald (Garden City, N.Y.: Anchor, 1975). It is relevant too that Hector's body is so horribly desecrated after his death. The ritual stabbing of his stripped corpse suggests the value an exhibition of wounds has in both Homer and *Coriolanus*.

38. Cavell's association of Virgilia with Volumnia, and his comment on Virgilia's silence, exemplifies what he himself, in his preface to *Disowning Knowledge*, identifies as the "male inflection" of essays written before his own formation of "a new set of natural reactions" in response to feminism and feminist criticism (x):

Again, the words "silent" and "silence" are beautifully and mysteriously associated, once each, with the women in his life: with his wife ("My gracious silence, hail!"); and with his mother ("He holds her by the hand, silent").

Toward both, the word of silence is the expression of intimacy and identification; but in his wife's case, it means acknowledgment, freedom from words,
but in a life beyond the social, while in his mother's case it means avoidance,
denial, death, and there is no life beyond the social. (167)

"He holds her by the hand, silent" is the stage direction that precedes Coriolanus's
capitulation to his mother's threats and entreaties in Act V. When he holds his
mother's hand, Coriolanus recalls Volumnia's appearance before him, together
with Virgilia and his own son, whose hand Volumnia, not Virgilia, holds and so
recalls himself to the meaning of being Volumnia's son. Certainly the word "silent"
refers not to Volumnia, who has done most of the talking in this scene, but to
Coriolanus, struck dumb by her terrible claims on him.

   39. *The Collected Plays of Bertolt Brecht*, ed. Ralph Manheim and John Willett
(New York: Random House, 1973), vol. 9, 179.

   40. *Language as Symbolic Action: Essays on Life, Literature, and Method* (Berkeley: University of California Press, 1968), 81–82; 95.

   41. Herbert Rosengarten and Margaret Smith, *Shirley*, xvi.

   42. *Brontë Society Transactions* 13, 68 (1958), 209.

   43. Igor Webb, *From Custom to Capital: The English Novel and the Industrial
Revolution* (Ithaca, N.Y.: Cornell University Press, 1981), 130–31.

   44. Burke, *Language as Symbolic Action*, 81–98:

But for our purposes the main consideration is this: Whereas a hostess or a
diplomat, or an ingratiating politician, or a public relations counsel might go
as far as possible towards *toning down* such situations, the dramatist must
work his cures by a quite different method. He must find ways to *play them
up*. In some respects, therefore, this play will require a character who is designed to help aggravate the uneasiness of the relationship between nobles
and commoners. (82)

Stanley Cavell's reading of Coriolanus's tragedy as his inability to achieve tragedy
persuasively argues that both the "logic" of Coriolanus's situation and his psychology prevent his death from being redemptive or purgative. Cavell makes Coriolanus's failure depend on his relation to and as food: "He can provide spiritual food
but he cannot make himself into food, he cannot say, for example, that his body is
bread" (161).

   45. Jameson, 54.

   46. *Myths of Power: A Marxist Study of the Brontës* (London: Macmillan, 1975),
47–48. See also Igor Webb: "It is precisely the sense of something disembodied,
of a force in the darkness, which adequately conveys the rupture of social convention, the break enacted in the extremity of armed conflict" (140).

   47. Quoted in Walter E. Houghton, *The Victorian Frame of Mind 1830–1870*
(New Haven, Conn.: Yale University Press, 1957), 306.

   48. Homans, *Bearing the Word: Language and Female Experience in Nineteenth-Century Women's Writing* (Chicago: University of Chicago Press, 1986), 199.

49. Armstrong, "The Rise of Feminine Authority in the Novel," *Novel* (1982), 137.

50. Burke quotes this passage from his essay on *Timon of Athens* at the end of his reading of *Coriolanus* in *Language as Symbolic Action*, 93.

Chapter 5

1. *Wuthering Heights*, ed. Hilda Marsden and Ian Jack (Oxford: Clarendon Press, 1976), 444. Subsequent references to passages in the novel itself are to the book, chapter, and page number in this edition, and appear in parentheses in my text.

2. *Wuthering Heights*, 444–45.

3. Letter to Richard Woodhouse (October 27, 1818) in *The Letters of John Keats*, 2 vols., ed. Hyder Edward Rollins (Cambridge, Mass.: Harvard University Press, 1958).

4. Leo Bersani applies this phrase to *Wuthering Heights* in *A Future for Astyanax: Character and Desire in Literature* (New York: Columbia University Press, 1984), 208.

5. Rachel M. Brownstein, "Representing the Self: Arnold and Brontë on Rachel," *Browning Institute Studies* 13 (1985), 11.

6. *The Brontës: Their Lives, Friendships and Correspondence in Four Volumes*, ed. Thomas J. Wise and John Alexander Symington (Oxford: Shakespeare Head Press, 1932), vol. 3, 68.

7. See *The Brontës: The Critical Heritage*, ed. Miriam Allott (London: Routledge and Kegan Paul, 1974), 160–70.

8. For a thorough analysis of arguments against the theater, see Jonas Barish, *The Antitheatrical Prejudice* (Berkeley: University of California Press, 1981). Barish points out how apparently contradictory prejudices against the theater manage to coexist, so that the theater is condemned both for allowing men to impersonate women and for bringing women on the stage to prevent their doing so, thereby bringing men and women together and allowing women to display themselves as actresses. His chapters on the Puritans and the antitheatrical prejudice in the nineteenth century provide an important social and political context for Brontë's treatment of the theater in *Villette*.

9. *Wuthering Heights*, 436.

10. See Nancy Chodorow's analysis in *The Reproduction of Mothering: Psychoanalysis and the Sociology of Gender* (Berkeley: University of California Press, 1978), and Margaret Homans's Lacanian application of Chodorow's theory to the birth of Catherine Linton in *Wuthering Heights*: "If the heir replaces the mother to the mother's disadvantage within the Law of the Father, it is also true that within Cathy's hallucinatory and extralegal understanding of maternity and childhood, the mother replaces the child. Dying in childbirth, Cathy becomes herself a child; the novel equates giving birth with her return to her own childhood" (*Bearing the Word: Language and Female Experience in Nineteenth-Century Women's Writing* (Chicago: University of Chicago Press, 1986), 81).

11. Margaret Homans's reading of a related passage, the one in which Cathy, during her final illness, recalls having made Heathcliff promise not to shoot lapwings, after he has set a trap over a nest of them, preventing the parent bird from feeding his/her young, argues that Cathy "implicates herself to some degree in the violence she recounts" but that her "main concern in the passage is with her protectiveness toward a vulnerable natural world that Heathcliff takes pleasure in victimizing." (*Bearing the Word*, 78–79). This reading violates what still seems to me the main dynamic of *Wuthering Heights* according to which actions are strong or weak rather than right or wrong, and protectiveness is one of the prerogatives of strength.

12. See "Master and Slave," 105–7, and Girard's note in *Deceit, Desire and the Novel: Self and Other in Literary Structure* (Baltimore: Johns Hopkins University Press, 1965).

13. Sarah Kofman, *The Enigma of Woman: Woman in Freud's Writings*, trans. Catherine Porter (Ithaca, N.Y.: Cornell University Press, 1985), 59–62.

14. Kofman, *Enigma*, 56–57.

15. Much of the history of *Villette* criticism, perhaps of criticism itself, could be summarized in the critics' confrontations with the haunting nun during the past two decades. Writing in 1966, E. D. H. Johnson remarked on the "uneasy silence" with which critics had passed over the nun and argued for the nun's "thematic function" in the novel while admitting "the ineptitude of its handling" and calling it an "artistic lapse" ("'Daring the Dread Glance': Charlotte Brontë's Treatment of the Supernatural in *Villette*," *Nineteenth-Century Fiction* 20 [1966], 325). In an otherwise very appreciative introduction to the 1972 Harper edition of the novel, Q. D. Leavis saw the nun as only a Gothic hangover and an attempt to forestall the complaint that the novel (like *The Professor*) would be lacking in "startling interest" or "thrilling excitement" (*Villette* [New York: Harper and Row, 1972], xxii–xxiii). In 1973, Charles Burkhart placed the nun in relation to Lucy's psychosexual development ("The Nuns of *Villette*," *Victorian Newsletter* 44 [1973], 8–13; and *Charlotte Brontë: A Psychosexual Study of Her Novels* [London: Victor Gollancz, 1973]). Feminist critics have placed her as the form of a vengeful repression (Mary Jacobus, "*Villette*'s Buried Letter," *Essays in Criticism* 28 [1978], 228) and one of Lucy's many buried selves (Sandra M. Gilbert and Susan Gubar, *The Madwoman in the Attic: The Woman Writer and the Nineteenth-Century Literary Imagination* [New Haven, Conn.: Yale University Press, 1979], 399–440) as well as a part of Brontë's "compelling narrative of a woman's accession to her proper place" because a form that "continually displaces identities and definitions" (Christina Crosby, "Charlotte Brontë's Haunted Text," *Studies in English Literature* 24 [1984], 715).

16. "The Life Cycle: Epigenesis of Identity," in Erik Erikson, *Identity, Youth and Crisis* (New York: Norton, 1968), especially 135–38.

17. "Analysis of a Phobia in a Five-Year-Old Boy" (1909b), quoted by Jean LaPlanche and J.-B. Pontalis (*The Language of Psycho-Analysis* [London: Hogarth Press, 1973]), 79.

18. "Charlotte Brontë's New Gothic," in *From Jane Austen to Joseph Conrad*, ed. Robert Charles Rathburn and Martin Steinmann, Jr. (Minneapolis: University of Minnesota Press), 1958, 128.

19. Crosby, "Haunted Text," 713.

20. I have profited from two articles on Rachel's impact on the Victorian writers in whose works she appears, Disraeli, G. H. Lewes, George Eliot, and Matthew Arnold, as well as Brontë. They are John Stokes's "Rachel's 'Terrible Beauty': An Actress Among the Novelists," *English Literary History* 51 (1984), 771–91, and Rachel M. Brownstein's "Representing the Self," 1–24.

21. Frances Ann Kemble, *Records of Later Life* (New York: Henry Holt, 1982), 244. A note that follows this letter revises Kemble's first impression in only one respect, granting Rachel the capacity to express tenderness and citing her performance in "Camilla" as evidence.

23. *Wuthering Heights*, 443.

24. Jacobus, "*Villette's* Buried Letter," 233.

25. *Lives, Friendships*, vol. 3, 290.

26. Quoted in *Critical Heritage*, 325.

27. Kemble, *Records*, 244.

28. The threat here has little in common with what Jonas Barish has described as the anti-theatrical prejudice, the fear of acting and actors because the impersonation of bad or inferior characters is morally harmful to the actor, endangering the integrity of the authentic self or signifying the absence of such integrity. See *The Antitheatrical Prejudice*, 307–10 especially. Also Martin Meisel, *Realizations: Narrative, Pictorial, and Theatrical Arts in Nineteenth-Century England* (Princeton, N.J.: Princeton University Press, 1973), 333.

29. As Eve Kosofsky Sedgwick points out, Brontë's characterization of the Vashti is indebted to Gothic formulas, and especially to the one according to which the countenance, often the brow, is impressed with a sign or inscription. See "The Character in the Veil: Imagery of the Surface in the Gothic Novel," *PMLA* 96 (1981), 260–67.

Chapter 6

1. "'Haworth Churchyard': The Making of Arnold's Elegy," *Brontë Society Transactions* 15, 77 (1967), 105–22.

2. March 21, 1853, in *The Letters of Matthew Arnold to Arthur Hugh Clough*, ed. Howard Foster Lowry (London: Oxford University Press, 1932), 132.

3. "Haworth Churchyard," in *Poems*, ed. Kenneth Allott (New York: Barnes and Noble, 1965).

4. E. C. Gaskell, *The Life of Charlotte Brontë*, ed. Alan Shelston (Harmondsworth: Penguin, 1975), 484.

5. For a full account of hypochondria's history in the eighteenth and nineteenth centuries, see John Mullan, *Sentiment and Sociability: The Language of Feeling in the Eighteenth Century* (Oxford: Clarendon Press, 1988).

6. Jacobus, "*Villette's* Buried Letter," *Essays in Criticism* 28 (1978), 229.

7. "*Villette* and the Conventions of Autobiography," *English Literary History* 46 (1979), 266, 277.

8. *The Brontës: Their Lives, Friendships and Correspondence in Four Volumes,*

ed. Thomas J. Wise and John Alexander Symington (Oxford: Shakespeare Head Press, 1932), vol. 2, 211–12.

9. Gaskell, *Life*, 348–50.

10. *Lives, Friendships*, vol. 3, 23.

11. Gaskell, *Life*, 390–93.

12. *George Eliot and Blackmail* (Cambridge, Mass.: Harvard University Press, 1985), 113.

13. George Eliot in a letter to Charles Bray (Sept. 26, 1859), quoted in Welsh, *George Eliot and Blackmail*, 131. Welsh is acute in connecting the secret identity of Marian Evans as George Eliot to the unsecret but improper identity of Marian Evans as Marian Lewes.

14. I am quoting D. A. Miller in *The Novel and the Police* (Berkeley: University of California Press, 1988), 16.

15. *Discipline and Punish: The Birth of the Prison*, trans. Alan Sheridan (New York: Random House, 1977), 192–93.

16. Translator's note, *Discipline and Punish*.

17. According to the *Supplement* to the OED, the verb "to surveil" or "surveille" is as recent as 1960.

18. D. A. Miller, in his discussion of *David Copperfield* in *The Novel and the Police*, makes the point that the characters of the novel, "however much the ethical content of their inwardness might differ," agree on a paranoid perception of the social world (204).

19. G. H. Lewes, *Edinburgh Review*, January 1850, xci, 153–73.

20. *Discipline and Punish*, 173.

21. *Lives, Friendships*, vol. 3, 60.

22. *Discipline and Punish*, 187.

23. Simon During, "The Strange Case of Monomania: Patriarchy in Literature, Murder in *Middlemarch*, Drowning in *Daniel Deronda*," *Representations* 23 (1988), 86–104.

24. *Boswell's Life of Johnson*, ed. George Birkbeck Hill (Oxford: Clarendon Press, 1934, rpt. 1971), vol. 1, 65–66.

25. *Boswell's Life of Johnson*, vol. 2, 423.

26. The distinction is analogous to the one Foucault makes between two approaches to disease, that of the hospital, which deals with "individuals who happen to be suffering from one disease or another," and that of the clinic, which deals with "diseases that happen to be afflicting this or that patient." See *The Birth of the Clinic: An Archaeology of Medical Perception*, trans. A. M. Sheridan Smith (New York: Random House, 1975), 59.

> In the hospital, the patient is the *subject* of his disease, that is, he is a *case*; in the clinic, where one is dealing only with *examples*, the patient is the accident of his disease, the transitory object that it happens to have seized upon.

27. *Discerning the Subject* (Minneapolis: University of Minnesota Press, 1988), 96.

Works Cited

Abrams, M. H. *Natural Supernaturalism: Tradition and Revolution in Romantic Literature*. New York: Norton, 1971.

Adelman, Janet. "'Anger's My Meat': Feeding, Dependency, and Aggression in *Coriolanus*." In *Representing Shakespeare: New Psychoanalytic Essays*. Edited by Murray M. Schwartz and Coppèlia Kahn. Baltimore: Johns Hopkins University Press, 1980, 129–49.

Alexander, Christine. *The Early Writings of Charlotte Brontë*. Oxford: Basil Blackwell, 1983.

Allott, Miriam, editor. *The Brontës: The Critical Heritage*. London: Routledge and Kegan Paul, 1974.

Argyle, Michael and Mark Cook. *Gaze and Mutual Gaze*. Cambridge: Cambridge University Press, 1976.

Armstrong, Nancy. "The Rise of Feminine Authority in the Novel." *Novel* 15 (1982), 127–45.

Arnold, Matthew. *The Letters of Matthew Arnold to Arthur Hugh Clough*. Edited by Howard Foster Lowry. London: Oxford University Press, 1932.

———. *Poems*. Edited by Kenneth Allott. New York: Barnes and Noble, 1965.

Austin, J. L. *Sense and Sensibilia*. Edited by G. J. Warnock. Oxford: Clarendon Press, 1962.

Baldwin, Robert. "'Gates Pure and Shining and Serene': Mutual Gazing as an Amatory Motif in Western Literature and Art." *Renaissance and Reformation* 10 (1986), 23–48.

Barish, Jonas. *The Antitheatrical Prejudice*. Berkeley: University of California Press, 1981.

Barthes, Roland. *Writing Degree Zero*. Translated by Annette Lavers and Colin Smith. London: Jonathan Cape, 1967.

Bate, Walter Jackson. *Samuel Johnson*. New York: Harcourt Brace Jovanovich, 1977.

Beauvoir, Simone de. *The Second Sex*. Translated and edited by H. M. Parshley. New York: Bantam Books, 1961, rpt. 1970.

Bersani, Leo. *A Future for Astyanax: Character and Desire in Literature*. New York: Columbia University Press, 1984.

Bogel, Fredric V. *Literature and Insubstantiality in Later Eighteenth-Century England*. Princeton, N. J.: Princeton University Press, 1984.

Boswell, James. *Boswell's Life of Johnson*. 6 vols. Edited by George Birkbeck Hill. Oxford: Clarendon Press, 1934, reprint 1971.

Brammer, M. M. "The Manuscript of *The Professor*." *Review of English Studies* New Series 2 (1960), 157–70.

Brecht, Bertolt. *The Collected Plays of Bertolt Brecht*. Edited by Ralph Manheim and John Willett. New York: Random House, 1973, vol. 9.

Briggs, Asa. "Private and Social Themes in *Shirley*." *Brontë Society Transactions* 13, 68 (1958), 203–19.

Brontë, Charlotte. *Jane Eyre*. Edited by Jane Jack and Margaret Smith. Oxford: Clarendon Press, 1969.

———. *Shirley*. Edited by Herbert Rosengarten and Margaret Smith. Oxford: Clarendon Press, 1979.

———. *The Poems of Charlotte Brontë: A New Text and Commentary*. Edited by Victor A. Neufeldt. New York: Garland Publishing, 1985.

———. *The Professor*. Edited by Margaret Smith and Herbert Rosengarten. Oxford: Clarendon Press, 1987.

———. *Villette*. Edited by Herbert Rosengarten and Margaret Smith. Oxford: Clarendon Press, 1984.

Brontë, Emily. *The Complete Poems of Emily Jane Brontë*. Edited by C. W. Hatfield. New York: Columbia University Press, 1941.

———. *Wuthering Heights*. Edited by Hilda Marsden and Ian Jack. Oxford: Clarendon Press, 1976.

Brownstein, Rachel M. "Representing the Self: Arnold and Brontë on Rachel." *Browning Institute Studies* 13 (1985), 1–24.

Burke, Kenneth. *Language as Symbolic Action: Essays on Life, Literature, and Method*. Berkeley: University of California Press, 1968.

Burkhart, Charles. *Charlotte Brontë: A Psychosexual Study of Her Novels*. London: Victor Gollancz, 1973.

———. "The Nuns of *Villette*." *The Victorian Newsletter* 44 (1973), 8–13.

Burney, Frances. *The Diary and Letters of Madame D'Arblay*. Edited by Charlotte Barrett. London: Bickers and Son, n.d., vol. 2.

Carlisle, Janice. "*Villette* and the Conventions of Autobiography." *ELH* 46 (1979), 262–89.

Carlyle, Thomas. *Sartor Resartus*. New York: Harper and Brothers, 1848.

Cavell, Stanley. *Disowning Knowledge in Six Plays of Shakespeare*. Cambridge: Cambridge University Press, 1987.

Chase, Richard. "The Brontës: A Centennial Observance." *Kenyon Review* 9 (1947), 487–506.

Chitham, Edward. "'Often Rebuked . . . ': Emily's After All?" *Brontë Society Transactions* 18, 93 (1983), 222–26.

Chitham, Edward and Tom Winnifrith. *Brontë Facts and Brontë Problems*. London: Macmillan, 1983.

Chodorow, Nancy. "Gender, Relation, and Difference in Psychoanalytic Perspective." In *The Future of Difference*. Edited by Hester Eisenstein and Alice Jardine. Boston: G. K. Hall, 1980; reprint New Brunswick, N.J.: Rutgers University Press, 1985, 3–19.

———. *The Reproduction of Mothering: Psychoanalysis and the Sociology of Gender*. Berkeley: University of California Press, 1978.

Craig, G. Armour. "Private Vision and Social Order." In *Jane Eyre: An Authoritative Text, Backgrounds, Criticism*. Edited by Richard J. Dunn. New York: W. W. Norton, 1971, 471–78.

Crosby, Christina. "Charlotte Brontë's Haunted Text." *Studies in English Literature* 24 (1984), 701–15.

Darwin, Charles. *The Expression of the Emotions in Man and Animals.* Revised and abridged by C. M. Beadnell. London: Watts and Co., 1948.

de Lauretis, Teresa. *Alice Doesn't: Feminism, Semiotics, Cinema.* Bloomington: Indiana University Press, 1984.

Dickens, Charles *Little Dorrit.* Edited by John Holloway. Harmondsworth: Penguin, 1971.

———. *Oliver Twist.* Edited by Kathleen Tillotson. Oxford: Oxford University Press, 1982.

Douglas, Mary. *Natural Symbols: Explorations in Cosmology.* New York: Random House, 1979.

———, editor. *Rules and Meanings: The Anthropology of Everyday Knowledge.* Harmondsworth: Penguin, 1973.

During, Simon. "The Strange Case of Monomania: Patriarchy in Literature, Murder in *Middlemarch*, Drowning in *Daniel Deronda.*" *Representations* 23 (1988), 86–104.

Duthie, Enid. *The Foreign Novels of Charlotte Brontë.* New York: Barnes and Noble, 1975.

Eagleton, Terry. "Class, Power and Charlotte Brontë." *Critical Quarterly* 14 (1972), 225–36.

———. *Myths of Power: A Marxist Study of the Brontës.* London: Macmillan, 1975.

Eliot, George. *Middlemarch.* Edited by W. J. Harvey. Harmondsworth: Penguin, 1965.

Ellmann, Mary. *Thinking About Women.* New York: Harcourt, Brace and World, 1968.

Empson, William. *The Structure of Complex Words.* New York: New Directions, 1951; reprint Ann Arbor: University of Michigan Press, 1967; 3rd edition Totowa, N. J.: Rowman and Littlefield, 1979.

Erikson, Erik H. *Identity, Youth and Crisis.* New York: Norton, 1968.

Ewbank, Inga-Stina. *Their Proper Sphere: A Study of the Brontë Sisters as Early-Victorian Female Novelists.* Cambridge, Mass.: Harvard University Press, 1968.

Foucault, Michel. *The Birth of the Clinic: An Archaeology of Medical Perception.* Translated by A. M. Sheridan Smith. New York: Random House, 1975.

———. *Discipline and Punish: The Birth of the Prison.* Translated by Alan Sheridan. New York: Random House, 1977.

Fowler, O. S. and L. N. *New Illustrated Self-Instructor in Phrenology and Physiology.* London: W. Tweedie, n.d.

Freeman, Janet H. "Speech and Silence in *Jane Eyre.*" *Studies in English Literature* 24 (1984), 683–700.

Freud, Anna. *The Ego and the Mechanisms of Defence.* Translated by Cecil Baines. New York: International Universities Press, 1946.

Freud, Sigmund. *Beyond the Pleasure Principle.* Translated and edited by James Strachey. New York: Norton, 1961.

———. *The Standard Edition of the Complete Psychological Works of Sigmund Freud.* Translated by James Strachey et al. London: Hogarth Press and the Institute of Psycho-Analysis, 1953, vols. 14 and 17.

Gallagher, Catherine. *The Industrial Reformation of English Fiction: Social Discourse and Narrative Form, 1832–1867*. Chicago: University of Chicago Press, 1985.

Gaskell, E. C. *The Life of Charlotte Brontë*. Edited by Alan Shelston. Harmondsworth: Penguin, 1975.

Gilbert, Sandra M. and Susan Gubar. *The Madwoman in the Attic: The Woman Writer and the Nineteenth-Century Literary Imagination*. New Haven, Conn.: Yale University Press, 1979.

Girard, René. *Deceit, Desire, and the Novel: Self and Other in Literary Structure*. Baltimore: Johns Hopkins University Press, 1965.

Gould, Stephen Jay. *The Mismeasure of Man*. New York: W. W. Norton, 1981.

Greenblatt, Stephen. *Renaissance Self-Fashioning: From More to Shakespeare*. Chicago: University of Chicago Press, 1980.

Gregor, Ian, editor. *The Brontës: A Collection of Critical Essays*. Englewood Cliffs, N. J.: Prentice-Hall, 1970.

Heilbrun, Carolyn. *Toward a Recognition of Androgyny*. New York: Knopf, 1973.

Heilman, Robert B. "Charlotte Brontë's New Gothic." In *From Jane Austen to Joseph Conrad*. Edited by Robert Charles Rathburn and Martin Steinmann, Jr. Minneapolis: University of Minnesota Press, 1958, 118–32.

Homans, Margaret. *Bearing the Word: Language and Female Experience in Nineteenth-Century Women's Writing*. Chicago: University of Chicago Press, 1986.

Homer. *The Iliad*. Translated by Robert Fitzgerald. Garden City, N. Y.: Anchor, 1975.

Horney, Karen. "The Value of Vindictiveness." *American Journal of Psychoanalysis* 8 (1948), 3–12.

Houghton, Walter E. *The Victorian Frame of Mind 1830–1870*. New Haven, Conn.: Yale University Press, 1957.

Jacobus, Mary. "*Villette's* Buried Letter." *Essays in Criticism* 28 (1978), 228–53.

James, Henry. *Henry James: Literary Criticism*. Edited by Leon Edel. New York: Viking Press, 1984, vol. 1.

James, William. *The Principles of Psychology*. Edited by Frederick H. Burkhardt et al. Cambridge, Mass.: Harvard University Press, 1981, vol. 2.

Jameson, Fredric. *The Political Unconscious: Narrative as a Socially Symbolic Act*. Ithaca, N. Y.: Cornell University Press, 1981.

Jay, Elisabeth. *The Religion of the Heart: Anglican Evangelicalism in the Nineteenth-Century Novel*. Oxford: Clarendon Press, 1979.

Johnson, E. D. H. "'Daring the Dread Glance': Charlotte Brontë's Treatment of the Supernatural in *Villette*." *Nineteenth-Century Fiction* 20 (1966), 325–36.

Jones, John. *John Keats's Dream of Truth*. London: Chatto and Windus, 1969.

Kaplan, E. Ann. *Women and Film: Both Sides of the Camera*. New York: Methuen, 1984.

Keats, John. *The Letters of John Keats*. Edited by Hyder Edward Rollins. Cambridge, Mass.: Harvard University Press, 1958.

Kemble, Frances Ann. *Records of Later Life*. New York: Henry Holt and Company, 1982.

Kofman, Sarah. *The Enigma of Woman: Woman in Freud's Writings*. Translated by Catherine Porter. Ithaca, N.Y.: Cornell University Press, 1985.

Kucich, John. "Passionate Reserve and Reserved Passion in Brontë." *ELH* 52 (1985): 913–37.

———. *Repression in Victorian Fiction: Charlotte Brontë, George Eliot, and Charles Dickens.* Berkeley: University of California Press, 1987.

Laplanche, Jean and J.-B. Pontalis. *The Language of Psycho-Analysis.* Translated by Donald Nicholson-Smith. London: Hogarth Press, 1973.

Lawrence, D. H. *Phoenix II: Uncollected, Unpublished, and Other Prose Works.* Edited by Warren Roberts and Harry T. Moore. New York: Viking Press, 1968.

Leavis, F. R. *The Great Tradition.* London: Chatto and Windus, 1948.

Leavis, Q. D. Introduction to *Villette*, New York: Harper and Row, 1972.

Lentricchia, Frank. *Ariel and the Police: Michel Foucault, William James, Wallace Stevens.* Madison: University of Wisconsin Press, 1988.

Lewis, C. S. *A Preface to Paradise Lost.* New York: Oxford University Press, 1966.

Lodge, David. *Language of Fiction: Essays in Criticism and Verbal Analysis of the English Novel.* New York: Columbia University Press. 1966.

Marks, Elaine and Isabelle de Courtivron. *New French Feminisms: An Anthology.* Amherst: University of Massachusetts Press, 1980.

Martin, R. B. *The Accents of Persuasion: Charlotte Brontë's Novels.* London: Faber and Faber, 1966.

Maynard, John. *Charlotte Brontë and Sexuality.* Cambridge: Cambridge University Press, 1984.

McKeon, Michael. *The Origins of the English Novel, 1600–1740.* Baltimore: Johns Hopkins University Press, 1987.

Meisel, Martin. *Realizations: Narrative, Pictorial, and Theatrical Arts in Nineteenth-Century England.* Princeton, N. J.: Princeton University Press, 1973.

Merleau-Ponty, Maurice. *The Primacy of Perception, and Other Essays on Phenomenological Psychology, the Philosophy of Art, History, and Politics.* Edited by James M. Edie. Evanston, Ill.: Northwestern University Press, 1964.

Michie, Helena R. *The Flesh Made Word: Female Figures and Women's Bodies.* New York: Oxford, 1987.

Miller, D. A. *The Novel and the Police.* Berkeley: University of California Press, 1988.

Miller, J. Hillis. *Fiction and Repetition: Seven English Novels.* Cambridge, Mass.: Harvard University Press, 1982.

Moglen, Helene. *Charlotte Brontë: The Self Conceived.* New York: Norton, 1976.

Moi, Toril. *Sexual/Textual Politics: Feminist Literary Theory.* London: Methuen, 1985.

Mullan, John. *Sentiment and Sociability: The Language of Feeling in the Eighteenth Century.* Oxford: Clarendon Press, 1988.

Mulvey, Laura. "Visual Pleasure and Narrative Cinema." In *Visual and Other Pleasures.* Bloomington: Indiana University Press, 1989, 14–26.

Nussbaum, Felicity A. *The Autobiographical Subject: Gender and Ideology in Eighteenth-Century England.* Baltimore: Johns Hopkins University Press, 1989.

Peters, Margot. *Charlotte Brontë: Style in the Novel.* Madison: University of Wisconsin Press, 1973.

Plath Sylvia. *Collected Poems*. Edited by Ted Hughes. New York: Harper and Row, 1981.

Poovey, Mary. *The Proper Lady and the Woman Writer*. Chicago: University of Chicago Press, 1984.

Quirk, Randolph. *A Comprehensive Grammar of the English Language*. London: Longman, 1985.

Ratchford, Fanny Elizabeth. *The Brontës' Web of Childhood*. New York: Columbia University Press, 1941.

Rich, Adrienne. *Of Woman Born: Motherhood as Experience and Institution*. New York: Norton, 1976.

———. *On Lies, Secrets, and Silence: Selected Prose 1966–78*. New York: W. W. Norton, 1979.

Rigby, Elizabeth. "*Vanity Fair*—and *Jane Eyre*." *Quarterly Review* 84 (Dec. 1848), 153–85.

Roberts, Doreen. "'Jane Eyre' and the 'Warped System of Things.'" In *Reading the Victorian Novel: Detail into Form*. Edited by Ian Gregor. New York: Harper and Row, 1980, 131–49.

Roper, Derek. "The Revision of Emily Brontë's Poems of 1846." *The Library* Sixth Series 6 (1984), 153–67.

Rutter, D. R. *Looking and Seeing: The Role of Visual Communication in Social Interaction*. New York: John Wiley, 1984.

Sabol, C. Ruth and Todd K. Randar. *A Concordance to Brontë's Jane Eyre*. New York: Garland Publishing, 1981.

Sadoff, Dianne. *Monsters of Affection: Dickens, Brontë, and Eliot on Fatherhood*. Baltimore: Johns Hopkins University Press, 1982.

Sandler, Joseph, with Anna Freud. *The Analysis of Defense: The Ego and the Mechanisms of Defense Revisited*. New York: International Universities Press, 1985.

Sedgwick, Eve Kosofsky. "The Character in the Veil: Imagery of the Surface in the Gothic Novel." *PMLA* 96 (1981), 260–67.

———. *Between Men: English Literature and Male Homosocial Desire*. New York: Columbia University Press, 1985.

Shakespeare, William. *The Complete Works of William Shakespeare*. New York: Random House, 1939.

Showalter, Elaine. *A Literature of Their Own: British Women Novelists from Brontë to Lessing*. Princeton, N.J.: Princeton University Press, 1977.

Shuttleworth, Sally. *George Eliot and Nineteenth-Century Science*. Cambridge: Cambridge University Press, 1984.

Skinner, Quentin. "Language and Social Change." In *The State of the Language*. Edited by Leonard Michaels and Christopher Ricks. Berkeley: University of California Press, 1980, 562–78.

Smith, Paul. *Discerning the Subject*. Minneapolis: University of Minnesota Press, 1988.

Spivak, Gayatri. "Three Women's Texts and a Critique of Imperialism." *Critical Inquiry* 12 (1985), 243–61.

Stokes, John. "Rachel's 'Terrible Beauty': An Actress Among the Novelists." *ELH* 51 (1984), 771–91.

Tillotson, Kathleen. "'Haworth Churchyard': The Making of Arnold's Elegy." *Brontë Society Transactions* 15;77 (1967), 105–22.

———. *The Novels of the Eighteen-Forties*. Oxford: Clarendon Press, 1954.

Vargish, Thomas. *The Providential Aesthetic in Victorian Fiction*. Charlottesville: University of Virginia Press, 1985.

Webb, Igor. *From Custom to Capital: The English Novel and the Industrial Revolution*. Ithaca, N. Y.: Cornell University Press, 1981.

Welsh, Alexander. *From Copyright to Copperfield: The Identity of Dickens*. Cambridge, Mass.: Harvard University Press, 1987.

———. *George Eliot and Blackmail*. Cambridge, Mass.: Harvard University Press, 1985.

Westkott, Marcia. *The Feminist Legacy of Karen Horney*. New Haven, Conn.: Yale University Press, 1986.

Willett, Flora Katherine. "Which Brontë Was 'Often Rebuked'? A Note Favouring Anne." *Brontë Society Transactions* 18, 92 (1982), 143–48.

Williams, Raymond. *Culture and Society 1780–1950*. New York: Harper and Row, 1958.

———. *Keywords: A Vocabulary of Culture and Society*. London: Hogarth Press, 1976.

———. *The English Novel from Dickens to Lawrence*. London: Hogarth Press, 1984.

Wise, Thomas J. and John Alexander Symington. *The Brontës: Their Lives, Friendships and Correspondence in Four Volumes*. Oxford: Shakespeare Head Press, 1932.

Woolf, Virginia. *A Room of One's Own*. New York: Harcourt, Brace and World, 1957.

———. *Collected Essays*. New York: Harcourt, Brace and World, 1967, vol. 1.

Yaeger, Patricia. *Honey-Mad Women: Emancipatory Strategies in Women's Writing*. New York: Columbia University Press, 1988.

Zeitlin, Froma I. "Playing the Other." In *Nothing to Do with Dionysus? Athenian Drama in Its Social Context*. Edited by John J. Winkler and Froma I. Zeitlin. Princeton, N.J.: Princeton University Press, 1990, 63–96.

Index

Abrams, M. H., 75
Armstrong, Nancy, 123, 182n.33
Arnold, Matthew, 10–11, 143–44, 145, 146, 158
Austen, Jane, Charlotte Brontë's criticism of, 3, 25–27; Woolf's comparison of Charlotte Brontë to, 10; G. H. Lewes's response to, 24
Austin, J. L., 59–60, 70

Barish, Jonas, 187n.8, 189n.28
Barthes, Roland, 26
Bate, Walter Jackson, 11
Bayne, Peter, 141
Beauvoir, Simone de, 16
Bentham, Jeremy, 151, 154
"Biographical Notice of Ellis and Acton Bell," 16–18, 21, 125
Brecht, Bertolt, 109, 113
Briggs, Asa, 111, 183n.3
Brontë, Anne, 1–2, 20, 25, 148
Brontë, Charlotte: as a woman writer, 3–4, 10–11, 13–16, 31–33, 128–29; and special pleading, 11–13, 18–20; and pseudonym, 13, 130–31, 147–48; on *Wuthering Heights*, 17–18, 125–42; on Emily Jane Brontë, 17–21; letters mentioned, 20, 22–23, 25–26, 31–33, 34, 60–61, 139–41, 143–45, 147–48, 155, 177n.21; on G. H. Lewes, 22–24; on Jane Austen, 3, 25–27; and eyesight, 28, 60–61; and early writing, 30–33, 34, 61; Matthew Arnold's response to, 143–44. *See also* "Biographical Notice of Ellis and Acton Bell"; "Editor's Preface" to *Wuthering Heights*; *Jane Eyre*; "Master and Pupil"; "Roe Head Journal"; *The Professor*; *Shirley*; *Villette*; "A Word to the 'Quarterly'"
Brontë, Elizabeth, 1–2
Brontë, Emily Jane, 1–2, 17–18, 19–21; as Heathcliff's creator, 125–26. *See also* "Biographical Notice of Ellis and Acton Bell";

"Editor's Preface" to *Wuthering Heights*; *Wuthering Heights*
Brontë, Maria (sister), 1–2
Brontë, Patrick, 1–2, 12, 28, 59; Mary Taylor's view of, 15; on the ending of *Villette*, 145
Brontë, Patrick Branwell, 1–2, 33
Burke, Kenneth, 110, 124, 186n.44
Burney, Frances, 9
Bunyan, John, 31

Carlisle, Janice, 145–46
Carlyle, Thomas, 80, 102–3, 118
Cavell, Stanley, 90, 99, 185–86n.38, 186n.44
Chase, Richard, 83–84
Chitham, Edward, 20
Chodorow, Nancy, 37–38, 176n.13
Clough, Arthur Hugh, 143–44
Coleridge, Hartley, 61
Cowper, William, 102
Craig, G. Armour, 84, 180n.9
Crosby, Christina, 135

Darwin, Charles, 27, 99
Dickens, Charles, 6, 14, 24, 65–66
Douglas, Mary, 27

Eagleton, Terry, 42, 115, 178n.27
"Editor's Preface" to *Wuthering Heights*, 10, 16, 125–26, 170
Eliot, George, 29, 46, 148–49, 150
Eliot, T. S., 86
Ellmann, Mary, 24
Empson, William, 7, 9–10, 16
Erikson, Erik H., 134

Félix, Rachel (Élisa- or Élisabeth-Rachel Félix), 139–42
Fielding, Henry, 24, 26
Foucault, Michel, 146, 149–51, 155, 190n.26
Freud, Anna, 8, 172n.13
Freud, Sigmund, 8, 37, 68, 83–85, 93, 102, 131–34, 172n.13
Fuller, Margaret, 144

This book has been set in Linotron Galliard. Galliard was designed for Mergenthaler in 1978 by Matthew Carter. Galliard retains many of the features of a sixteenth century typeface cut by Robert Granjon but has some modifications that give it a more contemporary look.

Printed on acid-free paper.